P9-DNE-997

THE
HEART
OF
REMARRIAGE

GARY & GREG
SMALLEY
WITH
DAN & MARCI CRETSINGER

Regal

From Gospel Light
Ventura, California, U.S.A.

Published by Regal
From Gospel Light
Ventura, California, U.S.A.
www.regalbooks.com
Printed in the U.S.A.

All Scripture quotations, unless otherwise indicated, are taken from the *Holy Bible,*
New International Version®. Copyright © 1973, 1978, 1984 by International Bible Society.
Used by permission of Zondervan Publishing House. All rights reserved.

Other versions used are
AMP—Scripture taken from THE AMPLIFIED BIBLE, Old Testament copyright © 1965,
1987 by the Zondervan Corporation. The Amplified New Testament copyright © 1958,
1987 by The Lockman Foundation. Used by permission.
CEV—Contemporary English Version. Copyright © American Bible Society, 1995.
ESV—Scripture taken from the *English Standard Version,* Copyright © 2001. The *ESV* and
English Standard Version are trademarks of Good News Publishers.
THE MESSAGE—Scripture taken from *THE MESSAGE.* Copyright © by Eugene H. Peterson,
1993, 1994, 1995. Used by permission of NavPress Publishing Group.
NASB—Scripture taken from the *New American Standard Bible,* © 1960, 1962, 1963, 1968, 1971,
1972, 1973, 1975, 1977, 1995 by The Lockman Foundation. Used by permission.
NCV—Scriptures quoted from *The Holy Bible, New Century Version,* copyright © 1987, 1988,
1991 by Word Publishing, Nashville, Tennessee. Used by permission.
NKJV—Scripture taken from the *New King James Version.* Copyright © 1979, 1980, 1982 by
Thomas Nelson, Inc. Used by permission. All rights reserved.
NLT—Scripture quotations marked *NLT* are taken from the *Holy Bible, New Living Translation,*
copyright © 1996. Used by permission of Tyndale House Publishers, Inc.,
Wheaton, Illinois 60189. All rights reserved.
TLB—Scripture quotations marked (*TLB*) are taken from *The Living Bible,* copyright © 1971.
Used by permission of Tyndale House Publishers, Inc., Wheaton, IL 60189. All rights reserved.

© 2010 Gary Smalley and Greg Smalley.
All rights reserved.

Library of Congress Cataloging-in-Publication Data
Smalley, Gary.
The heart of remarriage / Gary Smalley, Greg Smalley.
p. cm.
ISBN 978-0-8307-4677-4 (hardcover)
1. Remarried people—Religious life. 2. Remarriage—Religious aspects—
Christianity. I. Smalley, Greg. II. Title.
BV4596.R45S52 2010
248.8'44—dc22
2010008360

1 2 3 4 5 6 7 8 9 10 11 12 13 / 20 19 18 17 16 15 14 13 12 11 10

Rights for publishing this book outside the U.S.A. or in non-English languages are
administered by Gospel Light Worldwide, an international not-for-profit ministry.
For additional information, please visit www.glww.org, email info@glww.org, or write to
Gospel Light Worldwide, 1957 Eastman Avenue, Ventura, CA 93003, U.S.A.

To order copies of this book and other Regal products in bulk quantities,
please contact us at 1-800-446-7735.

Gary Smalley:
*To my faithful assistant, Sue Parks, who has helped in writing
this book with her many life stories and discerning insight.*

Greg Smalley:
*I dedicate this book to my wife, Erin. Thank you for loving me deeply from
your heart. I could not have written this book without your encouragement,
support and sacrifice. You are my best friend and the love of my life.
Also, to our four children: Taylor, Maddy, Garrison and Annie.*

Dan and Marci Cretsinger:
*To our dear friend Doris Haynes. We are ever grateful for her friendship.
She saw something in us that we thought had died, and God used her to pull us out
of the pit of guilt and help us forgive ourselves and move forward in faith and love.
She has been with us through many rough times, always there to encourage and
remind us of God's great promises to His children. She has inspired us, prayed for
us and counseled us, and we have healed and grown in our marriage and our faith.
Thank you, Doris. Thank you, Beth Moore, who wrote* When Godly People Do
Ungodly Things. *This book was a great tool in healing us. And to our children,
whom we love so dearly: Rachel, Michael, John, Dana and Sam.
Thank you for your forgiveness and love.*

Contents

Introduction: The Heart of Remarriage 7

Part One: Heart Matters

1. Remarriage: It Starts with Your Heart.................................17
2. Battered Hearts Need Safety 34
3. Healing Your Own Heart First 47
4. Beliefs That Build a Satisfied Heart in Remarriage 71
5. Keeping Each Other's Hearts Safe.....................................87
6. Preparing Hearts for Remarriage 107

Part Two: Roles in Remarriage

7. The Heart of a Remarried Husband 123
8. The Heart of a Remarried Wife.....................................141
9. The Heart of a Remarried Dad and Stepdad....................154
10. The Heart of a Remarried Mom and Stepmom 180
11. The Hearts of Children and Stepchildren in Remarriage 198
12. Open Hearts Toward Former Spouses............................217

Part Three: Heart Changers

13. Heart Checkups...230

Acknowledgments 252
About the Authors...253

The Heart of Remarriage

When Matt and Mandy decided to get married, they vowed to do it right. They would love each other till death parted them, and get married in their church in a ceremony witnessed by friends and family. Excitedly, the couple booked their wedding date in the chapel and planned their reception. Mandy bought a beautiful wedding gown, and the pair picked out rings. They lined up their premarital counseling appointments and showed up a few minutes early for the first session, eager to hear the words of wisdom their pastor would impart for their blessed union.

They entered the pastor's office, where the men shook hands and clapped each other lightly on the back, and Mandy gave the pastor a light hug. Then the couple sat down in chairs across from this man they respected—and waited.

Suddenly, the atmosphere turned slightly awkward. The pastor cleared his throat, obviously trying to find the right words. Matt and Mandy looked at each other anxiously. You see, Matt and Mandy were each getting married for the second time. She wasn't the young first-time bride, but a divorcée with an ex-husband living two states away and two small children. Matt had a former wife who now attended church across town, and three kids who went back and forth between mom and dad. The comfortable, wood-paneled church office suddenly began to feel stifling.

This scenario, or something like it, happens in churches every day. Well-meaning couples who have experienced the pain of leaving a marriage or losing a spouse through death or divorce want to get married for the second (or more) time, and well-meaning, caring pastors and ministers feel uneasy or don't have the right tools to counsel them on how to do it. Couples on the brink of remarriage desperately need wisdom, and their damaged hearts long for a blessing. They've heard the warnings of family and friends. They already know the odds against a second marriage making it. They live daily with the pain of "friends" who gossip, judge or simply no longer invite them over since their marriage ended.

Still, Christian couples who believe that God has offered them a new chance at love for a lifetime make joyful plans for remarriage. They want to build a family that will honor God, and they desire to be used by Him as a living picture of redemption. They need acceptance and solid advice, and they turn to their churches to receive it.

Often, the pastor isn't sure how to give it—the advice or the blessing. After all, praising the two for remaining sexually pure before the union doesn't exactly fit, and talking about how the marriage will change when children enter the picture usually doesn't apply. (Been there, done that.) Finances are muddied with child support coming and going, and simple suggestions for better communication hardly cover the sticky circumstances remarried couples will face, with former spouses who create chaos and children who may hate their stepparent. Plus, most loving pastors have counseled hundreds of marriages in trouble and watched remarriages fall apart right and left. They feel torn between hoping this union will last for the sake of all the kids involved and wanting to say, "Are you *sure* you want to do this?" (the polite version of shouting, "Run for the hills!"). They want to provide wisdom but aren't sure what are the right words to say.

When premarital sessions are over, couples smile and shake hands with their pastor again, but the smiles are now strained, and all feel relieved to be parting. The three may engage in a few more of these stilted conversations before the wedding, most likely never getting past the past and on to issues of the heart that could bring healing. Instead of getting a good start for a healthy remarriage, couples often feel guilty or frustrated at the lack of empathy and understanding. And pastors and lay pastors who care about these couples and want to marry them with a blessing may feel like they have failed to give hope, wisdom and solid resources to give remarriages a great start.

That's why we wrote *The Heart of Remarriage*. This book has a multifold purpose: to teach loving couples how to heal their own hearts from trauma associated with the death or divorce from a spouse; to give already remarried couples practical tools for keeping their hearts open to each other along this complicated journey; and to provide heart insight to loving pastors, lay pastors, counselors and even small-group leaders who want to give advice filled with God's wisdom that will help remarrying couples make it not only to the altar, but also through a fulfilling marriage that lasts the rest of their lives.

No Apologies Necessary

We believe that there is no need for Christians who have divorced or lost a spouse, or remarried after that loss, to feel like they need to apologize. Yes, the Bible says God hates divorce. But it also says He despises lies, and He isn't too pleased with envy, disobedience or rebellion either. Sin is sin, and when divorced people face judgment from their fellow Christians, or when pastors don't have the right words to minister to two wounded people now coming together in remarriage, hearts that need to heal can become hardened.

When did we forget that Romans 3:23 says, "for *all* have sinned and fall short of the glory of God" (emphasis added)? Traditional family members' sins are just as real as the sins of those in second marriages and blended families.

In *Divorce and Remarriage: A Redemptive Theology*, author Rubel Shelly puts it this way:

> Divorce is offensive to God, yet pardonable like any other sin. In many cases, divorce is indefensible, bringing serious consequences to adults and children. It should not be taken lightly. Yet to deny someone full forgiveness and the right to live life to the fullest in Jesus Christ denies the healing power of the Cross. God brings light out of darkness. His redemptive work in the lives of imperfect people restores the hearts of men and women and turns them back toward him. His grace forgives and transforms.[1]

Isn't that wonderful? God's grace forgives and transforms you, just as it does anyone who accepts salvation through Jesus Christ. Through Christ's sacrifice on the cross and our acceptance of that gift, God's grace redeems imperfect people, whether they are widows, pastors, divorced men, counselors, ex-wives or remarried husbands, so that we all have a "hope and a future" in Christ (Jer. 29:11).

Helping Hardened Hearts Heal

We wrote this book because we want hardened hearts to heal. We want remarriages to get off to a healthy start and spouses' hearts to stay open to each other, to their children and stepchildren, to their extended families and to their Christian friends and church family. We want pastors and small-group leaders to have the right words to help hearts heal and new families form. We know that God has a plan for every remarriage between two people who love Him and want to live called according to His purpose (see Rom. 8:28). As authors of many books on relationships and leaders of thousands of marriage workshops, we (Drs. Gary and Greg Smalley) will share our personal stories of watching people heal after divorce or the death of a spouse. We will give you practical tools for harnessing hope and seeing your remarriage flourish.

We have also partnered in the writing of this book with Dan and Marci Cretsinger, a remarried couple approaching their 15-year-marriage mark. Dan and Marci got their first marriages and divorces all wrong; yet today they are a picture of God's grace and redemption. They freely admit to the shame, guilt and serious consequences they and their families experienced after they left their first marriages for each other. However, they also stand as an example of hope and restoration in Christ. Their remarriage is a beautiful picture of what God can do with broken, sinful hearts and lives when they open fully to Him.

Heart Exams

The Heart of Remarriage is designed first and foremost to help couples examine their hearts, so that they can learn to open them fully and embrace the intimacy and wonder that remarriage can bring. Second, the content of this book is created to be a much-needed and overdue resource that church leaders and pastors can use to help remarrying couples work through their heart issues before they become heart blockages that keep their marriage from thriving. While many couples remarry with children still at home, and the challenges that come with forming a stepfamily are many, we won't focus this book on surface solutions. We believe that most relationship problems stem from clogged, closed hearts. If spouses in remarriage learn to open their hearts and let love flow, many stepfamily problems will be solved.

This book will show what closed hearts look like and what open hearts look like, how spouses can transform their beliefs and hearts with the Word of God, how broken hearts can be healed and how remarried couples can find true intimacy. It will then take a look at what open, loving hearts look like in the roles of remarried husband and remarried wife. Finally, we will shine a spotlight on how these united, open hearts can work together in the roles of mom, dad, stepmom, stepdad and even with their former spouses.

In short, *The Heart of Remarriage* will help you understand why you, your family or your congregants feel like you do, act like you do and react like you do in remarriage, and how these patterns are tied to old wounds and emotional habits. Plus, we'll give you ways to understand motivations, personalities and gifting, while meshing those with the unique motivations, personalities and gifting of each member in a remarried family.

We hope this book gives you and your family so much encouragement and so many practical tools that the pages become dog-eared from reading it time and again. We want your marriage not only to succeed but to thrive and to be a picture of God's grace and redemption. We know it can be all that!

As Natalie Nichols Gillespie, a mom and stepmom of nine, wrote in *Stepfamily Success*:

> Being part of this unique kind of family situation is a tremendous gift, privilege, and blessing. Don't let anybody tell you otherwise. . . . It has opened my eyes to more lessons about grace, mercy, and true love than I ever dreamed possible. . . . Yes, the pressure can be enormous, but that same pressure can mold your stepfamily into a new creation, one that glorifies Christ and loves one another.[2]

To the pastors and ministers who care deeply for the remarrying couples all around you, we want to encourage you too. We want to provide some valuable insight into the challenging landscape of remarriage so that you can help the members of your congregation who are taking that journey. We commend you for picking up this book. We appreciate your open heart for those who love Him and feel called to move beyond their past and create a new marriage. We are grateful that you will help get these marriages off to a great start and that you have a heart to see each member of your congregation fully healed and plugged into the Body of Christ.

We believe that God forgives everyone who comes to Him. He forgives the imperfect people in remarriages just as He does the imperfect people in first-time marriages. Ron Deal sums it up perfectly:

> Remarriage ministry does not diminish God's intent for the home any more than a ministry to alcoholics encourages drinking.

Remarriage ministry simply responds to broken lives, as Jesus did to the woman at the well (John 4), with grace and compassion. In addition, it calls couples to honor their remarital covenant and to live holy lives starting from today. It also equips them to do so, thereby preventing further divorces, building stronger families, and stopping the generational cycle of divorce.[3]

Collective Wisdom

Before writing this book, we surveyed hundreds of remarried couples regarding the most critical issues they faced, and the collective wisdom of these couples will allow you to acquire crucial knowledge and skills from those who have been through the same circumstances. It's like getting knowledge handed down by generations of scholars. We are going to give you advice from people like Dan and Marci, who have learned how to have a *great* remarriage and stepfamily. It's like getting tomorrow's newspaper today and being able to avoid the stock market crash or to cash in on the profits because you already know whether it will close up or down.

Furthermore, for years, we Smalleys have worked with couples in crisis that came to us in a last-ditch effort to save their rocky marriage. We achieved a lot of success with these at-risk couples by doing just one thing: bringing some safety into their marriage relationship. By the time they came to us, their hearts had totally closed to each other. And do you know the only way to get two closed hearts to open? They must begin to feel safe. So everything we did was designed to help these people feel safe again so that their hearts would once more open to each other.

You can benefit tremendously from their difficult learning curve. If you learn *now* how to make your hearts safe, you can build a rock-solid marriage that will bless you and others for generations. Open hearts are the key, and everything we offer in this book is designed to help your stepfamily feel just a little bit safer so that your hearts will stay open to each other, whatever circumstances come your way.

In each chapter, you'll find the following:

- **Heart Monitors:** Questions to ask yourself, your spouse and other members of your family. These questions also work well for spiritual leaders to pose to couples in small groups and counseling settings.

- **Heart Protectors:** Questions at the end of each chapter designed to help a couple think about the state of their own and each other's heart, and to promote dialogue so they can understand and prepare for the "heart attacks" they may face.

- **Heart Healers:** Actions that can be taken to heal a heart after conflict or from past emotional wounds.

Are you ready to tear down the walls, open the door to your heart and watch the healing and love flow? That is exactly where we want to begin our journey together. Let's get right to the heart of remarriage, so that you can learn how to make your marriage feel like the safest place on earth.
Enjoy the adventure!

Gary and Greg Smalley and
Dan and Marci Cretsinger

Notes

1. Rubel Shelly, *Divorce and Remarriage: A Redemptive Theology* (Abilene, TX: Leafwood Publishing, 2007), p. 37.
2. Natalie Nichols Gillespie, *Stepfamily Success* (Grand Rapids, MI: Baker Publishing Group, 2007), p. 51.
3. Ron L. Deal, "Redeeming the Remarried," *Christianity Today*, October 2007, p. 3.

PART ONE

HEART MATTERS

Remarriage: It Starts with Your Heart

A heart at peace gives life to the body.
PROVERBS 14:30

In our (Drs. Greg and Gary Smalley) years of counseling couples and holding marriage workshops, we have interacted with hundreds of husbands and wives who were absolutely convinced that nothing could make their marriage better. They swore they had tried everything to fix it, but nothing worked. There was nothing else they could do. They were angry, despairing, bitter and weary. They just wanted to be *done*.

Is that where you are in your remarriage or stepfamily? Have you been struggling to feel accepted and loved? Do you feel hopeless about getting your spouse and children on the same page, or trapped in the losses of your past, or mired in anger and bitterness over the way you or your kids are being treated? Maybe you picked up this book because you are thinking about remarrying or marrying someone who has been married before, and you've heard the horror stories and warnings not to do it. Are you afraid of what remarriage will bring?

Our co-authors, Dan and Marci Cretsinger, came to the very brink of giving up on their remarriage, many times; but as they'll share in personal stories throughout this book, when they put into practice the truths we're going to share, they overcame the anger, jealousy, bitterness and estrangements that were tearing their marriage and stepfamily apart. Today, their marriage is stronger than ever. How did they do it? It started with their hearts.

What if we told you that we believe that love, satisfaction and joy in your remarriage are only a heartbeat away? Well, maybe not just one heartbeat, but it's absolutely true that the quality of your remarriage is all determined by the state of *your* heart. It's easy to blame your mate, your children or stepchildren or your previous spouse for all of your problems; but the truth is that the quality of your life and your relationships stems from your own heart.

Here's the key: If your heart has an OPEN sign in the window, you are overflowing with love. If painful relationship experiences have flipped that sign over to the CLOSED side, you're out of the love business. It's that simple.

In many a remarriage, a couple gets together thinking that their hearts are wide open to each other and will stay that way. In reality, their heart signs may say OPEN, but the doors are actually locked. When their dream of putting together a perfect stepfamily is quickly shattered, the fantasy bubble bursts, and 7 out of 10 stepfamilies pull apart.[1]

You can be the one to beat the odds. We know you can. If you learn the importance of the state of your heart and how to open it and protect it so it can remain open, your remarriage can make it for a lifetime. Once you begin to understand the power of your heart, you can equip yourself with tools to harness painful or troublesome emotions and improve the level of peace, joy and satisfaction in your remarriage. You'll have the ability to better manage every remarriage challenge that comes your way.

Your Heart: The Vital Center of the Real You

Why is the heart so important? Because it is the part that connects us with a holy, living God. Several years ago, I (Greg) asked hundreds of married couples to define "heart." Here are some of my favorite responses:
The heart is . . .

- The wellspring of life
- A reflection of the true self
- The core of a person
- The deep center of our life
- The innermost part of the human personality
- Me
- The place we connect to God and others
- The essence of who we are
- The source of our real character

• The executive center of a human life. The heart is where decisions and choices are made for the whole person.[2]

This list makes it abundantly clear that nearly everyone instinctively recognizes that the heart is the fountain from which the true nature of a person flows. Several affirming statements are made in Scripture about the heart (emphasis added):

Above all else, guard your heart, for it is the *wellspring of life* (Prov. 4:23).

For out of the *overflow of the heart* the mouth speaks (Matt. 12:34).

A good man out of the *good treasure of his heart* brings forth good things, and an evil man out of the evil treasure brings forth evil things (Matt. 12:35, *NKJV*).

But what *is* the heart? Our favorite definition of the heart is *the vital center of the real you*. Another way to look at the heart is through the analogy of the "Holy of Holies." In the Old Testament tabernacle, there was an inner room called the Holy of Holies, or the Most Holy Place. It was God's special dwelling place in the midst of His people, a place that no ordinary person could enter. In fact, anyone who entered the Holy of Holies, except for the high priest, would die. And even the high priest, God's chosen mediator for His people, could only pass through the veil and enter it once a year, on a prescribed day called the Day of Atonement. And the high priest had to undertake some meticulous preparations: He had to wash himself, put on special clothing, bring burning incense to let the smoke cover his eyes from a direct view of God, and bring blood with him to make atonement for sins.[3]

It has been said that a rope was even tied around the priest's ankle before he went behind the veil, so that his body could be dragged out if God struck him down because something was not done properly. This is how sacred and precious the Holy of Holies was.

Our hearts are just as sacred. For those who have accepted Christ, our hearts are now the inner dwelling place of the most holy God. They are just as precious as the Holy of Holies, but how many of us treat our hearts that carefully? Many of us ignore, reject, abandon, judge and abuse our hearts. We are careless with the most valuable part of who we are.

You may be wondering how all of us missed this message of the importance of the heart. Why don't we spend more time at church, in marriage books or at marriage conferences talking about our hearts? For years at the Smalley marriage seminars we've conducted, we've asked the men to raise their hands if they grew up in a home in which their dad or significant male role model taught them how important the care of their hearts are in life and in their relationships. Never have we had a number greater than 2 percent to 3 percent of the hands go up. Then we ask the women to raise their hands if their moms or significant female role models taught them about their hearts and showed them how to take great care of them. Again, never more than a few percent of the women raise their hands.

The fact that our hearts are so important seems like such a simple truth, and it's true that the evidence is all around us. Yet somehow, most of us have missed this. What's going on here? I think John Eldredge, bestselling author of *Waking the Dead,* summed it up well:

> The enemy knows how vital the heart is, even if we do not, and all his forces are fixed upon its destruction. For if he can disable or deaden your heart, then he has effectively foiled the plan of God, which was to create a world where love reigns. By taking out your heart, the Enemy takes out you, and you are essential to the Story. Once you begin to see with the eyes of your heart, once you have begun to know it is true from the bottom of your heart, it will change everything. The story of your life is the story of the long and brutal assault on your heart by the one who knows what you and your marriage could be and fears it.[4]

Now do you see how the evil one wants nothing more than to keep your heart closed to God and to others—especially to your spouse? But once you learn to unlock the door of your heart and throw it wide open to God's love, your life and your remarriage can be radically transformed.

King Solomon gives us the first key we need to unlock the power of our heart. Solomon is universally considered to be the wisest man who ever lived. During his reign as king of Israel, God blessed him with a great amount of wisdom and wealth. Solomon wrote the book of Proverbs, which contains hundreds of pieces of wisdom that are still effective today. Some of the most fascinating proverbs King Solomon offered were about the heart. Consider Proverbs 14:30, "A heart at peace gives life to the body," or Proverbs 20:5, "The purposes of a man's heart are deep waters, but a man of understanding draws them out."

When the wisest man who ever lived tells you that something will give you life or instructs you to do something "above all else," those words are probably principles that you should pay close attention to. But why did Solomon focus so much on the heart? What does the state of the heart have to do with remarriage? In a word, *everything*.

To understand where Solomon was coming from, you need to understand what a wellspring is. A wellspring is a fountain or spring of water that never ends. It is a source of continual supply of a life-giving substance. King Solomon is saying that our hearts are a never-ending supply of something extremely important—something that gives us life.

What does your heart supply? Let us show you through a story about Greg's little girl on her first day of kindergarten.

The State of Your Heart

My daughter Taylor's first day of kindergarten was one I will never forget. My wife, Erin, and I stood on the corner of our street, waving as the school bus drove off with our little girl. Erin was weeping, and I had to get her into the house before the neighbors started to think I was doing something horrible to her. At the end of the school day, I went outside to welcome Taylor home from her first day of school. I was standing on the front porch waiting for my precious daughter when I saw the bus pull up. I couldn't wait to hear all about her first day. When the bus finally stopped, and all the kids jumped out, I was shocked by what I saw. Taylor exited the bus holding hands with a boy! I'm sure my jaw hit the ground, because I think I choked on a bug. I couldn't believe it. My little girl was holding hands with a boy. A BOY!

Instead of reacting, I gave Taylor the benefit of the doubt. *It must be a bus buddy assigned by the driver*, I reasoned.

But as the other kids dispersed, not only did Taylor keep holding this kid's hand, but also she began running up the sidewalk, right toward me. Suddenly, my five-year-old daughter yelled out, "Hi, Dad! This is Hank. We're in love, and we're going to get married!"

And with that bit of good news, I think I started to gag. At least, that's what it sounded like. After regaining my composure, and with the prematurely premarital couple standing before me, I decided to have a little bit of fun with them.

"So, you guys are in love?" I asked.

"Uh-huh," Taylor affirmed.

"And you're going to get married?" I queried.

"Uh-huh," they both agreed, nodding their heads.

"Being five and all," I said, holding back a smile, "where will you guys live?"

They looked at me, back to each other and shrugged their shoulders. Taylor dragged Hank to the side of the porch so they could huddle up and discuss my question. I could barely make out what they were saying. Then they both turned, and Taylor said, "Dad, if it's okay with you and Mom, Hank and I would like to live out in the backyard in the Little Tikes house [one of those plastic playhouses for preschoolers]."

"Sure," I said, and grinned, "Mom will love having you so close. We can visit any time we want [like real in-laws do]. Although you'll have a sweet place to live, you will need stuff to go into your house. I'd like to get you something special. We'll call it a housewarming gift. What kind of stuff will you need to survive our cold Missouri winters?"

Once again they looked at me, back to each other, shrugged their shoulders and this time walked to the side of the porch together. As I watched them confer, I realized that it wasn't a good sign when your five-year-old and her "fiancé" solve problems better than you and your wife do. (But that's a whole different book!)

When they finished, my future son-in-law stepped up and said, "We decided that we need three things."

Wow, I thought, *they've simplified their lives to three things.* "All right, lay them on me."

Hank stood straight and looked me in the eyes and said, "We need the TV and the remote [that only counted as one thing, apparently], a roll of toilet paper and a box of Lucky Charms."

As I thought about Hank's requests, I realized they made perfect sense. As a guy, I could live for months (well, until the Lucky Charms ran out) off those three things alone. So I high-fived him and welcomed him into the family. Over the next several weeks it felt very strange to watch how my little girl related to Hank. Actually, it was kind of creepy how they always seemed to be together, laughing and playing.

And then it happened.

I returned home from work one evening to find Taylor weeping in her room. I quickly discovered that Hank had broken up with her. The engagement was officially off.

After I silently looked up to the heavens and gave thanks, I comforted my daughter. I'll never forget what she said. As my precious Taylor lay on my arm, she looked up at me and cried, "Daddy, I loved him so much. [I'm not sure, but I may have gagged again.] But he hurt me so bad. I hate him now, and I want him to die!" (In case you were wondering, she gets that from Erin's side of the family.)

I've often thought about that moment and the passion that infused what Taylor said. Not so much because I fear for my own safety if she gets mad at me, but because it's the same thing that I've watched adult couples go through.

Isn't it interesting that earlier that very same day, Taylor was in love with Hank (as much as a five-year-old girl can be)? But once she was hurt, she definitely did not feel that love for him anymore. Now she wanted him dead. What happened to Taylor in those 12 hours? The same thing that happens to couples all around the world when they go through marriage problems and no longer feel love toward each other: *Taylor's heart slammed shut against Hank. In fact, if it could have slammed shut on his head, it would have.* That's it. That's the problem. A closed heart.

Closed Hearts

Most married couples just assume they will always be "in love" with each other. But those whose marriages end in divorce learn that their assumption was wrong. Painfully, excruciatingly wrong. Not many divorced people go into marriage the first time expecting it to be perfect, but they probably didn't think there would come a time when they felt no love at all for their spouse. It's like the Righteous Brothers' song, "You've Lost That Loving Feeling." They went into marriage with open, loving hearts; but one day, usually after months or years of heart-hardening events, the door of one heart or both spouses' hearts slammed shut. *Wham!* Every loving feeling was gone. Just like Taylor's experience, the emotional wounds they experienced cut off their love supply. Their hurts clogged their hearts.

There may have come a day in your previous marriage when you realized that you no longer loved your spouse. Maybe it was your former spouse who said the terrible words: *I don't love you anymore.*

There are hours, days and even years when couples lose that loving feeling—they don't feel any love at all toward their spouse. The difficulty is the confusion this produces: *Does the absence of the feeling of love mean that something is wrong with me? Is it my spouse? Perhaps the problem is our marriage? Maybe we weren't supposed to be married. Maybe he isn't my soul mate. Maybe there is some other person roaming the world, looking for me, but now I'm not available!* Sounds crazy, huh?

In every couple's relationship, there will be times (even for the briefest moments) when partners do not feel love for each other. In remarriage, the trick is not to let those moments convince you that you've made a huge mistake. There will be moments, even seasons, when emotions don't match the words in those wedding vows. Perhaps you feel that way right now. Everyone experiences lonely, empty feelings at one time or another in marriage. What needs to happen in those times is that couples consciously work toward bringing back the loving feelings. As a matter of fact, this is the most common question we hear from couples who come to us for marriage counseling: *Can you help us feel in love again?* The question can take many forms and slight variations:

- *Is it possible to awaken feelings of love for my husband in my heart?*
- *Can you help me feel love again for my wife?*
- *How can I restore the love in my marriage?*
- *Is it too late to rekindle our love?*
- *How can I bring healing and restoration of love and trust to my marriage?*
- *Can I ever love her again?*
- *Is it possible to rediscover the passion we once had for each other?*
- *Can you help me feel like something besides his roommate?*

In the end, every couple is asking for the same miracle: *Help us find that loving feeling again!* And guess what? In our work with couples, when we hear, *I don't feel love for my spouse anymore,* we just blow right by it.

You're probably thinking, *What? How can you simply let that go? Isn't feeling out of love with your spouse a huge problem?* Not really. It's not that we ignore the fact that someone does not feel "love" for his or her spouse. Instead, we know from experience that they are expressing the symptom, not the root issue. We know that they need to shift paradigms (or look at their situation differently). Instead of discussing their feelings of love, or lack thereof, we usually ask them something that really gets them thinking. We ask, *Where does love come from?*

When you look at love from that perspective, feelings are taken out of the spotlight. Love is not about chemistry or magic. Humans cannot generate love. A person's inability to create feelings of love for a spouse is not a sign that something is wrong with either person or with the marriage. It doesn't mean that the mate is unlovable, that the marriage is broken or that the spouse isn't their "soul mate." (In fact, we hate that term!) It is simply the reality that no love originates from humans. But very few of us are taught that freeing truth.

Cut out colored paper hearts and write a Scripture on each one that speaks about the heart. Post the hearts on a bathroom mirror, your computer monitor and other conspicuous places around your home.

God is the author, creator and generator of love. Love comes from God, and God is love (see 1 John 4:7-8). As a matter of fact, the only reason we can love at all is because He first poured His love into us (see 1 John 4:19). The point is that none of the love we talk about, write about and sing about comes from us. We do not create a single drop of love. It all comes from God.

By design, here is how the cycle of love works: When we open our hearts to God, we receive His love. He then fills our hearts abundantly full of His love (see Rom. 5:5). Once our hearts are full of God's love, we then can open our hearts and share love with others.

The Cycle of Love

We open our hearts to God   God fills our hearts with love   We share love with others

God's love feels good to me, and I am a conduit to pass it on to others. When I engage God and my spouse with an open heart, the flow of love is full and complete. God's love is the never-ending supply that flows through our hearts as a "wellspring." This is how we can live out the greatest commandment to "love God with all our *heart*, soul, mind and strength, and love others as we love ourselves" (our paraphrase of Mark 12:30-31). The key is to understand that the ultimate source of love is from God. We cannot even love God until He fills our hearts with His love. The condition for loving others is to first experience God's own love. Listen to 1 John 4:7-19:

> Dear friends, let us love one another, for love comes from God. Everyone who loves has been born of God and knows God. Whoever does not love does not know God, because God is love. This is how God showed his love among us: He sent his one and only Son into the world that we might live through him. This is love: not that we loved God, but that he loved us and sent his Son as an atoning sacrifice for our sins. Dear friends, since God so loved us, we also ought to love one another. No one has ever seen God; but if we love one another, God lives in us, and his love is made complete in us.
>
> We know that we live in him and he in us, because he has given us of his Spirit. And we have seen and testify that the Father has sent his Son to be the Savior of the world. If anyone acknowledges that Jesus is the Son of God, God lives in him and he in God. And so we know and rely on the love God has for us.
>
> God is love. Whoever lives in love lives in God, and God in him. In this way, love is made complete among us so that we will have confidence on the day of judgment, because in this world we are like him. There is no fear in love, but perfect love drives out fear, because fear has to do with punishment. The one who fears is not made perfect in love. We love because he first loved us.

The bottom line is that when people say they no longer feel love for their spouse, the problem isn't a lack of love. God is love, and His love is always available (a never-ending wellspring). God's love is like air—it's all around us. God's love flows through us when we open our hearts. When couples think they've "lost that loving feeling," we assume that they have closed the door to their hearts. But most people don't know this, so they often give up on the marriage. Dan and Marci did. They gave up on their 20-plus-year first marriages and divorced their spouses for each other. They thought love was the "feelings" they experienced together of being understood—feelings of chemistry and open communication.

"I was a Christian and had worked in women's ministry and led Bible studies for years," Marci shares. "But I felt that I was trapped in a loveless, hopeless marriage. We didn't know how to open our hearts to each other. Our communication was only on the surface because we had erected emotional walls around our hearts as protection. These walls had been constructed from years of misunderstanding, unforgiveness, passivity and sarcasm. I felt helpless, and he did too, because no matter what we tried—counseling, marriage seminars, books—the right tools weren't there. We spent years living more as roommates than as a married couple. We weren't even intimate for the last seven years."

 Make a compilation disc of (or download to your iPod) your favorite love songs (happy ones, not break-up songs!) and worship tunes. Turn on the music while you make dinner, run errands or work out.

At that time, Marci's heart was so boarded up and closed off to her husband that she could barely feel love at all, only frustration and hopelessness. This is an extremely dangerous place to be in a marriage; it's the time to be most aware that the devil desires to bring total destruction. What Marci and her husband did not realize is that people are not the creators of love. God is love. We'll say it again: *No love comes from us. We love because God first loved us.* Unfortunately, Marci and her first husband aren't the only ones who have experienced this shutdown without the revelation that might have reopened their hearts. Most couples don't understand it. All you have to do is look at the reasons for divorce that people usually cite:

- We're not compatible.
- Our differences are killing us.
- He had an affair.
- She has too many unrealistic expectations.
- We fight and argue constantly.
- We have nothing in common.
- I can't stand his personality quirks.
- We rarely have sex.
- All he does is work.
- We have no money.
- I feel like I'm living with a roommate.
- I finally found my "soul mate" (and it's not my spouse).
- Her parents are driving me crazy.

Certainly these types of circumstances strain marriages, but we assert that these are secondary problems. The real issue is that hearts have closed to each other. Let us say it one more time: The real issue isn't "love"; it's the state of the heart.

Is there an OPEN or CLOSED sign hanging in your heart's window?

This is the common thread in the marriages of nearly every hurting couple we've worked with—a shut-down heart. A heart completely disconnected from the heart of his or her spouse. People often use other words to describe a dead heart: detached, indifferent, numb, lifeless, heartless, lonely, emotionally unavailable, hard-hearted.

It's like something Tin Woodman said in L. Frank Baum's classic novel *The Wonderful Wizard of Oz:*

> It was a terrible thing to undergo, but during the year I stood there I had time to think that the greatest loss I had known was the loss of my heart. While I was in love, I was the happiest man on earth; but no one can love who has not a heart, and so I am resolved to ask Oz to give me one.[5]

Herein lies the real problem. When our hearts shut down (especially to our spouse), then God's love is no longer flowing through us. This is why someone says he or she doesn't feel "in love." If your heart is closed, then you have shut out God's love. You can't feel love, because the floodgate is locked down tight. This is what is actually happening when people do not "feel" love, especially in marriage. They have simply closed their hearts to their mates. Jesus said, "Moses permitted you to divorce your wives because your *hearts were hard.* But it was not this way from the beginning" (Matt. 19:8, emphasis added).

Watch The Wizard of Oz *and listen for the Tin Man's words about the heart. Talk to each other about the state of your heart. When has it felt the most open? When did it feel the most closed? Invite discussion about what not having a heart (or having a closed heart) feels like.*

Recognizing this truth can be extremely freeing. Instead of putting your efforts and energies into doing something you have zero ability to do (create love), now you only need to focus on the condition of your heart. Is it opened or closed? If you put a lid on the top of your heart, you shut yourself off from God as well. When your heart is closed, you don't get filled up with God's love; therefore, you don't have anything to give out. You can't love God, yourself or others.

Obviously, God will continue to love you and others, because He doesn't need us to fulfill His promises. But He wants us to be a part of the process. He invites each of us to connect to Him with an open heart so that we can reap the benefits when He uses us to love others. When you open the flood-gates of your heart for His love to pour through, you receive things like patience, kindness, encouragement, humility, politeness, selflessness, self-control, forgiveness, rejoicing with the truth, protection, trust, hope and perseverance (see 1 Cor. 13:4-7).

While no human being can manufacture any love, the good news is that we can choose the state of our hearts. God created us with the capacity to choose to open our hearts to Him—and to others. We can't always choose our relationships—we didn't choose our parents or siblings or children—but we *can* choose who we open and close our hearts to. First and foremost, we get to choose whether or not we want to open our heart to a relationship with Christ. "Here I am! I stand at the door and knock. If anyone hears my voice and opens the door, I will come in and eat with him, and he with me" (Rev. 3:20).

What "door" is He knocking on? He's knocking on the door of your heart. Christ is a gentleman. He doesn't break down the door; instead, He knocks and waits patiently. You choose whether or not to open the door, and you choose when you slam it shut. No one closes your heart down.

People do things that hurt us, and we sometimes react by shutting down. But it's still our choice. That's great news. It's our choice. It's *your* choice.

What does a closed heart look like? Signs of a closed heart include these characteristics:

- Distance or unavailability (emotional wall)
- Apathy or lack of interest
- Numbness, lethargy or lifelessness
- Selfishness or self-centeredness
- Insensitivity or being uncaring (heartless)
- Harshness, meanness or cruelty

If your heart is closed right now, that's okay. We're not here to force you to open your heart to anyone. If your heart is closed, we're sure it's closed for good reasons. Instead, we just want you to move forward with an understanding of the truth about love and the way it works. We want you to embrace what is really going on, to recognize that if you have a hard time "feeling" love, your heart may be closed to some degree. In the end, if you desire intimacy in your remarriage, it requires an open heart. We want to explore with you exactly what it takes to have a heart that is fully open and available to God and others (especially to your spouse), and we'll provide the tools you need to get there.

An Open Heart

By now, it should be clear that one of the greatest truths about relationships is that in order for you to get exactly what you most desire within your remarriage—intimacy, deep connection, emotional closeness, understanding, empathy, kindness, appreciation, love, affection, encouragement, care, tenderness, passion, adventure, and so on—your heart *must* have the OPEN sign hanging in the window.

 Imagine your heart with a CLOSED sign hanging across it. Now picture a hand turning the sign over to the OPEN side.

This is why the apostle Peter urged, "Love one another deeply, from the heart" (1 Pet. 1:22), and the apostle Paul encouraged the new Christians in Corinth, "We have spoken freely to you, Corinthians, and *opened wide our hearts to you*. We are not withholding our affection from you, but you are withholding yours from us. As a fair exchange—I speak as to my children—*open wide your hearts also*" (2 Cor. 6:11-13, emphasis added).

Open wide your heart and love deeply from the heart. That's wonderful advice from two of our greatest spiritual fathers.

Signs of an open heart include:

• Connectedness or involvement
• Interest, focus or attentiveness
• Energy, passion or being full of life

- Unselfishness, considerateness or thoughtfulness
- Sensitivity, compassion, a caring attitude or empathy
- Gentleness, kindness or tenderness

That brings me back to my daughter Taylor. Even at five years old, she allowed the door of her heart to slam shut after it was hurt by Hank. In kindergarten, that might not seem like a big deal. In marriage, however, when two hearts shut down to each other, it can cause the death of a family. And when a marriage dies, no one wins except Satan.

Dan and Marci experienced that truth when they fell in love and left their first spouses for each other. Marci knew she was sinning, and she and her new husband, Dan, paid an excruciating price for their sin.

"Both Dan and I had spent years in what felt like loveless, empty marriages," Marci shares. "Still, I knew it was wrong. It was wrong to fall in love with Dan, but my heart was shut down to my first husband. I remember looking through a family photo album during the time when I knew I was falling in love with Dan and weeping over those family pictures, bitterly torn. I felt like I could not go on anymore if I had to face another 20 years in that hopeless marriage."

Marci left her husband, and Dan left his wife. The two married a short time after their divorces were final and spent the first seven years in remarriage experiencing the agony of the fallout.

"We lost everything," Dan says. "We lost our finances, our families, our children, our homes. Marci's church pastor and friends turned their backs on her. I became very angry and took it out on Marci. Our kids almost drove us apart. It was a terrible, terrible time."

"I wouldn't recommend it to anyone," Marci says. "The guilt was enormous. I thought of suicide all the time. I cried and had nightmares every day for the first seven years of my remarriage. I knew that divorcing my husband for another man was wrong, but I had no idea of the devastation it would cause."

When they strengthened their relationship with God and learned how to open their closed hearts to each other, Dan and Marci's marriage began to get better. God forgave their sins the moment they asked for His precious forgiveness. They were covered by His grace and mercy, but it still took a tremendous amount of time for their hearts to heal. A closed heart keeps God's most precious gift—His love—from flowing through us and into our most important relationships.

And now these three remain: faith, hope and love. But the greatest of these is love (1 Cor. 13:13).

Spouses must remember to guard their hearts, for hearts are the wellspring of life and love in remarriage. In the next chapter, we'll take a look at one vital element that remarried hearts require in order to keep their core connected to God and to each other.

HEART MONITORS

1. Take a few minutes to evaluate where your heart is in your remarriage. Is it shut down completely? Is it fully open? Is it closed to some members of your stepfamily but open to others? If so, why?

2. What does it take to keep your heart open?

3. What are three things that you think have caused you to shut the door to your heart?

4. Did your parents or significant parental role model raise you with the knowledge of how important the care and keeping of your heart is? If so, what protective measures did you take? If not, how do you feel about your heart after reading this chapter?

5. What are four of the Bible verses that talk about the heart? Which verse is your favorite, and why?

HEART PROTECTORS

If your hearts are not completely shut to one another, talk with your spouse about the importance of the heart, and then explain to your children and stepchildren what you have learned. Concentrate on learning together how to keep your hearts open to God's love so you can let it flow through you to others.

If the heart of your spouse or your own heart has been completely closed, begin to pray that God will show you ways to crack it open. Be patient!

List some of the hurts and fears that cause you to shut your heart against your spouse. Examine the list closely. Are any of your spouse's actions being done with malice, or does he or she just have some personal habits that annoy you? Sort out the deliberate injustices from the quirks, and try not to take the quirks so personally.

Notes

1. Ron L. Deal, "The Stepcouple Divorce Rate May Be Higher Than We Thought," Successful Stepfamilies: Christian Resources for Church and Home. http://www.successfulstepfamilies.com/view/176.

2. Dallas Willard, *Renovation of the Heart: Putting On the Character of Christ* (Colorado Spring, CO: NavPress, 2002), p. 30.

3. "The Holy of Holies and the Veil," The Tabernacle Place, 2006. http://www.the-tabernacle-place.com/tabernacle_articles/tabernacle_holy_of_holies.aspx.

4. John Eldredge, *Waking the Dead: The Glory of a Heart Fully Alive* (Nashville, TN: Thomas Nelson, 2006), pp. 34-39.

5. Frank L. Baum, *The Wonderful Wizard of Oz* (New York: HarperCollins Publishers, 2000).

2

Battered Hearts Need Safety

For we are God's [own] handiwork (His workmanship), recreated in Christ Jesus,
[born anew] that we may do those good works which God predestined (planned
beforehand) for us [taking paths which He prepared ahead of time], that we should
walk in them [living the good life which He prearranged and made ready for us to live].
EPHESIANS 2:10, *AMP*

For a remarried couple or a couple approaching remarriage, Ephesians 2:10 just rings with hope, doesn't it? Isn't that exactly what anyone would want—to put the troubles of the past behind so that one can do "good works" and live the "good life which He prearranged and made ready for us to live"? It can happen, but we believe it happens best only after people learn the secret of success in every relationship. We consider this the best-kept secret we have ever discovered to help us create genuine, loving relationships with our mate and family. The secret is this:

Hearts need safety in order to open.

That can be a tall order in remarriage. Hearts need safety to open, and hearts that have experienced loss, betrayal and pain feel anything but safe. We humans all bring wounded—or worse, closed—hearts full of emotional baggage into our relationships, and that causes trouble. The baggage can be especially heavy for those who have had a marriage end through death or, like Dan and Marci, through divorce. Picture an old suitcase with scrapes and tears in the fabric from years of misuse, clothes and toiletries poking out at odd angles. That's where many of our hearts are. There are bits of past relationships sticking out here, insults from childhood poking out there, and scrapes and tears all over the place.

See if you can relate to some of these statements by people who experienced the loss of a spouse to death or divorce:

He abandoned me. I don't know what to do with myself. I mourn deeply; I am hurt beyond words. I feel like I have died, for my old life is surely over now.

The entire picture of our future life, along with all the practical plans underway to enable and support that life, were suddenly derailed and empty.

I still feel it is my fault that he left. It still hurts today, big-time.

I'm still in shock. I'm not sure what is going to happen to me and who will take care of me.

I'm so worried about my ability to have a good relationship or successful marriage in the future.

During our separation and for a while after the divorce was final, I experienced so many frightening feelings of disorientation.

I couldn't even put my finger on the exact cause of why I felt so anxious. It felt like my brain was going to fly apart.

I experienced emptiness where there used to be love and laughter.

I felt lost and confused most, if not all, of the time. You feel crazy and stupid, and the worst part is that you think you may feel that way forever. At the same time, you're expected to hold a job, take care of the children, house, car and, possibly, your parents.

With that kind of raw pain, why would anyone want to remarry? Because hearts, even wounded and broken ones, were created to be loved. We long for acceptance, companionship and connection, because God designed us that way. But when battered hearts come together, they can remain partially closed, tentative about loving fully, afraid to expose themselves to the possibility of that intense pain again.

No matter what overall condition your heart is in, divorce or death has changed your life. It has changed you. It rocked your world and uprooted your security. To have a successful remarriage, you have to heal your heart.

The emotional foundation of your remarriage needs to be solid, with a firm sense of safety filling each member's heart chambers.

 Assure your spouse or spouse-to-be that your love and respect is unconditional and that you accept your spouse for who he or she is, who he or she was, and who he or she will be.

Loss, Pain and Change!

We often tell remarried couples that if we had only one hour to spend with them, we would use the entire time to talk about safety and open hearts—how to open your heart so that it's the safest place on earth for your spouse and kids to come home to. Why? Because the common denominator of an experience like divorce or the death of a spouse is *pain*—massive amounts of hurt, regret, sorrow, grief, anguish, agony, torture or any other variation of the word "pain." In addition to the loss and pain, you're also experiencing a massive amount of *change*. When you add emotional pain to change, it equates to feeling very unsafe. To understand what we're talking about, you merely have to think about the circumstances that were present when you got remarried and compare them to the events leading up to your first wedding day.

Remember back to your first marriage. After getting premarital counseling that actually seemed to fit, many couples experienced their dream wedding. They had looked forward to that special day for as far back as they could remember. Most were young (mid-twenties), blissfully in love, somewhat naïve, optimistic and idealistic. Everything felt perfect and wonderful, and nothing seemed impossible. In essence, most couples getting married for the first time believe they are participating in a very special relationship. Their enthusiasm and excitement about the relationship help couples resolve any reluctance about marriage. They were able to create such high expectations because they probably did these things:

- Ignored each other's flaws
- Believed that their spouse would make them whole and bring them true happiness
- Denied the possibility of any future conflicts or problems

- Placed each other on pedestals
- Gave unqualified attention and admiration to one another

Most people who are remarrying are a little more down-to-earth. They're not total relationship cynics or overly pessimistic about love, or they wouldn't dare head for the altar again. However, most couples are well aware that remarriage will introduce challenges that were not present in their first marriage, even if they aren't quite clear on what the biggest difficulties will be. For example:

- Remarried couples often feel reluctant and insecure.
- Remarried couples can feel inadequate and fear failing in another marriage.
- Remarried couples are often still dealing with strong emotions like resentment, jealousy and rejection.
- Society has a negative perception of remarriage. Newly formed families may feel inferior and often hide from the world.
- The family hierarchy is reversed, with the new spouse often lower on the hierarchy than the children.
- There are many loyalty conflicts.
- Roles in remarriage can be very confusing.

Phew! And remarried couples are supposed to hang on to the Ephesians promise of the "good life"? That can seem like a very tall order in the wake of challenges, losses and pain that create an environment in which everybody feels emotionally *unsafe*. And changes that produce insecurity inevitably lead to *conflict*. Let us reassure you of one thing right up front: *The presence of conflict in your remarriage is 100 percent natural and normal.* It is virtually impossible to avoid bumping into differences of opinions, beliefs and behaviors as you deal with all of the remarriage and stepfamily issues.

 The presence of conflict in your remarriage is 100 percent natural and normal.

As a remarried couple endures arguments, disagreements, fights, struggles or whatever you want to call them, their sense of being emotionally

unsafe heightens. And the real danger in not being prepared for all this conflict is that it leads to a divorce rate that is higher for second marriages than
for first marriages; and the highest of all for those remarriages that include
minor-age children. We don't want this to happen to you! And it doesn't
have to. In fact, we believe that Christian remarried couples and the church
bodies and leaders who love them can turn the tide of remarriage statistics.

We want stability and peace to reign supreme inside the walls of your
heart and your home. We want you—no, we *need* you, as a fellow member
of the Body of Christ—to be able to do the "good works" God has planned
for you. (After all, your good works might be directly beneficial for us, and
we don't want to miss out!) You can and will do those good works, if hearts
heal and remain tender and open. Again, we want your heart to be the
safest place on earth, so that you can be blessed by the benefits a healthy
marriage and family have to offer.

What? We can hear you thinking. *You're admitting that there are advan-
tages that can come with being part of a remarriage?*

Yes, absolutely.

There are incredible benefits that come with remarriage. This is part
of God's redemptive promise. Check out these six amazing benefits that remarried couples can experience:

1. Second marriages can be more fulfilling than first ones because individuals have the ability to learn from their past mistakes, are older, more experienced and better prepared. They
   don't want to fail again, so they try harder; and they are not as
   idealistic and unrealistic about what to expect.

2. Partners in remarriage often appreciate each other more, because they know what it has been like to be betrayed or bereft.
   They know how hard it is to go it alone after being married and
   are grateful for the new, committed relationship they've created.

3. Remarried couples can let go of the guilt, fears and stress associated with raising children in a single-parent home. A healthy
   remarriage can fulfill the deep emotional needs of children and
   adults as effectively as a healthy traditional family can—those
   needs to nurture one another by providing safe refuge, comfort, encouragement, companionship, loving confrontation,

affirmation, stimulation, affection, a sense of belonging, acceptance, laughter and unconditional love.

4. Remarriage provides the couple with physical, emotional, mental and spiritual intimacy and outlet. If the first marriage was
   riddled with conflict, then a healthy remarriage can help build
   new bridges of trust.

5. Remarriage gives single parents someone to share the work-
   load; the new spouse also can serve as a sounding board.

6. Remarriage creates a foundation for new friendships and ministry opportunities.[1]

Isn't it awesome what God can do through pain and brokenness? Now
add your own benefits to the list. What positives have been added to your
life since you became a couple? What benefits have your children received?
Pastors, what blessings do you see coming from the remarriages in your
church? The benefits can be big, but they are based on one condition: Remarriages must be healthy. Families must be healthy. In order for second
marriages and beyond to be healthy, members must feel safe.

Safety: The Big Factor

Every remarriage is destined to take one of two paths: It will either succeed or fail. Period. In fact, in every interaction between spouses, each has
a choice to make: Partners can either move toward creating and maintaining a safe environment, or they can fall into the trap of reacting to one another in ways that make their relational environment feel insecure and
unsafe. Although it takes many things to create and maintain a marriage
that thrills, one big factor is emotional safety.

Why is emotional safety so important? Why should couples and counselors focus on it as being vital in a remarriage?

Emotional safety is crucial because the heart is the epicenter of life and
relationships. Proverbs 4:23 makes this very clear by stating, "Above all
else, guard your heart, for it is the wellspring of life." When the heart feels
safe, it opens. When the heart feels fear or senses a threat, it closes. Both
safety and fear set in motion chain reactions that lead to very different

outcomes. When people feel safe, they are naturally inclined to open their hearts—and intimacy occurs naturally. In the upcoming chapters, we will show you ways to facilitate open, healthy hearts.

Make a list of your deepest fears. Now "answer" those fears with the promises of God. For example, under "I am afraid that my spouse might leave me, and I'll be all alone," you might write Joshua 1:5: "I will never leave you nor forsake you."

Adam and Natalie Gillespie started their remarriage by driving away from their beautiful wedding reception with cans bouncing off the back end of the car and their combined five kids (then ages 18 months to 13 years old) packed into the backseat. On their wedding night, the couple tucked the baby and their three elementary-aged kids into bed, then the groom fell asleep on the living room sofa while the bride and her new stepdaughter watched a movie. Natalie knew it would have been awkward to have a "real" wedding night with a 13-year-old just down the hall, but it was still a little bit of a letdown, an inauspicious beginning that only hinted at the enormous storm that would soon bear down on this new family.

In their first two years of marriage, Natalie juggled classes toward her master's degree, two part-time jobs and the schedules of five kids who attended three different schools. Natalie's vibrant, 54-year-old mother was diagnosed with cancer and died shortly after the couple's first anniversary, and Adam's mother passed away just six months later. Adam tried to keep his business afloat, as his former wife dragged him into a bitter custody battle. The members of this family found themselves court-ordered to visit psychologists' offices, courtrooms and police stations. Guardian ad litems, social workers, detectives and truancy officers interviewed them. They fought false allegations of child abuse and accumulated tens of thousands of dollars in legal fees.

Then the emotional storm picked up speed, trying to uproot everything in sight. Adam's nine-year-old daughter suffered a brain aneurysm and nearly died, and the couple became unexpectedly pregnant. When Natalie sat down to share the news about the baby with her husband, she burst into tears.

"I didn't feel emotionally safe at all, and I just didn't think I could take any more," Natalie shares. "After more than a year of running ourselves ragged trying to make ends meet and keep the kids stable, Adam's and my relationship just didn't feel the same. I knew I still loved him and that he loved me, but we fought over money, the kids and especially his former wife and the havoc she was wreaking on our household.

"Plus, we both still had wounds from the betrayals we experienced in our first marriages and resulting divorces. We didn't know it then, but we were haunted by what I now call the 'Ghosts of Relationships Past,' which caused us to react unfairly to each other at times. It was an absolutely agonizing beginning—when we had been convinced we were a perfect match!"

Adam and Natalie Gillespie were propelled almost immediately into a series of circumstances that could have torn their new family from its tentative foundation. Instead, the external forces battered their hearts—but ultimately drove them to their knees. "There was so much pressure from the outside that it knocked us to our knees in prayer," Natalie says. "We had to rely on God to save our family—because we sure couldn't do it on our own."

The couple tried to create a safe environment by attending workshops on the effects of divorce on children and taking a 16-week parenting course that taught them how to present a united front to their kids. But it was a lesson on Love Languages that finally reassured Natalie their hearts could heal and become safe places where they could all reside.

"I knew that we loved each other in a way neither of us had experienced in our first marriages, but it just didn't feel like it did in the beginning," she admits. "Looking back on it, I realize that I didn't feel entirely safe. I wasn't trusting Adam with an open heart, and I know he hadn't given me all of his, either. Then we learned about Love Languages. When we were dating, we pretty much covered all the bases. Once we were married, I settled into loving Adam in ways that would make *me* feel loved, and he did the same. Because we're opposites in our Love Languages, this didn't work very well.

"Once we learned what the other needed to feel loved, we became much better at loving each other well. It still wasn't easy, but it opened our hearts to each other again. By keeping our focus on God, our marriage and our kids—in that order—we somehow stood firm."

Today, the Gillespies recently celebrated 14 years of marriage and have experienced many of the benefits, not just the trials, of remarried life. The custody battle ended years ago, Adam's daughter fully recovered from her aneurysm and recently graduated from university, and the unexpected baby is now their charming 12-year-old son. The Gillespies have further expanded their family by adopting three daughters from China over the last five years.

"We're not perfect, but Adam and I work hard to keep our hearts safe and open to each other," Natalie says. "When we do, we can show others that there is light at the end of the dark tunnel of divorce. We are living proof that God can redeem any situation for His glory."

What Is Emotional Safety?

When people feel safe in any relationship, they open their hearts and reveal the "real" them. That's the very definition of intimacy, feeling free to open up and reveal who we really are, knowing that the other people around us will love, accept and value us, no matter what.

In other words, we hold out our hearts and say, "Here is who I am emotionally, psychologically, spiritually and mentally. I want you to know my heart and soul. I want you to get to know who I am and appreciate who I am and value who I am. I am a very fascinating person and it will take you more than one lifetime to understand all of who I am!"

We feel emotionally safe with someone only when we believe that he or she will handle our heart—our deepest feelings and desires—with genuine interest, curiosity and care.

Are you starting to see the problem here for those who remarry? Partners can probably count on one hand the relationships they've had where they felt genuinely safe to open up and share who they really are. Most of us have very few people to whom we have entrusted our deepest dreams and thoughts. God designed us to hunger for intimacy and deep connection, to connect with others and experience relational intimacy, especially in the key human relationship with a spouse. Yet many of us struggle with various aspects of intimacy because it requires openness—and openness makes us instantly vulnerable. We know from experience that when we lay ourselves open, we can get hurt. Over time, especially if trust has been broken frequently, hearts close and disconnect from others. We're not quite sure what people will say or do, or how they'll use what they learn about us. Avoiding intimacy keeps us from feeling hurt, humiliated, embarrassed. But it's a false sense of security or emotional safety, because we were created to connect.

In spite of the risks, an intimate relationship offers enormous benefits. Intimacy creates the ideal opportunity to love deeply and be loved. It gives us a significant sense of belonging, a clear sense of purpose in life, the ability to make a major difference in another's life and a way to fully express the best of who we are. We have discovered that the foundational component to fostering intimacy is a totally safe environment—physically, intellectually, spiritually and emotionally.

 Pray daily for your spouse and with your spouse. Kneel by your bed together, even when you don't feel like it.

If people know their hearts are safe, they are naturally inclined to be open and to connect with others. Openness is the default setting for human beings. No state of being takes less energy to maintain than openness; you just have to be relaxed, be yourself. Maintaining defenses, walls, force fields and fortresses, however, takes tremendous energy. As a result, when people feel truly safe, they prefer to be open and use their energy to deepen their relationships and enjoy life.

Couple Focus: Create Safety

For remarried couples, creating safety will help build open relationships that will naturally encourage growth in the new family. It will help build marriages in which spouses will feel cherished, honored and fully alive. Safety sets a soothing tone that will allow family members to feel relaxed and refreshed.

In the movie *Twister*, there is a scene right at the end as the movie credits begin to roll that illustrates what we mean. The end of the film shows the hero and heroine passionately hugging outside of a majestic, old farmhouse, right after surviving an F-5 tornado. As the two characters affectionately embrace each other, the camera angle changes from a close-up shot of the weary lovers to an aerial shot of the farmhouse and surrounding landscape. As the credits roll, the view pans further and further out until it looks like you're in an airplane flying over the farm. Then you see it—the best part of the entire movie—the path of the tornado. It's an awesome sight. This F-5 twister (with wind speeds around 261 to 318 MPH that lifted homes right off their foundations) traveled right over the old farmhouse.

In the wake of the twister, there are no trees left standing, and all you see is a dirt path carved through the cornfields. You can see that this extremely wide tornado path engulfed the farmhouse, but it remained standing. Sure, it's missing some shingles and it's probably going to need a fresh paint job, but it survived the tornado in one piece. I (Greg) will never forget the scene. The old house looked so warm and inviting with its huge front porch, rocking chairs and large shutters flanking the bright windows. I've never thought about farming, but seeing that house made me want to start planting corn. It was all because of that house. I wanted to be there, sitting on the porch swing with my wife, watching our children play.

Why did that farmhouse affect me so much? Because it made me feel safe.

If a storm of that magnitude couldn't knock it down, nothing could. That's where I wanted to raise my family—somewhere safe and secure like that old farmhouse. Remarried couples have survived their own tornadoes of loss and change. Now imagine remarried spouses opening their hearts to love each other so that their marriage stands as steadfast as that majestic farmhouse, with both partners feeling safe and secure in each other's love.

If that sounds like paradise, maybe it's because Eden was a supremely safe place. Our relationship with God will always be the safest relationship we will ever experience. God's heart is always open, His love is always available and He always has our best interests in mind. We love how King David described how safe he felt with God:

> The LORD is my light and my salvation—whom shall I fear? The LORD is the stronghold of my life—of whom shall I be afraid? . . . One thing I ask of the LORD, this is what I seek: that I may dwell in the house of the LORD all the days of my life, to gaze upon the beauty of the LORD and to seek him in his temple. For in the day of trouble he will keep me safe in his dwelling; he will hide me in the shelter of his tabernacle and set me high upon a rock (Ps 27:1,4-5).

Before they sinned, Adam and Eve felt no fear. They enjoyed an amazingly intimate relationship with God and each other. The couple felt so close that God described them as "one flesh" (Gen. 2:24). Nothing came between Adam and Eve—not insecurities, not sharp differences of opinion, not even clothes! They were completely open with each other—no walls, no masks, no fear. And their relationship blossomed.

Isn't that a marvelous vision of marriage?

We want couples to learn how to create a safe home environment that will enable their remarriages to flourish and grow, and for their churches and church leaders to love and guide them through it. We want the focus to be on creating a partnership of two hearts that feels like the safest place on earth. We want to help couples put a hedge of protection around their households, one that allows them to experience the natural trial and error of two families coming together in such a way that it feels really good to everyone. We want hearts to feel as safe and sturdy as that old farmhouse.

 Watch the movie Twister *together. Look for the last scene. Capture the vision of you, as a couple, standing as firm as that farmhouse.*

Outside of a personal relationship with the Lord Jesus Christ, there is no relationship more important than marriage—and a great marriage requires proper training, skill acquisition and knowledge. This entire book is built around making remarriage safer, so that hearts can remain open and handle any storm they will face in the future. The safety that is fostered in remarriage will help everyone rebuild with hope and energy. When a remarried couple believes that they can not only survive, but also thrive, they forge deep connections and create a lasting legacy for their family.

What is the first step in building hearts that feel like the safest place on earth? The answer just might surprise you.

HEART MONITORS

1. On a scale of 0 to 10 (with 10 being the most safe), how safe is your relationship for both you and your spouse? How about for your children and stepchildren?

2. In what ways have you made it unsafe? In what ways can you increase the safety level?

3. How do you most often damage the safety of your relational environment?

4. How do you tend to respond when you feel unsafe in your relationships?

HEART PROTECTORS

Look at your schedule for the next few days or week. What events do you see that might cause conflict? Talk to your spouse now about these potential "hot buttons." Acknowledge that they might create friction, and you'll alleviate some of it right up front!

Set ground rules around your "fighting style." For example, agree to avoid cursing, direct insults, physical aggression (never okay) and throwing things. Come up with a code word or phrase that will allow one of you to walk away to calm down if things get too heated, without the other spouse feeling abandoned.

Note

1. L.A. Kurdeck, "Relationship Quality for Newly Married Husbands and Wives: Marital History, Stepchildren, and Individual-preference Predictors," *Journal of Marriage and the Family*, 1989, vol. 51, pp. 1053-1064. D. H. Demo and A. C. Acock, "Singlehood, Marriage, and Remarriage," *Journal of Family Issues*, 1996, vol. 17, pp. 388-407. M. Ihinger-Tallman and K. Pasley, "Stepfamilies in 1984 and Today: A Scholarly Perspective," *Marriage and Family Review*, 1997, vol. 26 (1/2), pp. 19-40. E. M. Hetherington, W. G. Clingempeel, E. R. Anderson, et al, "Coping with Marital Transitions: A Family Systems Perspective," *Monographs of the Society for Research in Child Development*, 1992, p. 57 (2/3).

3

Healing Your Own Heart First

If your heart is broken, you'll find God right there;
if you're kicked in the gut, he'll help you catch your breath.
PSALM 34:18, *THE MESSAGE*

The front porch of my (Greg's) home in Arkansas seems to be a bird sanctuary. Erin and I spend a lot of time trying to get rid of the barn swallows that nest near the top of our front entryway. We'll get rid of one, and it seems like the next morning there are new birds building a new home. I can't figure out how they build their nests so fast. Our front porch represents the barn swallow version of *Extreme Home Makeover*. It drives us crazy. The main frustration isn't the fact that they build nests; it's that they dive bomb us every time we walk out the front door. Barn swallows are like kamikaze pilots. We don't really even need a doorbell anymore, because when people come over, you can hear the screams of terror as they flee from the kamikaze birds.

To be honest, however, I respect our fearless squatters because they epitomize the concept of guarding your heart. They fiercely protect their homes and vigilantly care for their young, and I believe that guarding our hearts is about learning how to fiercely protect and care for this very center of our being. Until you know how to take care of your own heart, especially if it's been broken time and time again, you can't open it fully and properly to love your spouse or family. Therefore, the first step in building a relationship that feels like the safest place on earth is to first make your own heart healthy.

Taking Care of Your Own Heart

Most marriage, remarriage and stepfamily books go to great lengths to show you how to invest in the other people in your family, how to give of yourself and pour out your own heart. That's not our advice. At least not yet.

We believe that your journey toward feeling safe and having a healthy remarriage begins with taking care of your own heart first. *What? That doesn't sound very Christian, to put myself first,* you might be thinking. But, yes, you read that right. Before you can love others effectively, you have to feel safe. And before you can feel safe, you have to know exactly how to take care of your own heart. When we share this truth, most people look at us like we're speaking a foreign language (which probably isn't a bad analogy, because taking care of our own hearts is foreign to most of us).

What about you? Did you grow up in a home where your parent(s) taught you how to care for your own heart—how to effectively deal with the hurt, pain and difficulties that came your way as a child, an adolescent and as a teen? We honestly have never had anyone say, "Absolutely, my parents taught me precisely how to deal with my emotions—pain, anger, frustration, conflict, hurt, disappointment, fear, and so forth—in only healthy ways." Most of us didn't learn how to do what King Solomon told us to do, which is to "guard our hearts." As a matter of fact, if we heard that phrase at all, it was usually from our youth pastor when he was giving the sexual purity talk.

Certainly sexual purity is an important part of guarding our hearts, but it is only one part of the meaning behind Solomon's words. We believe that guarding your heart is so much more than keeping pure sexually. It's much more like watching the way those barn swallows guard their nests. It's about learning what to do with painful emotions, how to heal after hurt, fear, frustration or disappointment. It's about being a barn swallow for your heart, vigilantly caring about it and fiercely protecting it.

 Maintain a close connection with God through prayer. Prayer is a great way to open your heart and keep it open.

You will never feel truly safe in any relationship until you are confident in your own ability to guard and care for your own heart. The foundation of a great marriage is a couple with open hearts, so that God's love can flow through them. Thus, it's not selfish or self-centered, but necessary and healthy, to learn how to take great care of your heart. Only by investing in your own heart will you be able to keep it open, so that you can minister to your spouse's heart. Then both of you can help heal the rest of the hearts in your stepfamily.

Healthy Boundaries or Emotional Distance?

One way to protect your heart is to set emotional boundaries with people or retreat behind an emotional wall when someone makes you feel emotionally unsafe. That would be fine, except that God doesn't want our hearts hidden behind a wall or locked away inside an emotional fortress. He wants our hearts wide open so He can love people through us, especially our spouse. If all we learn to do when people hurt us is to put up a wall, we cannot live out the Greatest Commandment. How can we love God and others if our hearts are boarded up? If they are closed for business? We can't.

 Practice forgiving quickly, so you don't hold on to resentment and bitterness.

Feeling free to open up and reveal who you really are is a wonderful idea, but it can be very difficult for spouses in a second marriage or beyond. Why? Because life has already proven itself to be full of pain and heartbreak. Most of us have allowed our hearts to take a lot of abuse—without properly dealing with the pain, hurt, frustration and fear we have encountered.

For example, as boys grow up and become men, many of us learned along the way that "real men don't cry" or that our feelings were "wrong," "crazy" or even "stupid." In a general sense, young boys are taught that hurt should never be displayed. Consequently, men often end up "disconnected" from their emotions.

In contrast, young girls often feel invalidated emotionally, and they are taught (especially through movies, television and romance novels) to follow their emotions with reckless abandon. Both sexes encounter major relational issues, and neither learn how to properly care for their hearts. Instead, people experience a variety of the following kinds of "heart attacks":

- They ignore their emotions and think their way through life.
- They completely trust their emotions and feel their way through life.
- They throw open their hearts to anyone, any time.
- They open their hearts to no one, no time.
- They criticize themselves.
- They "stuff" their feelings.

- They judge themselves.
- They minimize their pain and hurt.
- They numb out.
- They make terrible choices (e.g., alcohol, drugs, affairs).
- They mistreat their bodies (e.g., gluttony, cutting, anorexia).
- They act out sexually.

All of these "heart attack" behaviors lead to relationship dysfunction. Some of these behaviors have led spouses to divorce. Some of them
are causing dysfunction in remarriages now. All of them create blockages that keep God's love from flowing into and out of our hearts. In the
past, we never considered whether or not we were taking good care of
our hearts. As a matter of fact, we'd have thought you were weird if you
had asked us about the state of our hearts. It took us a long time to realize that you can't feel safe with others until you first feel like you are
keeping your own heart safe.

 *Develop a close circle of trusted mentors. Everyone needs wisdom from
those who have already traveled the road ahead and can be trusted with
heart-level issues.*

Feeling safe with yourself is really about trust: Do you trust yourself
to take good care of your own heart? The romantic myth in our society
is that we will find someone who will take care of us, who will treat us
like we deserve to be treated, who will guard and protect our hearts for
us. However, people will always let us down. No one can be 100 percent
safe and trustworthy. It's just not possible.

So in those moments when your spouse is not trustworthy or safe,
the question is: What will you do with your own heart? Will you take
care of it or will you ignore it? Will you minimize the pain or neglect
the "attack" altogether? If you choose to ignore or neglect your heart
pain, then your heart will soon shut down. Only when you act protec-
tively and take care of your heart will the blockage clear so that love
can flow freely.

In the process of healing your heart, where do you start? You start
with yourself.

How Do I Love Me? Let Me Count the Ways

A healthy, open heart—one that is nurtured and protected—is the key to living out the Greatest Commandment to love God and love others. We are not commanded to love ourselves, because when Christ says to love your neighbor "as yourself," He assumes that you are already doing that job. He created us to love ourselves, but many of us fail miserably. Learning to take care of your heart begins with how you perceive your own value and worth.

1. Recognize Your Own Value

You recognize your own value when you perceive and treat yourself like an incredible gift from God. Each of us has immeasurable value because we are unique, divine creations. If you believe that you are a priceless treasure, your life—and the lives around you—will be better for it. Jesus said, "Where your treasure is, there your heart will be also" (Matt. 6:21).

When you do not value yourself, your heart remains closed against your own worth, which hinders your relationship with God and others. Ask yourself these questions: Do you think of yourself as valuable? Do you like yourself? Do you accept yourself? Do you forgive yourself? How do you treat yourself? Do you speak to yourself harshly or kindly?

The reason these questions are so critical is that Scripture says we are to love others *like* we love ourselves. If you don't even like yourself, how can you possibly love your spouse?

 Accept and believe sincere compliments and affirmations. It's okay to receive when others praise you.

When you consider yourself a treasure, your heart will follow—and so will your words and actions. Conversely, if you consider yourself a piece of junk (or worse), your heart, words and actions will demonstrate that fact. When you do not value your uniqueness, when you do not see yourself as God's priceless work of art, hardness of the heart sets in. And we already know that hardening of the heart is the kiss of death to relationships. Again, a closed heart disconnects us from relationships with God, others and ourselves.

If you have ever doubted your value, then consider in the following verses how your heavenly Father describes you:

- You may not know Me, but I know everything about you (see Ps. 139:1).
- You were made in My image (see Gen. 1:27).
- In Me you live and move and have your being (see Acts 17:28).
- You are My offspring (see Acts 17:28).
- I knew you even before you were conceived (see Jer. 1:4-5).
- I chose you when I planned creation (see Eph. 1:11-12).
- You were not a mistake, for all your days are written in My book (see Ps. 139:16).
- I determined the exact time of your birth and where you would live (see Acts 17:26).
- You are fearfully and wonderfully made (see Ps. 139:14).
- I knit you together in your mother's womb (see Ps. 139:13).
- I brought you forth on the day you were born (see Ps. 71:6).
- You are my treasured possession (see Exod. 19:5).

In order to take care of your heart properly, it's critical that you get your sense of value from the Lord. His view is the most accurate, never portraying you better than you should appear, but always revealing the true beauty inside you. This is exactly what the Scriptures say: "The LORD does not look at the things man looks at. Man looks at the outward appearance, but the LORD looks at the heart" (1 Sam. 16:7). Christ sees us as we really are.

In his bestseller *The Purpose-Driven Life*, Rick Warren lays out this description of how God views you:

> You are not an accident. Your birth was no mistake or mishap, and your life is no fluke of nature. . . . Long before you were conceived by your parents, you were conceived in the mind of God. He thought of you first. . . . He custom-made your body just the way he wanted it. He also determined the natural talents you would possess and the uniqueness of your personality. . . . Most amazing, God decided how you would be born. Regardless of the circumstances of your birth or who your parents are, God had a plan in creating you. It doesn't matter whether your parents were good, bad, or indifferent. God knew that those two individuals possessed exactly the right genetic makeup to create the custom "you" he had in mind. They had the DNA God wanted to make you. . . .

God never does anything accidentally, and he never makes mistakes. He has a reason for everything he creates. . . . God was thinking of you even before he made the world. . . . This is how much God loves and values you![1]

In order to capture this God's-eye view, we need to heed the advice of the apostle Paul: "I pray also that the eyes of your heart may be enlightened" (Eph. 1:18). We need our hearts to see what God sees when He looks at us.

How do you see yourself? As precious? As priceless? Do you honor yourself? Honor is a way of accurately seeing the immense value of someone made in God's image. God created you as a one-of-a-kind individual with unique gifts and personality. He sees each of us as precious and valuable. When you catch a glimpse of how God sees you, you are protecting and caring for your heart. When you recognize and affirm your own value, you create a safe environment that encourages your relationships to grow.

Marci thought she would never be useful to God again after she divorced her husband and remarried. She saw herself as a spiritual outcast, a "scarlet" woman, because she had left her marriage and her two teenage sons.

"It took years before the turning point came and my heart really began to heal," Marci shares. "I remember one thing that really was a breakthrough for me in healing my heart. We had joined a small group of very nice people, but we were the quiet ones in the group. We really didn't talk much. One week, I shared some of our story of our divorces. Later, one of the women said to the group, 'It's obvious that God is not done with Marci yet.' You can't imagine how much that meant to me. It gave me hope."

Marci could not affirm her own value because she no longer recognized it. But she is a person God sees as having limitless value. You are too. God created you to be worthy of greatest honor. Remember that before you can be safe with yourself, you must recognize and embrace your own value: For where your treasure is, there will your heart be also (see Matt. 6:21).

"I thought God would never let me teach again, that He could no longer use me," Marci says. "I was divorced, I left my family, and I wasn't doing well in my second marriage at that time. I felt like I had no value. Then someone on staff at my new church helped restore my heart. He asked me how I introduced myself to people. He asked me if I said, 'Hi, I'm Marci. I'm divorced. I have five kids.' He made me examine how I presented myself, then he said that the truth was that none of the descriptions I used really mattered. 'What does matter is that you are a child of God, and that's who you really are,' he said. I then started hearing other truths in worship songs, truths like the fact that God has called me by name and that He calls me friend. God used different things to start giving me hope and heal my heart."

2. Give Your Heart a Voice

Not only did God create our emotions, but He also made our hearts the source of our emotions. Chip Dodd, in *The Voice of the Heart*, explains this perfectly: "Feelings are the voice of the heart, and you will not have fullness until you're adept at hearing and experiencing all of them. When you are not aware of your feelings, your life is lived incompletely. Whenever you don't feel, you are blocked from living life to the fullest. Wherever you lack awareness of your heart, no room exists for God."[2]

The heart expresses itself through a wide range of emotions. According to the Bible, your heart can experience positive emotions like joy, gladness, cheerfulness, merriment, wisdom, steadfastness, valiance, purity, nobility, creativity, courage, conviction, faith, hope and love. Our heart can also feel many troublesome emotions like anger, anguish, fear, woundedness, sadness, grief, brokenness, division, foolishness, fright, anxiety, faintness, cowardice, forgetfulness, numbness, hatred, stubbornness, sorrow, pride, hardness, wickedness and perversity.

Emotions are, by definition, irrational and illogical. They are only feelings, and they are not, in and of themselves, right or wrong, good or bad. Instead, they are a great source of *information*. God designed emotions to provide essential information regarding our needs, desires and beliefs. They should not be stuffed or ignored. Neither should they be followed blindly. Instead, they give us clues and insight about ourselves—feelings are the barometer of the heart.

 Try different techniques to manage your emotions, such as praying, taking deep breaths, stretching, listening to music, exercising and talking to your spouse.

When we feel lonely, our need for connection with other people is unmet. When we feel afraid, our need for safety is unmet. When we feel rejected, it is our need for acceptance that is unmet. In essence, emotions are a natural part of our God-given design that serve the good purpose of providing us with valuable information.

Many people are not aware of what is going on inside of them emotionally, so they miss these clues about themselves. For example, you might be hesitant to take action because of the fear of failing. You might not open up around people because you're afraid of being hurt. You might be resistant to sharing the desires of your heart for fear of being rejected. When the heart is silenced, you are deprived of a rich resource for growth and relationship.

The most effective way to identify your feelings is through emotional education. Simply put, you need to develop a "feelings" vocabulary. Some of you are probably thinking, *But isn't the point to understand* why *we are feeling the way we do?* No. It's actually more important to know *what* you're feeling than to determine the reason why you feel it. We all need to experience and express a wide range of emotions, not just the pleasant ones. Otherwise, we develop only a limited awareness of who we are, and we are severely limited in our ability to learn important emotional lessons.

If you're not sure how to identify your feelings, a good place to start is to simply ask yourself, *What am I feeling?* As you do this, remind yourself that you're after information. Don't judge your emotions; instead, see them as a source of information. Then ask yourself, *What are my emotions trying to tell me?* What could it mean, for example, if you are feeling stressed out, worried, sad, fearful, hurt or frustrated?

Once you identify your feelings, at this stage you have to figure out what to do with them. Don't try to "fix" how you feel. In this moment, just work on learning how to accurately pinpoint your emotions. You may want to ask yourself the following questions:

- Do I pay a lot of attention to how I feel?
- Do I notice my emotions as I experience them?
- What emotions do I frequently experience?
- What emotions are easy for me to express?
- What emotions are difficult for me to express?
- What emotions did I see expressed in my family growing up?
- What emotions were never expressed in my family growing up?
- Can I accurately name my feelings?
- Do I pay attention to the thoughts, beliefs and actions that could be causing how I feel?

- Do I understand how my feelings influence my thoughts and actions?
- Am I aware of how my emotions impact my spouse and family?

It's extremely important to be able to identify your emotions. If you have a hard time coming up with precise "feeling words" or can't put a name to what you are feeling, you may want to use a "feelings list." Here are five major categories of emotions that can vary greatly in their intensity:

Anger	Joy	Sadness	Hurt	Fear
frustration	contentedness	depression	loneliness	uncertainty
annoyance	peace	anguish	homesickness	worry
bitterness	relaxation	distress	abandonment	anxiety
irritation	cheerfulness	despair	embarrassment	fright
disgust	satisfaction	melancholy	shame	nervousness
exasperation	excitement	grief	guilt	terror
bothered	enthusiasm	helplessness	foolishness	agitation
fury	ecstasy	hopelessness	humiliation	concern
rage	happiness	misery	pain	phobia

The best way to use this list is to accurately identify your feelings on a daily basis. This may sound too elementary, but we know that it works. It won't take you long to develop a richer emotional vocabulary. Not only will you get better at expressing a wider range of emotions, but you will also better experience the flavor, intensity and richness of your feelings. It will definitely add "spice" to your life and remarriage.

Remember, God is the creator of emotions—they were His design. Not only does God have deep feelings Himself, but He also created us to experience emotions. They exist to provide us with a valuable stream of information that helps us understand ourselves and nurture our hearts.

3. Deal with the Lies that Have Been Written on Your Heart

We all have wounds. Different authors or psychologists might call them hurts, lies, fears, arrows, messages . . . but they all have the same effect on our hearts. Life events work to create wounds. As Marci experienced after her divorce, painful hurts, lies and messages try to define who we are. When these wounds occur on a heart level, the results are profound, impacting the way we treat ourselves and our marriage.

The enemy cunningly uses our life circumstances (divorce or the death of a spouse) and significant interactions to wound our hearts. Over the years, we have heard hundreds of life stories and the subsequent wounds produced:

- Sandy's mom was always conscious of her appearance. She was quick to point out when Sandy gained a few pounds, always ready to tell her she would never find a good man if she was fat. The enemy deeply etched this lie on Sandy's heart: "Your value is based on your appearance."

- The divorce was sudden. Bob did not even know his wife was unhappy. Maybe if he had been a better husband, then he could have kept them together. Instead, he clearly heard the enemy say, "You are not good enough."

- On the day of the Presidential Physical Fitness test in sixth grade, Andy was not able to do a single pull-up or sit-up. Everyone laughed at him. The enemy told him, "You are a failure."

- Heather's husband left her for another woman. The enemy lied, "You will always be abandoned by the people you love."

- Chris's dad was the life of the party, fun and engaging. But he could also be volatile and angry. Chris could never predict which mood his dad would be in. The enemy convinced him, "You are powerless."

- From as far back as Jill could remember, her dad said hurtful things and made cutting remarks. Jill heard the enemy say, loud and clear, "You have no value."

- Becky always felt a little different from the other kids at school. No one sat with her at lunch, hung out with her during recess or hardly even talked to her. She left middle school with a clear message from the enemy, "You will always be alone."

As you can see, the Father of Lies can and will use any circumstance (divorce, sporting events, jobs, school experiences, home environment) and anyone (parents, teachers, friends, classmates, employers, former spouses) to deeply wound our hearts.

So that you can spot his tricks from this day forward, here is a review of just how he works:

1. The enemy uses life circumstances to create heart wounds.
2. The wounds come with messages that tell us something about ourselves (e.g., "You are not valuable").
3. These messages become deeply etched on our hearts without our awareness.
4. The messages are lies. They are not true. (You really are valuable, but the lie tells you otherwise.)
5. The lies engraved on our hearts affect how we see ourselves and how we interact with God and others.

Why does Satan go after our hearts? *Because the heart is the wellspring of life and relationship.* Whatever happens in the heart affects every other aspect of our lives. King Solomon wisely wrote that as a man thinks in his heart, so he *is* (see Prov. 23:7). Thus, the battle is over the control of our hearts. God wants our hearts to be filled with the truth that we are one-of-a-kind treasures that He handcrafted for a divine purpose. The enemy wants us to feel cheap, empty and useless. He lies to us and wounds us in order to close us down and shut us off from God and others. He knows that marriages cannot succeed and families cannot thrive when hearts are shut down.

 *Try to journal your feelings. Research shows that when you write something down, your brain doesn't have to remember it. It's like going to the store with a shopping list. If you write down what you need, you don't have to constantly review the list in your mind. If you journal your feelings, you don't have to dwell on them, like poking your tongue again and again into a sore tooth.*

The lies, wounds and messages written on our hearts have far-reaching ramifications. Let's look back at the people listed previously in this chapter and see how the enemy's messages impacted their lives and relationships:

- Sandy (My value is based on my appearance) has suffered from a string of eating disorders. She is passing her unrealistic expectations about body image to her kids.
- Andy (I'm a failure) works 16-hour days in the business world. He hates his job, but he is determined to prove that he can be successful.
- Bob (I'm not good enough) is always trying to "earn" his wife's love, and he gets extremely defensive when she points out anything he's done wrong.
- Heather (I'll be abandoned) is constantly afraid that her husband will leave her. When they fight, she often disconnects first so she doesn't have to feel the sting of rejection.
- Chris (I am powerless) married a fun, successful woman. She gets angry and volatile, just like his dad. He is so used to the cycle that he takes whatever she dishes out, never saying a word.
- Jill (I have no value) constantly questions her husband. She is suspicious and believes he focuses more attention on his work than on her.
- Becky (I'm alone) clings to her husband and will do anything he asks. Their marriage is very codependent because she is paranoid that she will lose him.

These are stories we hear every day in this fallen world. We get hurt, and our wounds etch messages onto our very vulnerable hearts. The messages are lies, and the lies push us to behave in unhealthy ways. The lies are so powerful (and painful) that we eventually shut down our hearts to protect ourselves. With our hearts disengaged, our marriages suffer or end. Our families fail. Remarriages fare even worse if the cycle is not recognized and broken. Our job is to heal these wounds, so that we can get our hearts back open.

 Laugh out loud. Tell jokes and funny stories, watch sitcoms on TV or head out to a hilarious movie. Laughter warms hearts and keeps them wide open.

To combat the lies, you must first identify what wounds and messages have attacked your heart. None of us is immune to the enemy's lies and negative messages. Here is a list of the most common lies we find on people's hearts:

You are:

Worthless	Unlovable	Abandoned
Valueless	Unacceptable	Disconnected
Defective	Humiliated	Unwanted
Inadequate	Helpless	Unknown
Insignificant	Powerless	A failure
Ugly	Out of Control	Invalidated
Rejected	Controlled	Not good enough
Judged	Vulnerable	Ineffective
Unloved	Alone	

Your job is to identify which of these messages is etched on your heart. There may be more than one. That's okay. You may have something that is not on this list. That's okay too. The important thing is to identify the lies. How? Simply think back and identify any significant emotional traumas you can recall from your childhood through your teen years (teasing, disappointments, bullying, betrayal, traumatic events). Once you have identified the events and the messages they sent, you have to dig deeper to figure out how they impacted your heart. What did you feel (hurt and alone? angry and afraid?)? What did you say to yourself, or what message did you receive from the incident (e.g., "I am not acceptable")? Look back at the list and identify one or two messages that fit.

Now think about how these lies came back to haunt you in your adult life, especially if you experienced divorce. What messages were written or reinforced in your heart (e.g., failure, rejection, worthlessness, abandonment, inadequacy)?

These negative messages can be etched even more deeply by ongoing conflict. Think about a recent disagreement with your spouse. Look for evidence of the lies engraved on your heart. Did your wife make you fear abandonment, because your first wife left you? Did your husband make you feel rejected, like your classmates did in eighth grade? What were you feeling? Review the list above.

Spouses have a way of triggering these wounds deep inside us because our spouse is the closest person to us. Your husband or wife has been granted access to the most valuable and vulnerable part of who you are—

your heart. With all that access, your spouse has the greatest ability to do you harm—or help you heal.

 Learn to recognize and express your likes and dislikes. People tend to shut down when they don't know what they need or want.

We hope you have begun to identify the lies and messages that have wounded your heart. Now let's get to work allowing God to buff away those messages so that they no longer drive you to feel negative emotions and act in ways that close you down. Submitting to God's heart surgery to remove the lies gives you the freedom to open your heart back up again.

Successful heart surgery replaces the enemy's messages. Satan is the author of lies. Anything he writes on your heart, any message he creates, will not be true. You may be saying, *I see the message on my heart now, and I already know that it is not true. I'm cured!* Unfortunately, it is not that simple. You see, the message is etched on your heart. The fact that you recognize the lie is in your head. In a battle between your head and your heart, your heart will win every time. You cannot outsmart or outrun what is written on your heart. The Bible tells us that as a man "thinks in his *heart,* so he is" (Prov. 23:7, *NKJV*, emphasis added), not as a man thinks in his *head.*

The only thing that can get rid of the lies for good is God's truth.

 Write God's Word on your heart through Scripture memory.

When we approach God in prayer, we get to speak to Jesus and the Holy Spirit. That is really good news, because they know a thing or two about what is right and what is wrong. Jesus refers to Himself as "the way and *the truth* and the life" (John 14:6, emphasis added). After the resurrection, Scripture tells us that when Jesus told His friends about His imminent departure back to heaven, He comforted them with the news that He would send them a helper. "And I will ask the Father, and he will give you another Counselor to be with you forever—the Spirit of truth" (John 14:16-17). Isn't it great to know that the role of the Holy Spirit is to remind us of the truth of who we were created to be?

All you have to do to receive major heart surgery is to ask. Take each lie to the Lord in prayer and ask Him to reveal what is true about you. Ask Him to speak from His heart to your heart. Taking care of your heart means that you unclog each chamber from Satan's lies. "Then you will know the truth, and the truth will set you free" (John 8:32).

4. Don't Let People Be Your Source of Truth

Looking back, the most helpful way we've learned to care for our hearts is to take what people tell us to the Lord. In the past, when someone would criticize, judge, evaluate, critique or scrutinize us, or provide feedback or advice, or even share their opinions, we were likely to take their statements at face value, accept them as fact, and treat them as certainties. We allowed other people's words to become truth in our lives.

But people are just that—people—flawed human beings with sin natures. Simply because someone you know feels or believes something (especially something about you or your marriage), that doesn't make it "truth." People have their own expectations, family of origin issues, past experiences, beliefs, values, and so on, that *always* color their perceptions of the truth. It helps to remember that any time someone shares something with you. It is only from their point of view, influenced and intertwined with their own "stuff." Think of it as a big, twisted ball of fishing line. To untangle the truth from the "stuff," take what people say about you to the Lord. Don't allow people to be the source of truth in your life.

 Keep your life in balance, with a good mix of hard work and pure fun, responsibility and rewards.

When Erin shares her feelings or frustrations about me (Greg), I listen to the best of my ability, and then I tell her that I will check out what she's saying with the Lord. I remember the first time I ever said this to her. She looked at me (you may know this look) and said, "This is just another clever ploy to get out of hearing me!" Although this was far from the truth, I knew that I probably deserved her skepticism. Instead of arguing with her, I went to the Lord in prayer. Later that day, I felt a real peace in my heart about what she had shared. Because I had taken it to the Lord, He now brought me to a place of conviction. I was quickly able to take responsibility for my choices. It's not our mate's job to convict us; that's God's role.

Even when someone comes to me and says, "The Lord told me to say this . . ." or "God revealed this to me," I am cautious. God certainly uses people to speak His truth into my life, but I am convinced that when we hear things from people (even apparent words from the Lord), we should always check them out by going straight to the source of truth. John 16:13 makes it pretty clear that Christ is this source: "But when he, the Spirit of truth, comes, he will guide you into all truth."

The Lord will always guide us to His truth if we ask Him. Even while people are in the middle of sharing something with you, you can be praying, "Lord, You hear what he is saying about me. Is this truth? What are You trying to teach me?" I have been doing this for several years now, and I consistently have experienced the Lord revealing His truth when I ask. Seek Him with an open heart and mind. He is always faithful.

Here are some ways to start applying your own "truth filter." First, humble yourself by admitting you don't have any hint of God's love or power within your natural self. You are nothing more than a beggar crying out to a holy God for His love and power. He gives you all of the tools and abilities to become like Him—holy. We are simply twigs, incapable of producing grapes, but He grafts us into Himself, the Vine, through grace. He then allows His "supernatural sap" to flow within us to produce the fruit of the Spirit: love, joy, peace, patience, and so on (see Gal. 5:22-23). That's the best deal in life.

After humbling yourself before God, He begins to fill you with the power of His Spirit. Then you have both the desire and the ability to love Him with all of your heart, soul, mind and strength (see Matt. 22:37-40). That love comes from Him alone.

Also, after humbling yourself, you have both the desire and the ability, because of His gifts to you of love and power, to love your neighbors as you love yourself. You can do that for others because the God of the universe is now filling you up with all of the fullness of Himself. And He is meeting all of your needs through His riches in heaven through Christ Jesus (see Phil. 4:19).

Finally, you now have His power and love to experience everything that happens to you as good or great. Life is full of bad things, good things and great things. The best news I have ever read is about how God works good into our lives through "bad" experiences. He uses all of our bad circumstances to transform us.

For example, as life throws me anything, I can expect everything to turn into good or great! So, life, bring it on! I'll rejoice, and again, I say that I will rejoice in everything that happens to me. I can give thanks for all things, for this is God's will through Christ Jesus (see 1 Thess. 5:16-18). Everything works together for my good because I love God, and I've been empowered to love others. Nothing is wasted; I'm never a victim.

When someone shares a "word from God" with you, apply these truths to it: Does it resonate with your spirit, with the words you know from the Bible? Hold it up to the light of specific verses, and you can trust His Word to illuminate what is real and what you are to do.

5. Treasure Hunt from Your Past

Everything that occurs in our lives and everything that we are (warts and all) has a hidden gift attached. It's the old adage that "every cloud has a silver lining" and the Scripture that states that all things work together for good for those who are called according to His purpose (see Rom. 8:28). It is true. Another way to take care of our hearts is to go "treasure hunting" in the painful experiences of the past and present.

> My life is but a weaving, between my God and me.
> I do not choose the colors, He worketh steadily.
> Oftimes He weaveth sorrow, and I in foolish pride,
> Forget He sees the upper, and I the underside.
> Not till the loom is silent, and shuttles cease to fly,
> Will God unroll the canvas and explain the reason why.
> The dark threads are as needful in the skillful Weaver's hand,
> As the threads of gold and silver in the pattern He has planned.

This anonymous poem beautifully illustrates one of the greatest things we can ever learn: the ability to find the hidden treasure buried within each difficult experience. The Scriptures assure us that trials and difficult times are unavoidable. Consider the message that the apostle Paul delivered in Romans 5:3-5:

> And not only this, but we also exult in our tribulations, knowing
> that tribulation brings about perseverance; and perseverance,

proven character; and proven character, hope; and hope does not disappoint, because the love of God has been poured out within our hearts through the Holy Spirit who was given to us (*NASB*).

Although we may work overtime trying to protect ourselves from pain, we'll never be able to isolate ourselves totally from being hurt by our own actions and the actions of others. Isolation isn't taking good care of our hearts. Openness is. Therefore, we need to learn how to take any negative experience and see the flip side.

When trials crash into our lives, we are instructed to rejoice (as soon as possible), knowing that trials bring about many wonderful things. It can be so beneficial to teach ourselves to say, "I'm grateful that I am going through this pain. I don't like it; I wish it wasn't here. But since it is here, and it's beyond my control, I want to express appreciation that God is with me in this." Being able to thank God in the midst of a trial is a sign of maturity and a healthy heart, because we realize that our pain is producing great things. We only grow out of pain. (We'll unpack this further in the next chapter.) When we are content, and life is good, what need do we have for God? When we experience tragedy and pain, we remember that we need to cling to Him for our very lives. Only people who experience need recognize the need for a Savior. If life is always grand, what do you need to be "saved" from?

 Make sure that your personality strengths do not become your weaknesses. If you are too outgoing, you might overwhelm others; if you overdose on perfectionism, you may seem rigid.

However, don't jump into "treasure hunting" too fast. When you experience loss, tragedy or pain, it is important to grieve. If you skip the grieving process, it's like looking for buried treasure without a map. Grieving provides us with the necessary time to prepare for finding the treasure.

The treasure hunt begins by listing the positive aspects you can now see in the past painful situations in your life. For example, a divorce or the death of a loved one can make you stronger, courageous, more loving, humbler, more mature, compassionate, thoughtful, gentle, careful, kind or patient. In fact, the things you like most about yourself probably developed as a direct result of trials. When we experience difficulties, God promises that He will make us complete (see Jas. 1:2-4).

In 1 Corinthians 13, we find the attributes of love. Notice that these characteristics are the same types of treasures that many people gain as a result of trials:

> Love is patient, love is kind and is not jealous; love does not brag and is not arrogant, does not act unbecomingly; it does not seek its own, is not provoked, does not take into account a wrong suffered, does not rejoice in unrighteousness, but rejoices with the truth; bears all things, believes all things, hopes all things, endures all things. . . . But now faith, hope, love, abide these three; but the greatest of these is love (1 Cor. 13:4-7,13, *NASB*).

In addition to these things, going through a trial almost always results in our becoming more sensitive and sympathetic, which is the basis of love. When life's challenges beat us up, we tend to become more sensitive. We become more compassionate, because now we know how other people feel when they suffer. We are much more caring, thoughtful and gentle. Trials tend to blast us out of our arrogance or complacency and into empathy. These are characteristics of love—compassion, kindness, patience and self-control. All of these things are birthed out of pain.

I (Gary) seek to find out what faith God has granted me in difficult situations to watch His purposes unfold, year after year. I'm now almost 70, and I'm more excited about today and the future than at any time before. My life is just starting, because every day is the first day of the rest of my life. I live with great hope about the present and the future.

Another benefit is that difficult experiences cause us to slow down and take stock of what's really important. People—our spouse and family—are the most important of all. They are the ones whose hearts God has entrusted to us. They are the ones He has called us to walk with through life. Difficulties can open our eyes to how valuable these relationships are.

Have you ever talked with a person who has gone through a heart attack? Afterwards, life is never the same. Someone who has had a heart attack will typically start exercising and losing weight, developing a stronger body than before. Heart attacks also help people become more loving. They are better able to relate to other people's pain. They have an instinctive sense of what others need because of the near-death experience they had.

Treasure hunting is not something we do for just a short time; we should continue to seek the treasure in each trial that comes. It's work that needs to continue until we feel the results of God's revelations and blessings from what was once our biggest source of pain.

6. Set Relationship Boundaries When Necessary

It's perfectly fine to set boundaries around relationships that are unhealthy. You're not building a fortress or retreating behind a wall. You are recognizing that getting too close to some people is toxic to your heart. Still, it is often difficult to know how to establish necessary boundaries in an effective way. An effective boundary is one that will take care of you and your heart in a way that best accomplishes your overall personal and relational goals. Thus, the critical initial question is: What am I wanting or trying to accomplish?

Without a clear answer to this question first, most people either build walls or barriers between themselves and the people or circumstances that are difficult or threatening (withdrawal), or they attempt to stop or change the behavior (control, manipulation). Either of these responses hurts relationships and shuts down your heart.

What you want to accomplish is the nurture and protection of your heart in such a way that it strengthens and builds even the most challenging relationship. This answer speaks to a deeper question: Ultimately, what does it look like to take good care of my heart?

The goal in setting boundaries with people is *to attempt to create a safe space that enables my heart to remain open to God, self and others*. The goal of maintaining an open heart is the essence of a Christ-centered boundary. A Christlike boundary will be characterized by love, honor and respect. It will also help you move toward, rather than away from, relationships. Therefore, it cannot involve withdrawal (which involves closing the heart and spirit), manipulation or control (which can shut down others' hearts and spirits).

 Keep short accounts by lovingly confronting others when you are hurt instead of ignoring the issue ("speaking the truth in love").

The way to establish a Christ-centered boundary is first to remind yourself that your goal is to create a space that enables you to keep your heart open to God, to yourself and to others (including those with whom you are setting boundaries). Next, make a request regarding the behavior or circumstances that are making it difficult for you to keep your heart open. Remember that the response to a request can be no. If no is not acceptable to you, you are actually making a demand, not a request. Finally, establish a contingency plan in case the other person denies your request. This is an action you can take that moves you to a physical, emotional or spiritual space that best facilitates your heart opening. You can even set healthy boundaries in marriage to help eliminate heart-damaging patterns. Dan and Marci experienced this when Marci set a healthy boundary to protect her heart from Dan's anger.

"Dan and I had a very unhealthy communication pattern during the first eight years of our marriage," Marci says. "He carried a lot of anger and hostility toward me as a result of family frustrations and guilt. The only way I knew how to respond to his anger was to withdraw. God was working in my heart, because I was sick and tired of fighting and desperately wanted things to change. I prayed and asked God to give me understanding and wisdom as to how to respond to Dan. In His still, small voice, God whispered what I needed to hear, and I was prepared the next time Dan lost his temper with me.

"My heart was fighting for our marriage. So from my heart, I responded in a sweet and calm manner, 'Dan, you don't need to yell at me. I'm your wife, your best friend and your lover. I'm on your team, and I'm sick of the devil trying to divide us. Please, talk to me in a way that honors our marriage and God, and let's try to get along.' It worked! Dan immediately calmed down and responded in a wonderful manner. I had to set a boundary, but the boundary was really against the devil, not my husband. I wanted Dan to understand that it was us against him, not us against each other."

Marci's response to Dan deflated his temper because she didn't accuse or respond with anger. Remember, a boundary is anything you set in order to keep your heart open. Setting a boundary with your former spouse, for example, might require you to say something like, "I really want to understand you so we can communicate about what's best for our kids, but I'm not okay with direct insults. I'm willing to listen to you if you are willing to share your feelings in a way that honors both of us."

This is "Christ-centered," because when someone is being verbally abusive, your heart is going to shut down. A closed heart is not what God desires for us. Make a request that will allow your heart to remain open. If the other person chooses not to honor your request, then you might need to walk away or hang up the phone. Let the other party know that you are open to listen when he or she is willing to treat you in a loving way.

It All Begins with You

In marriage, you realize very quickly that you cannot control anyone else. You are ultimately in charge only of you. That's why the best place to start making positive changes in your remarriage is in your own heart. Like the barn swallows on Greg's front porch, you need to become vigilant—even fierce—about weeding out the lies and preventing any new blockages from clogging your heart's love flow.

Now that you know how to pay close attention and protect your heart, you can keep it fully open and filled abundantly with God's love. You are precious, one of a kind. Out of all the billions of people in the world, God carefully crafted together you and your spouse's particular combination of talents, gifting, skills, temperaments, personalities and even flaws. Your marriage is designed to be a learning, nurturing, growing environment filled with open hearts that can abundantly outflow love to others. It's not an impossible dream. But it all begins with you.

Think about the love between a parent and a newborn child. The parent recognizes immediately how valuable and vulnerable that little person is and vows to care for that baby, pay attention to her, protect her, nurture her and love her. Make those same vows now to your own heart. You and your marriage deserve it.

HEART MONITORS

1. What were you taught as a child about how to handle your emotions? Were you taught to hide them or to put on a show? How is that affecting your remarriage?

2. What "messages" have been etched by the enemy on your heart? How much "surgery" do you still need to erase them?

3. List at least five of your very best qualities. How did you feel as you wrote that list?

4. How often do you recognize your emotions and the information they are giving you? How can you become more attuned to your feelings?

5. Who are the experienced, trusted mentors in your life? How have they helped your marriage?

6. What have your "treasure hunts" of past hurts uncovered? What benefits can you now see as the result of the three biggest trials, tragedies or traumas you have experienced?

HEART PROTECTORS

Before any future interaction with someone whose relationship with you has not been healthy, set boundaries. Practice how your conversation might go and what your "escape hatch" will be.

Carry a notepad for one week and write down as many feelings as you can (and what triggered or inspired them). After seven days, examine your list for any patterns you see. Did you experience negative feelings at regular times of the day (when you were hungry or tired, perhaps)? Did food affect your feelings? Do particular people lift your spirits or shut you down? Make any changes that will foster better feelings and a healthier heart.

Praise your spouse. Name five or six ways that your mate was uniquely created, "fearfully and wonderfully made."

Notes

1. Rick Warren, *The Purpose-Driven Life* (Grand Rapids, MI: Zondervan, 2002), pp. 22–24.
2. Chip Dodd, *The Voice of the Heart: A Call to Full Living* (Nashville, TN: Sage Hill Resources, 2001), p. 35.

4

Beliefs That Build a Satisfied Heart in Remarriage

And do not be conformed to this world, but be transformed by
the renewing of your mind, that you may prove what is that good
and acceptable and perfect will of God.
ROMANS 12:2, *NKJV*

You have learned some of the ways you can protect and guard your heart, the wellspring of life, and help you feel safe so that you can love openly and fully. But you can't do it all on your own. The best way to build a satisfied heart in remarriage is to transform your beliefs so that permanent change takes place in your heart and is then reflected in every part of your thoughts, words and actions. That's powerful, and we've discovered that it works.

Let us share another story from the Smalley family. When my (Gary's) grandson Michael and I launched our own little scientific experiment on his behavior (with the permission of his parents, Kari and Roger, of course), I had no idea how it would turn out. But when Michael was 10 years old, I began to teach him to memorize just a few key Bible verses. Over the next two years, as we learned together, I watched Michael's life and mine become transformed. We were both amazed at the changes, and his parents couldn't thank me enough. This was a total accident. I had no idea that he and I would start changing as much as we did. My grandson's actions, words and thoughts changed from griping, whining and complaining at the age of 10 to tenderhearted gratefulness by the age of 12. By seeing the results of our little "lab experiment" in his life and my own, I became convinced even further how true God's Word is and how vital it is to learn it if we want our lives to change and our hearts to feel safe.

My time with Michael brought to life Hebrews 4:12, which says that God's Word is alive and powerful and sharper than a two-edged sword. Jesus says He is the "Word," and He became flesh and dwelt among us as a gift from God. He also said that if we know the truth (and part of the truth is that Jesus Himself is the Word), the truth will set us free. Memorizing His Word—hiding it in our hearts—is like tucking away Jesus Himself, who lives in us and dwells with us when we accept His gift of salvation. Memorizing the Word is an important aspect of keeping the wellspring of life flowing. It's a key component of that vertical connection, a personal relationship with God. When we are filled with the Word, which is Christ, we are filled with love, because God is love. Then and only then can we overflow His love to those around us.

In my own life over the past eight years, I have watched nearly 100 Bible verses transform my life in amazing ways, and I know they can transform the love and lives of couples who have remarried so that they have loving, satisfied, safe hearts.

Following her divorce, Marci found strength and comfort when she memorized God's Word. "The Scriptures felt like they were pumping new life into me, renewing my mind and healing my heart," she says. "There are so many verses I have come to love, but one of my favorites is Psalm 107:19-20, which says, 'They cried to the LORD in their trouble, and he saved them from their distress. He sent forth his word and healed them; he rescued them from the grave.' What tremendous hope those verses gave me when I was in the midst of despair!"

Here are some other verses that helped restore Marci's quality of life and heal her heart:

The LORD is gracious and full of compassion, slow to anger and great in mercy. The LORD is good to all, and His tender mercies are over all His works. . . . The LORD is near to all who call upon Him, to all who call upon Him in truth. He will fulfill the desire of those who fear Him; He also will hear their cry and save them (Ps. 145:8-9,18-19, *NKJV*).

For I know the thoughts that I think toward you, says the LORD, thoughts of peace and not of evil, to give you a future and a hope. Then you will call upon Me and go and pray to Me, and I will listen to you. And you will seek Me and find Me, when you search for Me with all your heart (Jer. 29:11-14, *NKJV*).

"This last verse has taken firm root in my heart," Marci says. "I believe it with all that I am. It has changed my beliefs and restored my heart. It is TRUE! I am no longer hopeless or helpless."

Hearts, Thoughts, Words and Actions

There is one powerful, life-changing, transforming biblical law that we have had the privilege to discover over these past few years that can keep hearts open and satisfied. As we have watched remarried couples discover this same truth, they soon learn that their new mate, their blended family, no longer control their moods or their quality of life. When you realize that your quality of life is in your own hands, not in the hands of others or even at the mercy of your circumstances, that revelation brings excitement and a sense of freedom and peace. This truth is . . .

Your heart is filled with your own personal beliefs.

That's it? You might be thinking, *Duh. Why should I get excited about that?* Hang in there while we reveal why this principle is so amazing.

Your beliefs—what you consider to be *true* for you—are what determine the quality of your own life. Your beliefs control what you think about, say and do; and what you think about, say and do are connected to the types of emotions you experience. Whether you are happy, sad, depressed, excited, discouraged, joyful or at peace, all of these feelings come to you via your thoughts, words and actions.

Jesus said in many verses that our thoughts, words and actions come out of our hearts. And our emotional state is almost always a reflection of our thoughts, words and actions. Look at Matthew 12:34: "For the mouth speaks out of that which fills the heart" (*NASB*). In Matthew 15:18, Jesus says, "But the things that proceed out of the mouth come from the heart" (*NASB*). In the next verse, He speaks about thoughts and actions when He says, "For out of the heart come evil thoughts, murders, adulteries, fornications, thefts, false witness, slanders" (v. 19, *NASB*). Although those Scriptures have always made sense to us, the apostle Paul also wrote something that caused our hearts to leap with joy when we read these words and connected the dots:

> If you confess with your mouth that Jesus is Lord and believe in your *heart* that God raised him from the dead, you will be saved. For it is

by believing *in your heart* that you are made right with God, and it is by confessing with your mouth that you are saved (Rom. 10:9-10, *NLT*, emphasis added).

Are you tracking with us yet? Your emotions are determined by your thoughts, words and actions. Your thoughts, words and actions come out of your heart. If your heart is filled with a belief in Jesus Christ, filled with the Word (Jesus and the Bible, the living Word of God), then your feelings are determined by what's in your heart, not by the words, thoughts or actions of anyone else, and certainly not by your circumstances! Isn't that wonderful? That simple truth can set you free from trying to manipulate the people and circumstances in your life. When you stop pursuing happiness and start pursuing God and His Word, you get joy—and that's a lot better than happiness. You will be able to love fully and receive love from an open, satisfied and safe heart in your remarriage.

 Draw a stick figure person. Write out Romans 12:2 somewhere on the figure and "connect" this verse to the figure's head and heart. Hang it on your refrigerator.

Conversely, whatever we spend a lot of time thinking about also affects the state of our heart. They go hand in hand. If you spend time dwelling on the things of God, then your heart, your actions and your emotions will reflect that. To make it even easier, there are fewer than 10 major beliefs or concepts that we believe you need to establish in your heart in order to be transformed in a mighty way. While I (Gary) have written a previous book and curriculum on these 10 transforming beliefs that help parents guard their children's hearts, for remarried couples reading this book, I want to give you the "vital two" of these beliefs that I believe will help your marriage greatly.[1] First, let's look at a practical example of how our beliefs propel our thoughts, words and actions.

Imagine that you are walking in your backyard and notice new buds forming on your rosebushes. You are focused on the beauty of these rosebuds as you walk toward the bushes, not noticing a snake coiled in the grass about three feet in front of your roses. As you are about to take another step, you see movement under your foot. That's when you see the snake, scream and try to get out of the way! Or you might see the snake, jump back to determine its type, suck in your breath and become very still. Whatever you do, your reaction to seeing the snake takes less time than the blink of your eye.

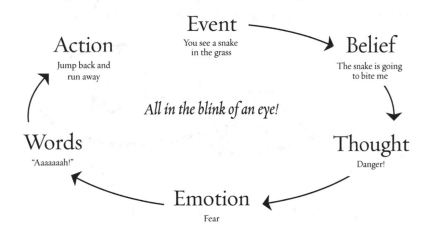

This circle is completed so rapidly that most humans aren't aware of it. And here's the key: Your reaction to the snake depends on what you *believe* about snakes. If you're like me (Gary), snakes don't faze you much. I was once stuck near a rattlesnake den at about the age of 10. My close friend and I thought that we would die, until we figured out how to move right past those "fall-blinded" rattlesnakes. After that experience, I had a fascination with snakes and began to learn which of the various snakes in the United States were poisonous and which ones were safe. In the rosebush scenario, I would have recognized immediately if that snake was safe or poisonous. Still, my response would have been to jump back in order to see what type of snake it was.

If you believe that snakes are creepy and dangerous, you may have thought "Danger!" and screamed and jumped and run in the opposite direction with your heart racing, especially if you've seen those snake shows on TV. All of those reactions would have happened in less than a second.

According to Dr. Bruce Lipton, world famous medical professor and human cell specialist, human *beliefs* are 10 million times more powerful at controlling our behavior than our *thoughts* are. You can think whatever you want, but your beliefs are always going to override your thoughts. You can wish for change, wish that you were happier, wish that you could get along better with your spouse, or wish that you were married to someone different, but no amount of wishing will change your behavior or emotions, because they are all determined by the *beliefs* that are already stored in your heart. Dr. Lipton also says that thoughts trump beliefs in the long run, because "new thoughts," thoughts you think over and over again, day after day, eventually change your old beliefs and establish new ones.

The Two Vital Beliefs

It makes sense, then, that in order to change your thoughts, behavior and even your feelings, you need to change your beliefs. The first and possibly the most important belief that can alter your life and remarriage for the better is this:

VITAL BELIEF NUMBER ONE:
*A loving relationship with God and His power in me
to love and serve others is far superior to the belief that
I need to gain more pleasure or have more fun.*

This belief is in direct contrast to the belief that most of us put first and foremost, whether we acknowledge it consciously or not. Most of us really believe that to have the best quality of life, we must have our share of pleasures, thrills, excitement, entertainment, fun and play time. We learn this from our family, teachers and friends. In short, we believe it's our personal, individual right to be happy, and that happiness will most surely come after we have experienced our share of pleasure. With that belief lodged in our hearts, we damage our relationships, especially our marriage relationship. In fact, I (Gary) would say that over the 60 years I have developed this belief in my own heart, it became the most destructive belief within me.

Why? Because this belief centers on self, and focusing on yourself never satisfies. If your basic belief is that you need pleasure, happiness or fun, then you will constantly feel like you don't have enough. You must chase more money, more recognition, more stuff, more everything in order to feel happy. Instead of good things, pursuing happiness through pleasure brings lust, anger and greed into our lives. When the belief that we must make ourselves happy is stored in our hearts from the time we are young and ambitious, every time we think about or act on this belief during our lifetime, we reinforce it. We cause it to grow. And instead of happiness, we get broken relationships, unhealthy addictions, anger, jealousy, envy and misery. We can have "everything" yet feel empty.

 Ask a close friend or mentor what he or she would say are your top beliefs and goals. What does this person see you spending time doing and discussing?

I remember sitting in the living room of a famous movie star who had just won an Academy Awards Oscar. She placed it on a large pedestal in her room, pointed to it and said these words that I will never forget: "I thought that this statue would finally bring me what I've looked for all my life. Instead, I'm depressed, confused, discouraged and without any hope that I'll find true happiness. Because if this isn't it, nothing else will match it."

I discovered the same truth in my fifties. I was making more money than I could spend, and it never, ever added anything to the quality of my life. I felt less, not more, fulfilled. I tried to manage all the rewards that God had given me, and it took so much time that I gradually walked away from the Rewarder. When I returned to seeking only God—to loving God with all my heart and not expecting anything or anyone else to complete me or make me happy—God began to fill me up again with all the fullness of Himself (see Eph. 3:16-20). What I started learning anew a few years ago is that believing in God is far more satisfying, exciting and joy-filled than seeking the pleasures that come from this world. Money, lustful thoughts, careers, even our children will never fulfill us. Our spouse can't complete us. Only God can. What I am now trying to keep firmly established in my own heart is the belief that loving God and loving others by serving them is 10 billion times more important than my own pleasures or entertainment. This belief lifts you up from expecting anything on this earth—even your spouse—to contribute to the quality of your life.

 Ask God to help you love Him first.

When you truly get that vertical connection, that belief that God is everything and that He is enough, you will almost immediately begin to notice that you won't be trying to change your mate anymore. You won't be frustrated or fearful over the amount of money you are making or the size of your house, apartment or tent. You won't try to live through your children or be angry with them for not living up to your expectations. You will be able to accept your family and friends as they are. Day after day, you'll rely only on God to fill you with the fullness of Himself.

Moving from Self to God

You cannot expect to change your negative, pleasure-seeking beliefs overnight, because it took years, probably even decades, for you to get where you are today. Maybe you had accepted Christ and thought you were loving God fairly well, but it didn't hit you until now how much you were actually living for yourself. To be brutally honest (and so that you will not be discouraged if your progress seems slow), it took nearly three years for me (Gary) to lose the lustful thoughts I had for women other than my own wife. It took daily effort to change my beliefs and transform my heart. But the effort has been more than worth it. Plus, to encourage you, I began to see a big change in terms of my battle with lust within the first two weeks.

You can change, too, and this heart transformation will radically improve your remarriage. It can transform *everything* about the quality of your life and bring a new, loving atmosphere into your home so that the hearts that dwell there feel safe. There are actually fairly simple steps to transforming the beliefs that have been controlling your thoughts and actions. These steps are formed from the Bible verse Romans 12:2, which says:

> And do not be conformed to this world, but be transformed by the renewing of your mind, that you may prove what is that good and acceptable and perfect will of God (*NKJV*).

Here are three simple ways that you can transform your beliefs. First, *memorize four powerful, life-changing verses.* By putting these four truths, this living Word, inside your mind and heart, you lay a foundation from which you can build your renewed belief in loving God and loving and serving others. These verses are the following:

1. The words of Jesus in Mark 12:30-31: "And you must love the Lord your God with all your heart, all your soul, all your mind, and all your strength. The second is equally important: 'Love your neighbor as yourself.' No other commandment is greater than these" (*NLT*).

2. The words of Paul to the church at Galatia in Galatians 5:13-14: "My brothers and sisters, God called you to be free, but do not use your freedom as an excuse to do what pleases your sinful self. Serve each other with love. The whole law is made complete in this one command: 'Love your neighbor as you love yourself'" (*NCV*).

As you memorize these four verses, ask God to illuminate His words. Look for words that are repeated and unpack the meaning of each one. For example, in the Mark 12:30-31 verses, "all" is mentioned three times. "All" means that there is no room for anything else, like expectations obtained from the things of this world. When you meditate on and memorize His Word, God will reveal His meaning for your life again and again for the rest of your days.

Second, do what David did in Psalm 1: *meditate on God's law.* In Psalm 1, it says that King David meditated on God's highest law day and night (the law of loving God with all his heart). When he did that, the Bible describes him as becoming like a tree planted by living waters. It also says that *all* he did prospered. Wouldn't we like that in our own lives? Meditating on God's law, the Bible, simply means repeating the words in the Bible verses and dwelling on the meaning of those words several times a day. I would encourage you to find a Bible commentary, a Bible concordance or other tools to look for what each word means in the verses you memorize. (You can also go to www.searchgodsword.com.) Read these verses in different translations, and ask God to illuminate His Word as you read, recite and repeat.

The truth of how powerful it is to learn God's Word is confirmed again in the famous words of Moses in Deuteronomy 6:4-9, which told the Israelites, God's people, that if they would brand on the hearts of their children and themselves that they should love God with all their heart, soul, mind and strength, then *all* that they would do in the Promised Land would prosper.

 Get a Strong's Concordance *or other Bible reference tools to help you dig deeper into the Bible.*

How did they "brand" this truth on their hearts? The Bible says that they were to repeat these words of God over and over again, when they woke up in the morning, when they sat down and stood up from eating, when they walked in and out of their houses. They were to repeat them as they walked along the path, and braid them in their hair along their temple and tattoo them on the back of their hands. That's a lot of "daily thought time" about the most important words that God ever spoke. Since those who believe in Him today are also His people, God designed us to repeat His most important truths every day, all day long, until those truths become our deep-rooted beliefs!

I (Gary) accidentally discovered this amazing truth when I was raising my three children. Almost every day, I asked my kids a question and had them answer it out loud. I asked, "Okay, kids, what's the greatest thing in life?" or "What's the most important thing that we can do in life?"

They would answer by saying, "Dad, we already know, it's honoring God and His creation. Okay, Dad, we know it now, we don't have to say it anymore." But I would always bring it up in different ways. Today, my children are in their late thirties and early forties, and all three honor God and honor His creation. It's a huge belief that is now "branded" on their hearts.

Third, *maintain an excited and expectant attitude of watching your life becoming transformed into the image of God.* It's important only that you notice the transformation; don't try to transform yourself. Just be excited and expect God to do great things in your life and with your beliefs as you brand His Word on your heart. You can't become like Christ through your own efforts. Rather, your job is to stay helpless, humble and in receiving mode, allowing the living, powerful, two-edged sword of the Word of God to work within you as you memorize and meditate every day, all day long.

Trust God's Word when He says that He blesses the humble and the poor in spirit. In other words, if you admit that you are a "beggar," helpless to create God's kind of love within you, He promises to give you His grace (His love and power freely given to you with no effort on your part). He can work in you and through you and bless you with more and more of His kingdom. Matthew 5:3 confirms this: "They are blessed who realize their spiritual poverty, for the kingdom of heaven belongs to them" (*NCV*).

Let the Holy Spirit, who lives within you, do His work within you daily. When you combine memorization and meditation on the Word of God with the power of the Holy Spirit working within you, your desire to love God more and to love others more will increase.

 Find 10 Bible verses that describe how the Holy Spirit works in you.

For example, when I sense that I am starting to have lustful thoughts about the "ideal" woman or when I get discouraged about a lack of money or become fearful that I am not getting my "share" of pleasure, I say to myself, *Okay, Smalley, do you want to keep growing the belief that lusting to use people and things is more important than loving and serving God and others?*

Which one is more important to God? That answer is a no-brainer. Today, I have God's power enabling me to say *no*. I now say, *I am going to starve that old, lustful, pleasure-seeking belief to death and watch the roots dwindle. Now I'm growing the best belief within me, God's belief, that I can love and serve Him and others.* That's what brings me high quality of life. That belief has proven so true. Jesus is right. He was dead-on. Loving others *does* fulfill all the Law and the Prophets.

The second major belief that can transform your remarriage is almost as powerful as the first one, but it's about as easy to swallow as cod liver oil. Read it, and then stick with us as we explain. Here it is:

VITAL BELIEF NUMBER TWO:
Bad times are good for you. All of the difficulties and conflicts that you face in your remarriage are actually, truthfully, beneficial for you.

Now don't throw this book across the room or start wondering what we've been smoking. We know that this second belief we want you to develop in your heart goes exactly against the grain of our human nature. And it is the direct opposite of what our culture has been teaching us our entire lives. The lie that most of us have been fed is the belief that *trials, difficulties and frustrations are all "bad" and should be avoided if at all possible.* That belief, my friend, comes straight from the "pit." In fact, that very belief causes us to violate the third commandment of God through Moses that says we are not to take God's name in vain. How? Well, when we curse God for allowing difficulties in our lives, when we beg God to reduce our trials or take them away altogether, we're calling Him a liar. When we think God was absent when we were born or when we decided to marry again or when something bad happens to us, we are taking Him in vain. The real truth is that we can thank God in all circumstances because Romans 8:28 says, "And we know that in all things God works for the good of those who love him, who have been called according to his purpose."

All things—your life, your remarriage, your children and your stepchildren. The death of loved ones, the financial crises you face. *All things.* They are good for you, because it is only through difficulties and challenges that you grow and God's love is perfected in you. It is in hard times that you desperately feel the need for a Savior to deliver you. The biggest traumas and tragedies tend to produce the most spiritual growth. So thank God, praise Him for the challenges in your remarriage. If you face them with Him, you'll be amazed at the eventual results.

Think about a trial in your past and what good came out of it. Share with your spouse what you learned and how you grew.

Other Bible verses show how beautiful lives become when hearts and beliefs are transformed. Trials are compared to trophies that give us more of His patience, character and hope, even when it doesn't *feel* like it. The Bible says there is nothing that makes a person more beautiful than a grateful heart, and that those who give thanks to God in all circumstances add bountiful health to their lives and bring encouragement to their families. On the flip side, it says that a griping, complaining mate is like a dripping faucet or irritating, clanging pipes. Which do you want to be?

According to the HeartMath stress management researchers in California, when people express gratefulness, it releases the healthiest hormones our bodies produce. When we complain, judge and criticize others, their research showed that our bodies release the most harmful hormones into our systems. Even our bodies respond to our beliefs![2]

By thanking God for the challenges you face in your marriage, you take another step toward changing from pleasure seeking to loving God and serving others. By embracing God's Word, allowing the Holy Spirit to work in you and developing a grateful heart despite trying circumstances, you will find a natural desire to love your spouse and family. When you desire to love, your emotions follow, and you will soon find yourself enjoying your remarriage fully.

Key Verses for Living the Two Vital Beliefs

We can say truthfully that these two vital beliefs—believing in God first to meet all our needs and fulfill us, and believing that bad times are actually good for us—have made a huge positive difference in our lives and marriages. As I (Gary) was writing this chapter, in fact, my wife and I received some "terrible" news. It was sad information. But I told the bearer of this news that I was finishing up a chapter on rejoicing in the middle of trials, and I put into practice those two vital beliefs once again. Four hours later, I was already feeling my emotions line up with my belief that all trials are worthy of praise and thanksgiving. I'm not up again instantly after hearing bad news, but in a few hours or days, I come full circle back to joy, because God is the source of joy. His truth about giving thanks is what brings me back to the best quality of life.

Give it a try in your life, but don't be discouraged if this new attitude does not come overnight. It sure didn't for me. It's tough to see things that hurt or anger us as "good." We much prefer whatever is easy and fun. But by burying God's Word within our hearts and allowing His Holy Spirit's power to work in us, we will experience change. By the day after my sad news, I had already experienced a number of opportunities to praise God for the event and to experience "the peace of God, which transcends all understanding," and which "guard[s] your hearts and your minds in Christ Jesus" (Phil. 4:7). It works every time, and I love it. It worked in my grandson Michael's life, even at the tender age of adolescence. I can guarantee it will work in your life and your remarriage, too.

Here are some of our favorite Bible verses that we used to transform our old belief that trials are "bad." If you memorize and meditate on any one of these verses or just a couple of them, within a few months you'll begin to notice that your attitude about the challenges life throws you will begin to change. You will find that it will become much easier to praise God during the pain of difficulties, and "you shall know the truth, and the truth shall make you free" (John 8:32, *NKJV*).

- Romans 8:28: "And we know that for those who love God all things work together for good, for those who are called according to his purpose" (*ESV*).

- 2 Corinthians 12:9-10: "But he said to me, 'My grace is sufficient for you, for my power is made perfect in weakness.' Therefore I will boast all the more gladly about my weaknesses, so that Christ's power may rest on me. That is why, for Christ's sake, I delight in weaknesses, in insults, in hardships, in persecutions, in difficulties. For when I am weak, then I am strong."

- Romans 5:3-5: "And not only that, but we also glory in tribulations, knowing that tribulation produces perseverance; and perseverance, character; and character, hope. Now hope does not disappoint, because the love of God has been poured out in our hearts by the Holy Spirit who was given to us" (*NKJV*).

- James 1:2-4: "Dear brothers and sisters, when troubles come your way, consider it an opportunity for great joy. For you know that when your faith is tested, your endurance has a chance to grow. So let it grow, for when your endurance is fully developed, you will be perfect and complete, needing nothing" (*NLT*).

- 1 Thessalonians 5:16-18: "Be cheerful no matter what; pray all the time; thank God no matter what happens. This is the way God wants you who belong to Christ Jesus to live" (*THE MESSAGE*).

Aren't those verses powerful? It's easy to see how dwelling on them day and night could transform our lives, isn't it? While I have fully outlined the two most vital beliefs that inspire transformation, there are several other beliefs I will touch on now. These are key beliefs that all followers of Christ should begin to brand on their hearts:

- Believe that loving God with all of your heart, soul, mind and strength is the highest and best belief you can brand upon your heart (see Matt. 22:36-40).

- Believe that Christ is the Son of God and He came to save us by His sacrificial death on the cross (see Rom. 10:9-10).

- Believe that God's Holy Spirit was sent so that we can have the strength with power and love that God designed us to have (see John 16:7-16; 1 Cor. 13:4-8).

- Believe that God gives His love and power freely to the humble, the helpless, the true spiritual "beggars" pleading for God's love and power. I beg God every day, from a position of helplessness, for His love and power to grow deeply within me (see Eph. 3:16-20).

When you meditate on key verses and center your thoughts on key beliefs, your old beliefs will pass away and everything will become new. And when both spouses in remarriage experience this transformation, nothing can tear them apart! Their hearts and home will truly be the safest place on earth for all of the members of their family. If my 10-year-old grandson's life and mine could be transformed by these verses and beliefs, yours can too.

HEART MONITORS

1. Do you have a personal relationship with God? If not, how can you start one today?

2. What beliefs have you been living by? After reading this chapter, what differences have you discovered between what you thought you believed and how you have actually been living?

3. What connection do you now see between your heart, your beliefs, your words, your thoughts and your actions? How are these all connected to your feelings about your spouse and family?

4. In what ways do you think that your marriage will improve if your beliefs are transformed? How will it make your family's hearts safer and more open?

HEART PROTECTORS

Ask God to forgive you for the times when you have sought your own pleasure and happiness instead of focusing on loving Him and your mate. Ask the Holy Spirit to work in you to transform your beliefs.

Discuss with your spouse the beliefs you have been living versus the ones you want to live. If your focus has been on your happiness or if you have tried to rely on your mate for fulfillment, ask your spouse to forgive you.

Set your watch, cell phone or other alarm to go off hourly for at least one day this week. Each time it does, repeat the key verses and two vital beliefs outlined in this chapter.

Memorize the key verses in this chapter. Set them to a familiar tune, recite them over and over or write them several times. Do whatever it takes to brand them on your heart.

Notes
1. Gary Smalley, *Change Your Heart, Change Your Life: How Changing What You Believe Will Give You the Great Life You've Always Wanted* (Nashville, TN: Thomas Nelson, 2008).
2. Marci Shimoff, "Happy People Know How to Let Their Heart Lead," Institute of Heart Math. http://www.heartmath.org/templates/ihm/section_includes/press_room/pdf/happy_people_know_how_to_let_their_heart_lead.pdf.

5

Keeping Each Other's Hearts Safe

Be completely humble and gentle; be patient, bearing with one another in love.
EPHESIANS 4:2

Remember that majestic old farmhouse from the movie *Twister* that we described earlier? We hope this is slowly becoming your vision for what remarriage can be. Your goal is to open your heart and the hearts of your family so that they feel like a safe haven, a place of warmth and security for all who enter. What will it take to accomplish this? One little phrase: *emotional security*. Next to your relationship with Christ and the transformation of your mind and beliefs, emotional security is the most important aspect of fostering a great remarriage.

The marital relationship is what makes or breaks a stepfamily. The husband and wife are the heart of every family, and we already know that the heart needs to remain wide open for love to flow through it. What does it take to keep the valves clear that's different from what you may have heard or read in other marriage seminars, conferences or books? Let us say it again: *emotional security*.

Here's what we mean: After you examine yourself honestly and allow God to perform the necessary surgery to clear any blockages (go back to chapters 3 and 4 if you need to review), your now wide-open heart has to feel safe in order to stay that way. Oftentimes, remarriage relationships feel anything but safe. The walls were raised on a foundation of loss and change. The yard is filled with emotional landmines, ready to be tripped at any moment by an inadvertent gesture, look or sharp tone that brings to mind a former spouse or painful divorce. *Wham!* Your heart's door slams shut, and the hard work must start all over again.

Since most remarriages take place after some sort of trauma (divorce or death), there is a built-in, underlying sense of insecurity. This is one of your primary battles. It's not a knock on remarriage. It's just what makes second unions and beyond unique from most first-married families. As if that's not difficult enough, add in the fact that these new marriages are situated directly in the path of oncoming "tornadoes" trying to rip them apart—tornadoes such as children still suffering from the effects of loss; former spouses who loathe the new spouse ('the intruder"); guilt over failed marriages; stepchildren who don't want a stepparent in their lives; birth children who get "buried" underneath the wreckage of prodigal stepkids; and let's not forget one of our favorites (heavy sarcasm here), the "ghosts" of marriages past that pop up at every turn! These are just a few of the common storms that barrel down on remarried couples. All of these situations and circumstances erode their sense of safety and security and send hearts back to square one.

Don't let the emotional funnel clouds on your horizon send you bolting behind emotional barricades. As a couple, you can stand firm, even against an F5 storm, if you put considerable effort and energy into making your hearts feel like the safest place on earth. Can you picture it yet? You and your spouse are curled up together on the porch swing of that old farmhouse, the one that has survived tornado after tornado. You are cuddling, talking and watching your children and stepchildren laugh and play. That's the picture to keep in front of you. That's the place where you want to raise your family—in an environment that is safe and secure—where hearts can feel safe and stay open.

The Open Heart

We hope you are getting sick and tired of the "open heart" message by now, because we certainly are trying to drive it home. *An open heart is the prerequisite, the requirement, for any healthy relationship—especially a remarriage.* Yet many of us struggle with the vulnerability that comes with a wide-open heart. It can feel risky and dangerous, especially when you've been let down before. As authors Arch Hart and Sharron Hart May explain:

> When a husband and wife love each other, they literally give their hearts to each other for safekeeping. This is such a delicate, trusting act that any violation or injury of this trust can cause the most painful of reactions. Imagine taking the very essence of your be-

ing—your heart—and placing it in the hands of your spouse. Your heart becomes your mate's to care for, safeguard, cherish and love. This necessitates a willingness to be vulnerable and take a bold, risky step. If your partner reciprocates, you both have chosen to risk being hurt, rejected and abandoned. Placing your heart in the hands of another is a giant step of faith. Afterward, you can only wait to see what your spouse will do with your heart. Your desire, of course, is that your spouse will be a safe haven for your heart. And that is your spouse's longing as well.[1]

When you give your spouse access to your heart, there's no guarantee how your mate will behave, what he or she will say or how your spouse will use what he or she learns about you. If trust has been broken before, allowing yourself to engage in that level of intimacy again takes a tremendous amount of heart work. But the benefits of a truly open and intimate remarriage are numerous. Intimacy creates the ideal opportunity to love deeply and be loved, to experience a significant sense of belonging, to make a major positive difference in another's life and to express fully the best of who we are. Isn't this what every couple wants to experience in marriage?

 Bring home flowers, candy or your spouse's favorite treat—just because.

To achieve this level of intimacy in marriage, we typically try to foster or create a deep connection. We invest time in learning each other's love language and emotional needs. We talk at a deep emotional level. We enjoy a satisfying sexual relationship. We go on romantic date nights. We give gifts like flowers, cards and boxes of chocolate. We attend relationship conferences and read marriage books. We join small groups and talk about our marriage. We try to nurture and care for our relationship the way we need to nurture and care for our hearts.

Although this sounds reasonable, these strategies don't always work. The reason that date nights, sex, emotional communication, love languages, flowers, cards and even chocolate do not result in true intimacy and deep connection is that we may still have a heart blockage created by our fear of being emotionally vulnerable and getting hurt again. At the same time that we are employing all the devices we can think of to get close to each other, we are also strategizing ways to keep from getting hurt. Our actions toward our relationship as a couple draw us together, while the individual protective measures we are raising push our hearts apart.

If you realize that you have been putting the kids ahead of your marriage, create couple time. Upon arriving home at the end of the day, set aside the first 15 minutes to connect with each other. Go for a walk, shut the bedroom door, do whatever it takes to secure that alone time to reconnect your hearts.

Here is what many spouses do to avoid opening their heart and getting hurt:

- They may hide by constantly withdrawing from people. ("You're always running away.")
- They may work hard to avoid emotional situations. ("You are constantly ducking me.")
- They may keep parts of their heart permanently shut down. ("You seem so guarded.")
- They maintain superficial connections. ("Our relationship seems so shallow. I never get to see the real you.")
- They use humor as a way to distract others. ("You're always making jokes.")
- They put on the happy face and pretend that all is well. ("You have on your fake smile again.")
- They find ways to distract themselves. ("You're such a workaholic" or "All you do is shop.")
- They deflect intimacy through conflict and negative interactions. ("All we ever do is fight.")
- They may get angry or demanding in order to control their level of vulnerability. ("You get so angry when I try to connect.")
- They overly invest in their children. ("You're always with the kids; you never have time for me.")
- They may become too needy, clingy or possessive. ("I can't believe how insecure you are.")
- They get anxious or have panic attacks. ("Why do you seem so nervous around me?")

- They limit their words and don't talk. ("You're always so quiet.")
- They maintain defenses, walls and force fields. ("It's like you're inside this huge castle; I never seem to have access to your heart.")
- They become more irritable, cold or sexually indifferent. ("You're never in the mood.")
- They turn to food for comfort and support. ("Are you eating again?")
- They seek outside relationships. ("All you do is hang out with your friends.")
- They project an image to get people to like and accept them. ("You seem so phony.")
- They may ignore or deny how they actually feel. ("You never share your feelings.")
- They isolate ourselves. ("It seems like you always hide out in your cave.")
- They become sick. ("You are always so depressed.")
- They attempt to numb or anesthetize their pain through drugs, alcohol or some other addiction. ("You just keep trying to drink your pain away.")
- They turn on themselves. ("You always beat yourself up.")
- They become bitter and resentful. ("You seem to hate that you married me.")
- They get involved in an affair. ("You were the last person I thought would ever be unfaithful.")
- They rely only on themselves. ("You're so self-reliant; you don't need me.")

All of these coping strategies severely limit the level of intimacy a couple can achieve in remarriage. It's awfully hard for your spouse to get close to you if you've barricaded yourself behind an impenetrable emotional wall.

In spite of the obvious risks, often compounded in remarriage by hurts from the past, it is vital for spouses to achieve open hearts and then foster deep connections with each other. Open, intimate hearts intertwine to form a bond that can withstand enormous amounts of pressure and stand the test of time.

Focus on Creating a Safe Marriage Environment

Intimacy occurs effortlessly and naturally when two hearts are open to one another. In its most basic sense, intimacy is the experience of being close to another person and openly sharing something with that person. This may or may not include words. It doesn't necessarily require work or effort. The best approach to fostering intimacy in remarriage is to focus on creating a safe environment for yourself and your spouse. When both of you feel safe, you will naturally be inclined to relax and to be open. Then, intimacy simply happens. It does not require effort or conscious attention.

Think about a time when your spouse hurt you. You instantly felt closed, shut down or disconnected. But have you noticed how quickly your heart reopened when the offender took responsibility for hurting you and sought forgiveness? You went from feeling completely closed to wide open in little more than a heartbeat. This is because openness is the default setting of our hearts. Our hearts were designed to be open. It's all the junk—lies, negative messages and hurtful behavior—that forces our hearts to shut down. But that isn't how God created us.

Emotional safety is the bedrock of a close, open, intimate marital relationship. In this kind of secure environment, the couple wants to stay in love and harmony and feel very protected, rather than vulnerable, with each other. Emotional safety will help you create a climate in which you can build an open relationship that will grow and flourish. It will help you and your spouse feel cherished, honored and fully alive.

Attend a marriage conference, join a couples' group, make time for daily devotions or take up a new hobby or activity together. While these aren't cure-alls for heart blockages, investing in your relationship and learning together make hearts feel safer.

In your quest to have a satisfying remarriage, we want to encourage you to make emotional safety a top priority—it must be the foundation for your family to survive.

What Does Emotional Safety Mean?

Most marriage books coach you on how to use a new therapy technique, unpack some latest bit of research or apply the five trendy steps or seven popular principles. What you really need is simply the know-how to create an emotionally safe environment.

We asked more than 1,000 couples who attended a recent marriage seminar to define "emotional safety." Here are some of their responses:

- Feeling completely secure
- Knowing that you are loved
- Being accepted for who you are
- Feeling relaxed and less tense
- Being cared for above anyone else
- Feeling free to express who you really are
- Being loved unconditionally
- Feeling confident and less insecure
- Feeling respected
- Being with someone who is trustworthy
- Feeling comfortable around that person
- Being there for me
- Being fully understood
- Feeling valued and honored
- Loving reassurance
- Feeling a deep sense that the relationship is solid
- Allowing ourselves to open fully to give and receive love
- Not being judged
- Seeing me for who I am
- Accepting my flaws as part of the whole package
- Maintaining an atmosphere of open communication

That's a pretty amazing list, isn't it? Wouldn't it feel wonderful to have all of these things as the foundation of your marital relationship? We define emotional safety as *feeling free to open up and reveal who you really are, knowing that the other person will still love, understand, accept and value you—no matter what.* Wow! I want that in marriage. Don't you?

 Try to come up with five personal questions to ask your spouse that you do not know the answers to, such as her most embarrassing moment or his most memorable meal. Other suggestions? Find out what celebrities your mate has met, how many (and what kind) of pets your partner had growing up and what your spouse has always secretly wanted to do.

You feel emotionally safe with someone when you believe that person will handle your heart—your deepest feelings and desires—with genuine interest, curiosity and tender, loving care. In other words, you hold your heart out to the person and say, "Here is who I am—emotionally, psychologically, spiritually and mentally. I want you to know my heart and soul. I want you to get to know who I am and appreciate who I am and value who I am. I am a very fascinating person who will take you more than one lifetime to understand!"

But you will never offer your heart or reveal who you really are if you don't feel that it is safe to do so.

What Makes People Feel Unsafe?

Have you ever been outside and noticed the pill bugs (also called roly-poly bugs)? They are fascinating little creatures, silver-gray little bugs that immediately roll up into a ball when they are touched.

One day, my daughter Taylor (who was one year old at the time) was playing with me in the backyard when she discovered a nest of roly-poly bugs. They were everywhere. She was so fascinated whenever she touched the bugs and they rolled up into little balls. Since Taylor loves anything round, she kept flicking the insects and squealing, "Ball! Ball!"

Before Taylor started playing, the bugs were completely open and vulnerable. When she started flicking them, they felt threatened. Their defense mechanism to the perceived safety threat was to roll up into tight balls. And once a roly-poly bug has balled up, it's impossible to force it back open. If you tried to pry it open, I'm almost certain the bug would die.

Our hearts are just like roly-polys. When we feel threatened or hurt, we shut our hearts down and curl them into tight little balls, because we don't feel safe in the situation or environment. This creates a real disconnect in our marriage. In order to keep emotional safety at a high level and avoid the "roly-poly syndrome," we need to take a look at the most common ways that we offend, frustrate and hurt each other. There are probably hundreds of catalysts for feeling unsafe, but we consistently see several issues that top the list. When we asked more than 1,000 couples, "What makes you feel unsafe in your marriage?" we weren't sure what would emerge as number one. This was the one thing that stood above the rest: *criticism*.

Criticism is the contaminant that can kill a marriage. Critical words spread throughout the relationship and choke out intimacy and connection. When we express disapproval of our spouse or our spouse's behavior by pointing out faults or shortcomings in a critical manner, we sit in judgment over our spouse. Rather than asking for a specific change, criticism is about *control*. It is about getting someone to do something we want. By criticizing, we attempt to coerce or manipulate our mate into submission. Criticism erodes the loving trust that keeps couples together. It wears us down and creates defensiveness and anger.

Before you speak to your spouse, test your words with the acronym HEAL. Will your words be Helpful, Encouraging, Affirming and Loving? If they don't pass the HEALing test, keep them to yourself.

In addition to criticism, here are other issues that can make your marriage relationship feel unsafe:

- Being physically abused, threatened or intimidated
- Feeling belittled
- Living with a spouse who repeatedly withdraws during conflict and never returns
- Telling hurtful jokes or sarcastic comments at a spouse's expense
- Being defensive
- Having your feelings, thoughts, beliefs and opinions judged
- Being ignored or minimized
- Acting out in anger
- Feeling controlled
- Being yelled at or spoken to with harsh words
- Breaking promises
- Constant nagging
- Feeling betrayed because private information was revealed without your permission
- Having the past brought up over and over
- Refusing to listen to you or seeming uninterested
- Being rejected or abandoned
- Never giving you the benefit of the doubt
- Deceiving you
- Being disrespected or dishonored

- Closing down emotionally
- Being teased
- Withholding affection or sex
- Cheating
- Being treated like your opinions don't matter
- Being verbally attacked
- Being unwilling to admit to wrongs
- Being forced to do something that you're uncomfortable with
- Being constantly "fixed" by your spouse
- Refusing to forgive
- Being embarrassed or humiliated in front of others
- Having your needs dismissed as unimportant
- Being unappreciated or taken for granted

Which behaviors cause your "Danger, Will Robinson!" sirens and flashing lights to go off? Do you recognize any items on the list that you have committed against your spouse that have resulted in your spouse feeling unsafe?

When we encounter these offenses, our hearts curl up like roly-polys. They may not close completely, but these attacks definitely set us back and take a toll on our marriage. Keeping hearts open to each other is vital. We need God's love constantly flowing between us. Otherwise, we won't feel love and we can't live it out in our stepfamily. We will never have the "farmhouse" type of safety we long for.

Now that you know the specific behaviors that create feelings of insecurity, let's turn our attention to the building blocks of safety in remarriage. You can help your spouse feel relaxed and secure in your relationship. In fact, it's easier than you may think.

Creating Safety in Your Marriage

When Martin and Lanna met and fell in love, they had two divorces and four children between them. The dating relationship went great, and the couple felt like they were strong enough to weather any storm that could come their way in remarriage. Now, only six months after the wedding ceremony, they aren't so sure. None of the kids is happy, and they fight with each other nonstop. This upsets Martin and Lanna, causing them to protect their biological children and square off against each another. Because of the division in the couple relationship, the kids are horribly resentful of their respective new stepparent. Martin and Lanna desperately desire peace in their new home. But tranquility constantly eludes them. Instead, it feels like World War III.

In order to make their hearts a place of emotional safety, Martin and Lanna are going to have to make the tough choice to put each other first—ahead of the desires of their children. While many first marriages make it for the sake of the children, many remarriages end *because* of the children. Creating safety in a stepfamily begins by nurturing the marriage relationship. *This is the highest priority in remarriage: The couple comes first!* As goes your marriage, so goes the family. The marriage relationship is the single most important factor in bringing stability and safety to a stepfamily.

Back your spouse in front of others, especially all of your children. Discuss any concerns privately. Your spouse will feel more secure with your support.

We're confident that every remarried couple would agree with this principle, so why is making the marriage a top priority so difficult on a daily basis? The reality is that since most remarried couples have parenting responsibilities already on their plate, they lose the opportunity to build the foundation of a successful marriage independently of children. It takes a lot of time and energy to make a remarried household with children run smoothly. In the process, remarried couples often place their own relationship on the back burner. They tend to neglect the marital relationship—thinking that since they are adults, they can wait—because they are so busy trying to meet all the kids' needs and move toward full family integration. If children are unhappy in the remarriage, their parents' feelings of guilt or loyalty can easily pull the couple apart.

The best way to stabilize a remarriage is for the couple to ensure that they develop a warm and satisfying relationship. We repeat: *No other human relationship takes precedence over your marriage relationship!* It is the couple relationship that helps the home run smoothly. There is no way around this truth. When remarried couples place the health of their marriage first, the research is overwhelmingly positive about marriage the second time around:

- Evidence exists that those who remarry have a better balance between self-interest and other-interest than they had in their first marriages. The husbands have learned to focus more on the interests of their wives, while the wives have learned something about the importance of caring for her own interests as well as those of her husband and family.[2]
- Research shows that husbands in remarried families contribute significantly more than husbands in first marriages to the household tasks of cooking, meal cleanup, shopping, laundry and housecleaning.[3]
- Because couples in second marriages tend to be older, have greater experience, have learned from past mistakes and are often better prepared, their relationship can be even more fulfilling than many first marriages.[4]
- While spouses in long-established stepfamilies view their marital relationship as just as happy as their first marriage, they also view their second marriage as more egalitarian in terms of housework and child care, more open and pragmatic and more willing to confront conflict.[5]
- Failure in a first marriage has no necessary bearing on the quality of a second marriage.[6]

It is vitally important for the marriage relationship to come first. It gives every family member the best chance for success at integrating into the new family formation. A good marriage does not ensure stepfamily satisfaction or contentment among the children, but without a strong marriage, all family members will continue to feel unsafe, making integration nearly impossible.

---

*Now that you know that your marriage must come first,
the key to creating safety is made up of an* attitude *and an* action.

Attitude: Recognize your mate's value.
Action: Treat your spouse in valuable ways.

Your Mate's Value

The primary attitude that will help your spouse feel emotionally safe is your assurance that you understand how incredibly valuable and vulnerable your mate is. This is the essence of *honor*. By honor, we mean the decision to place high value, worth and importance on your spouse by viewing your mate as a priceless gift and granting him or her a position in your life worthy of great respect. Honor is a gift we give to our spouse. It isn't earned by their actions or contingent on our emotions. We give them distinction whether or not they like it, want it or deserve it. We honor them whether we want to or feel like it. We just do it; it's a daily decision we make.

The apostle Paul encouraged the early Christians to honor each other when he wrote, "Be devoted to one another in brotherly love; give preference to one another in honor" (Rom. 12:10, *NASB*). What great marriage advice! The definition of honor we prefer is, "To give preference to someone by attaching high value to him or her." Honor has to be at the center of your remarriage, and it is not a difficult attitude to master or put into practice. Honor gives legs to the words, "I love you." It puts that statement into action.

I (Greg) watched the power of recognizing a mate's value this past Thanksgiving holiday. My family spent the holiday weekend with my parents. One of the things that I most appreciate about my parents is the honesty in their marriage. They've never claimed to have a "perfect" marriage and they don't shy away from working out their disagreements.

At one point during the visit, my parents got into a huge argument. I couldn't tell you now what it was about (I'm sure they don't remember either!). The funny part was watching a couple married for more than 45 years still get upset with each other. They were so frustrated with each other at one point that they both ran off to different parts of the house. Of course, all of the women followed my mother to provide emotional comfort and support. Since I was the only guy around, I figured I'd better chase after my father. But instead of empathy or emotional support, I reasoned that my dad needed to laugh.

As I trailed my father to his home office, I suggested what I thought was a very good idea: "Hey, Dad," I laughed, "since you've written like 50 marriage books, how about if I pull one off the shelf and read it to you? Maybe you've already written your way out of this situation." I thought my banter was quite funny. His office door slamming in front of my face indicated that he didn't agree with me. I let the situation calm down for a few minutes before I knocked.

"Come in," he reluctantly responded.

As I walked into his office, I found my dad sitting behind his computer. I wasn't sure what he was doing, but I assumed he was on the FOXNews site or something. However, when I walked up behind him, I was shocked to see what he was reading—a document titled, "Why Norma Is So Valuable." (My mom's name is Norma, in case you were wondering.)

"What are you reading?" I asked.

"Well," my dad began, "I've learned over the years that instead of sitting here thinking about how frustrated I am sometimes at your mother, I can remind myself of all the reasons why she is so precious and valuable to me. Years ago, I started writing them down. Whenever I think of something new, I just add it to my list."

As I looked at the screen, I saw that it contained hundreds of words and phrases describing my mom's value. It was amazing, one of the best ideas I've ever heard for recognizing someone's worth. Talk about creating safety!

The great news is that you can do the same thing for your spouse.

 *On a sheet of paper, list all the reasons why your spouse is so incredibly valuable to you. For example, you might write down a character trait, faith pattern, value, moral, parenting skill or job they do that you appreciate. This is a work in progress, so keep adding to your list.*

Here are some words to prime the pump:

Humble	Cooperative	Fun-loving	Inventive
Serious	Curious	Helpful	Studious
Resourceful	Dedicated	Determined	Friendly
Caring	Thoughtful	Neat	Daring
Generous	Brave	Lovable	Successful
Considerate	Funny	Witty	Imaginative
Creative	Loyal	Energetic	Gentle
Intelligent	Carefree	Calm	Joyful
Adventurous	Self-confident	Courageous	Ambitious
Patriotic	Imaginative	Detail-oriented	Faithful
Responsible	Independent	Organized	Cheerful
Happy	Honest	Unselfish	Mannerly
Loving	Hard-working	Respectful	

Review your list whenever you need to be reminded of your spouse's high value (like during an argument).

Now that you have the right attitude (and the list to prove it), you need to pair it with action. Attitude without action is meaningless. James 1:22 confirms it: "Do not merely listen to the word, and so deceive yourselves. Do what it says." Once you recognize your mate's value, you need to show it.

Action: Treat Your Spouse in Valuable Ways

If you want to make your heart and home feel like the safest place on earth, you must be able to convey through your words, actions and deeds how much you honor your spouse. This means that you learn how to handle your mate's heart—his or her deepest feelings, thoughts and desires—with genuine interest, curiosity and care. That's honor in action.

Remember the definition of emotional safety: feeling free to open up and reveal who you really are and know that the other person will still love, understand, accept and value you—no matter what. This is the essence of unconditional love. This is safety in action. We are safe when our spouses share their deepest feelings ("I feel worthless"), thoughts ("I'm tired of being hurt by my girlfriends"), opinions ("I think you're traveling too much"), hopes ("I would love to get a master's degree someday"), dreams ("I've always wanted to go on a medical missions trip"), fears ("I'm afraid that people will reject me"), hurts ("I've never told anyone this, but when I was young . . .") and memories ("I'll never forget when my father . . ."). Your spouse is safe, and you have created emotional safety, when you handle that delicate information in an extremely careful way.

We are gentle with each other's hearts when we are patient and kind (see 1 Cor. 13), when we are understanding and empathic. Another important aspect of safely handling someone's heart is when a spouse acts interested, uses good listening skills and asks pertinent questions. Curiosity is the lost art of wanting to find out more in order to better understand someone. Make it your goal to be curious about your spouse, and see how much more you'll begin to understand.

I want to treat my spouse in valuable ways, you might be thinking, *but how do I do it? I need specific examples.* Great! Here are some of the ways that spouses say their mates take action to make them feel valued and emotionally safe:

- Prays for me
- Helps challenge lies written on my heart
- Keeps track of my positive behavior—tries to notice what I do that pleases
- Does not judge my feelings, innermost thoughts, needs and desires
- Loves and accepts me unconditionally
- Accepts my influence (be teachable)
- Expresses love and appreciation with words
- Practices healthy communication
- Has the best interests of our relationship foremost in mind
- Is not self-centered or selfish
- Doesn't intentionally hurt me
- Gives me full attention and looks at me when I talk
- Allows me to enter his/her inner world—shares feelings, thoughts, fears, insecurities, flaws and weaknesses
- Shows genuine interest in what I share by listening
- Validates my feelings
- Is approachable
- Reassures me of his/her love
- Considers my point of view
- Is trustworthy
- Acts curious about me—asks lots of questions
- Provides physical affection, and not just before sex
- Spends time with me
- Constructively resolves our conflicts and arguments
- Serves me in ways that are meaningful to me
- Is honest and tells the truth
- Provides positive affirmation
- Has fun and laughs with me
- Honors my boundaries
- Never uses anything against me that I share in confidence
- Takes time to work through conflict
- Initiates alone time with me
- Decides on general household rules together
- Supports me when we're around the children
- Works out financial matters together
- Presents a united front with the kids
- Practices good communication skills with me
- Nurtures our friendship

- Never closes me out
- Regards me as important
- Tries hard to understand my feelings
- Is interested in my friends
- Asks for my opinion frequently
- Values what I say
- Protects me on a daily basis
- Is gentle and tender with me
- Develops a sense of humor
- Avoids sudden major changes without discussion and without giving me time to adjust
- Comforts me when I'm down emotionally; puts his/her arms around me and holds me
- Is interested in what I feel is important in life
- Corrects me gently and tenderly
- Allows me to teach him/her without putting up defenses
- Compliments me often
- Is creative when expressing love, either in words or actions
- Has specific family goals for each year
- Lets me buy things I consider necessary
- Is forgiving when I offend him/her
- Shows me he/she needs me
- Accepts me the way I am; discovers my uniqueness
- Admits mistakes; isn't afraid to be humble
- Defends me to others
- Allows me to fail, and then discusses what went wrong after he/she comforts me
- Rubs my feet or neck after a hard day
- Goes on romantic outings
- Writes me an occasional note telling me how much he/she loves me
- Surprises me with a card or flowers
- Expresses how proud he/she is of me
- Tells me how much he/she appreciates me
- Gives advice in a loving way when I ask for it
- Leads our family in our spiritual relationship with God
- Prefers me to others
- Takes time to notice what I have done for him/her and the family
- Brags about me to other people behind my back

- Tells me about his/her job
- Notices how I spend my day, at work or at home
- Learns to enjoy what I enjoy
- Disciplines the children in love, not anger
- Helps me finish my goals, hobbies or education
- Treats me as if God stamped on my forehead, "Handle with Care"
- Gets rid of habits that annoy me
- Is gentle and thoughtful to my relatives
- Doesn't compare my relatives with his/hers in a negative way
- Thanks me for things I have done without expecting anything in return
- Makes sure I understand everything he/she is planning to do
- Does little things for me—an unexpected kiss, coffee in bed
- Treats me as an intellectual equal
- Discovers my fears in life
- Sees what he/she can do to eliminate those fears
- Meets my sexual needs
- Finds out what makes me insecure
- Plans our future together
- Doesn't quarrel over words; tries to find hidden meanings
- Holds my hand in public
- Puts his/her arm around me in front of friends
- Tells me often that he/she loves me
- Remembers anniversaries, birthdays and other special occasions
- Gives me a special gift from time to time
- Shares the responsibilities around the house
- Doesn't belittle my characteristics
- Lets me express myself freely, without fear of being called stupid or illogical
- Carefully chooses words, especially when angry
- Doesn't criticize me
- Is sympathetic when I'm sick
- Calls me when he/she is going to be late
- Gives me special time alone with my friends
- Reads a book I recommend to him/her

As you can see from this extensive list, love really is an *action* verb. Safe people with open hearts can focus on how loving they can be rather than on how much love they need to receive. This is exactly what the apostle Paul was trying to communicate when he wrote, "After all, no one ever hated his own body, but he feeds and cares for it, just as Christ does the church" (Eph. 5:29). We need to feed and care for our marriage—to nourish and tend it.

Put the above list into action, as well as your own ideas, in order to create a blanket of emotional security and safety that will envelop your marriage. When you put each other first and carefully construct a haven for your hearts, you'll be swinging on the front porch of that old farmhouse before you know it!

HEART MONITORS

1. What relationship(s) has been given top priority in your family so far? Where does your marriage rank?

2. How can you give more time and attention to your marriage and let the kids know that from now on you will be putting each other first, without making them feel threatened or insecure?

3. What five character traits do you love best about your spouse? What five traits do you see as your strengths?

4. How can you keep criticism from contaminating your marriage? Come up with some creative ways you can eliminate this relationship killer.

HEART PROTECTORS

Name 10 ways your spouse could help you feel emotionally safe, honored and loved. Now list 10 things you think you could do to make your spouse feel safe, honored and loved. Exchange lists.

With your spouse, make a list of goals for your remarriage. Where do you want your relationship to be in one year? Five years? Ten? Your goals can be emotional, spiritual, physical and professional.

Get out your calendars and pencil in "couple time." Spend at least 15 minutes each day catching up conversationally. Try to have a date once a week or every two weeks, an overnight getaway once a month (or at least a quarterly weekend away) and an annual vacation.

Talk together about what you liked best about each other when you were first dating. What activities were special? What songs did you listen to? What romantic gestures made you feel safe? Go back to your beginning behaviors and woo your spouse again.

Notes

1. Dr. Archibald D. Hart and Sharon Hart Morris, *Safe Haven Marriage: Building a Relationship You Want to Come Home To* (Nashville, TN: Thomas Nelson, 2003), p. 28.
2. R. M. Smith, M. A. Goslen, A. J. Byrd and L. Reece, "Self-other Orientation and Sex-role Orientation of Men and Women Who Remarry," *Journal of Divorce and Remarriage*, 1991, vol. 14, no. 3, p. 32.
3. O. Sullivan, "The Division of Housework About Remarried Couples," *Journal of Family Issues*, 1997, vol. 18, pp. 205-223.
4. L. A. Kurdeck, "Relationship Quality for Newly Married Husbands and Wives: Marital History, Stepchildren, and Individual-preference Predictors," *Journal of Marriage and the Family*, vol. 51, pp. 1053-1064. D.H. Demo and A.C. Acock, "Singlehood, Marriage, and Remarriage," *Journal of Family Issues*, 1996, vol. 17, pp. 388-407. M. Ihinger-Tallman and K. Pasley, "Stepfamilies in 1984 and Today: A Scholarly Perspective," *Marriage and Family Review*, 1997, vol. 26 (1/2), pp. 19-40. E. M. Hetherington, W. G. Clingempeel, E. R. Anderson, et al, "Coping with Marital Transitions: A Family Systems Perspective," *Monographs of the Society for Research in Child Development*, 1992, p. 57 (2/3).
5. E. M. Hetherington, "Family Functioning in Non-stepfamilies and Different Kinds of Stepfamilies: An Integration," *Monographs of the Society for Research in Child Development*, 1999, vol. 64, no. 4, pp. 184-191.
6. D. R. Johnson and A. Booth, "Marital Quality: A Product of the Dyadic Environment or Individual Factors?" *Social Force*, 1998, vol. 76, pp. 883-905.

6

Preparing Hearts for Remarriage

There are three things that amaze me—no, four things that I don't understand:
how an eagle glides through the sky, how a snake slithers on a rock,
how a ship navigates the ocean, how a man loves a woman.
PROVERBS 30:18-19, NLT

We've spent a lot of time so far focusing on how important our heart is, how easily it has been wounded and shut down by events in our past, and how to reopen it again. We have learned how we can transform our beliefs and meditate on key Bible verses to change our lives. And in the last chapter, we unpacked many of the ways we can nurture and nourish each other's hearts in marriage so that they remain open, with love flowing freely. But right about now, we can hear you saying, *This is good stuff about the heart, Smalleys and Cretsingers, but I thought this book was going to focus on my remarriage. Seems like open hearts and love for God and others are important in any healthy, loving relationship. What makes remarriage different?*

Ah, we're glad you asked. If you are preparing for remarriage or helping couples prepare for remarriage, you need to know that there are many unique circumstances and situations that make remarried hearts more vulnerable to confusion, hurt, anger and conflict than hearts looking forward to being joined in a first marriage. If you're already remarried, you probably know exactly what we mean. (But don't skip this chapter, because we're going to outline ways to make sure your heart has healed so that your remarriage can last a lifetime.)

Closed for Business

When a marriage ends because of death or divorce, it leaves a void, an empty space in the heart, whether you experienced the loss or were the one who did the leaving. Regardless of how a marriage ends, it causes devastation, even when it is accompanied by a feeling of relief. The Bible says that when two people are married, they become "one flesh." If that is true, and we believe that all of God's Word is true, then when a marriage ends, it tears that one flesh apart. Ouch!

With a loss of such magnitude, people react in a variety of ways to try to fill the now-empty space inside or to dull the guilt and pain of the consequences that came with their actions. Some people numb the pain with alcohol, drugs, food, work, television or any other method or substance they can think of to escape. Some let their anger take over the space inside, growing roots of bitterness toward a former spouse or at God, and dead-bolting the door of their heart. The most common way that most people fill the void left by a spouse who is no longer there is to jump too quickly into a new romantic relationship.

 Talk to remarried couples about what they did right and wrong during their courtship. Find out how they feel they could have better prepared for remarriage.

The problem with all of these misguided efforts is that they cut off the healing process and keep the heart in pain—*but the one in agony doesn't know it!* The "good" feelings induced by alcohol, drugs and even food, or the emotional high of receiving affection and admiration from a new person, form a nice, neat scab over the heart's gaping wounds. But without taking time to clean out the heart first, the deep emotional wounds will eventually fester and hearts will become closed for business.

Shortcuts Short-Circuit Healing

There is no way to get around one universal truth: Healing takes time. Lots of it. In the national video-based series *DivorceCare*, founder Steve Grissom and other experts say it takes years, perhaps as many as five to seven years, to fully recover from divorce. Yet, in the United States, three-fourths of those who divorce legally remarry, and most of them do it within four years of their divorce. In fact, some statistics show that about one-third of those who divorce remarry within a year!

When crucial healing time is short-circuited by remarriage, the probability that the new marriage will fail increases greatly. Why? Because wounded, broken hearts can't really bond to another person until they are healed and transformed. Plus, remarriage comes with so much change and conflict that additional wounds are inflicted on spouses' hearts. In the midst of remarriage, there is no time to heal from the original hurts caused by divorce or death, let alone try to recover from the new hurts now piling up. Remarrying too soon after the end of a marriage is a recipe for disaster. *In fact, any new romantic relationship that comes within two years of the death of a spouse or divorce will most likely lead to additional pain, conflict and heart damage.*

> *When crucial healing time is short-circuited by remarriage, the probability that the new marriage will fail increases greatly.*

If you are reading these words as you prepare for remarriage, and it hasn't been two years or more since your divorce or the loss of your spouse, please don't think we are judging you or that you should put this book down now. And if you have already remarried soon after divorce, bear with us. You can still heal and have fully open, loving hearts in your remarriage. We just believe that it will be a far more difficult task for you to accomplish. You will have to work doubly hard, because when you are already in a remarriage, it is a challenge to love God first, then your spouse and kids, when you also need to heal your own heart. All of these will have to work in tandem, and it may feel like climbing Mt. Everest! It can be done, but it will be painful, perhaps excruciating at times.

 Adjust your expectations about the time it takes to heal. Don't try to rush the grieving and healing process.

If you are on the verge of remarriage or hope to remarry one day, you are in the best position possible to allow God to heal your heart. You have time to focus on Him, to allow Him and His Word to do the healing, transforming work on your beliefs and in your broken heart. Take that time! The years it takes to fully heal are not a curse of loneliness because your marriage ended. No, you should begin to see them as a time of exciting opportunity to rediscover (or discover for the first time) your relationship with God, to focus on the fascinating person He fashioned you to be and to create a life of surrender to God that will complement a future spouse, not depend on a new mate for happiness. Those who use healing time wisely find that their lives are fuller, richer and more satisfying when they enter remarriage. Plus, the hearts of their new spouses, children and stepchildren will be safer for it.

Got to Get Vertical

When a marriage ends in death or divorce, it is natural for spiritual questioning to take place. The emotions that flood us during personal loss cause us to want to know why this is happening to us. In chapter 5, we learned how important it is to start believing that difficulties are good for us. But in the midst of loss, it takes time to grasp that. It's hard to see the good in the death of a husband or wife you loved. Your heart may close because it doesn't want to experience the pain of death again. In divorce, hearts are damaged because they weren't handled carefully or treated well. Divorced spouses harden their hearts toward each other. And when love is gone, the chances are very good that the vertical heart connection between the spouses and God is broken too. After all, you can't be fully surrendered to God and hate Him for taking your mate, or love God and despise your mate.

All of the emotions churned up by loss, betrayal and the end of dreams and expectations have to be reconciled and released to God. That takes time. There isn't an instant or quick fix to a heart broken or torn apart by a marriage's end. God wants to heal hearts, but He can do it best when people take time to meditate on His Word; when they spend time in prayer; and when they actively seek Him and only Him for fulfillment.

Romance distracts the heart from God's healing. It focuses your time and energy on another human being instead of strengthening the vertical connection with God that is the vital foundation for new, lasting love. Romance feels good, but emotions are deceiving. The excitement that comes with a new romance can overshadow the heart work that needs to be done. It deadens the pain, when the pain of your loss or your actions needs to be felt and worked through with God. What would happen if you broke your arm and felt no pain? You would not realize that your broken arm needed to be taken care of, splinted or put in a cast. You would not treat it tenderly or minister to it, because you wouldn't realize that it was damaged. Eventually, you might even lose your arm because it wasn't given the time and attention it needed to heal. Romance can act like Novocain to broken hearts—and those hearts will have a much harder time healing.

The One and Only You

Psalm 139:14 says that we are each "wonderfully made," but we'll bet you didn't feel so wonderful after your marriage ended. In fact, if your marriage ended because your spouse left you, your self-esteem probably hit rock bottom. If the person who vowed to love you in every circumstance until one of you died has now left you, what's wrong with you? You may feel like you are 13 again, going through adolescence and wondering if your hair, nose, figure and other physical attributes are "good enough." You may think you must not be smart enough or talented enough. In short, you feel anything but "wonderfully made."

If you were the spouse who did the leaving, your guilt may be causing you to beat yourself up, convincing you that God could never forgive a sinner like you. If your spouse died, the anger you feel at the loss of your dreams may cause you to feel ugly or unwanted. The devil wants us to believe the lies that we are hideous, stupid, horrible, unforgivable, nasty people. But God says we were made in His image. His Word says that He sings over us, that He loves us. His Word calls those who follow Christ His "bride," and a bride is beautiful and beloved.

 Do something for yourself that makes you feel special. Take a hot bath, talk to an old friend, eat a rich dessert or dress up for dinner.

You need time after your marriage ends to rediscover the one and only you. This is your time to focus on yourself without the pressure of serving your mate. You can take the acting lessons you always wanted, cook new recipes, spend time with friends (of the same gender, please, so that romance doesn't enter the picture), join Bible studies, volunteer, go back to school, or learn a foreign language. If you are a single parent, the demands on your time are great, but you need to carve out time to get to know the wonderful human being whose face you see every morning in the mirror, bed-head and all.

You get the privilege of using the time you have before romance enters the picture again to like the person God created you to be, to get comfortable in your own skin. When you see yourself the way God sees you and learn to love the beautiful creation He made you to be, then you can love more clearly. Your heart will not be deceived into thinking it is "in love" with another person, only to discover too late that you were mostly infatuated with the way that person made you feel about yourself. You won't have to worry about using someone else for your own happiness, because you will be filled with the joy of knowing your true identity in Christ.

Ready for Reconciliation

Another reason why time is so important in the healing process is that God would prefer first marriages to reconcile. He hates divorce. We hate the consequences that divorce inflicts on spouses, children, families and friends. Ask most divorced people and they will tell you they hate divorce too, because they have experienced the consequences firsthand.

While it may seem impossible that your marriage could ever be reconciled after divorce, it can happen. If God heals hearts, and those hearts are transformed because of the new beliefs they have internalized through memorizing and meditating on God's Word, former spouses can reconcile and have a beautiful, fulfilling marriage. Because many people divorce based on their "feelings" (or lack thereof), and because feelings are cyclical (and deceiving), research has shown that even when a divorce occurs, there will most likely be a point in time (or many points in time) when each spouse wants to reconcile. The trick is getting those feelings in both people to line up at the same time. If spouses do not take time to heal before remarrying, the window of opportunity for reconciliation of the first marriage—no matter how unlikely you may think that is right now—closes. If either spouse remarries, that new marriage permanently ends the chance that the original marriage can be put back together.

 Pray that God will help you have the right feelings—whatever those may be— toward your former spouse.

If you want to live a life that is handed over to God and to His will, you have to be willing to ask Him if He wants you to reconcile with your former spouse, and you have to accept His answer, whether you like it or not. He may call you to a time of singleness that is much longer than you desire. He may ask you to never remarry, if remarriage would render you unable to fulfill His mission for your life or might interfere with your relationship with Him. He may want you to remain separated, rather than divorced, if your unbelieving spouse left you. He may ask you to forgive the spouse you loved deeply who betrayed you, and then ask you to trust that person with your heart again. We don't know the plan God has for you, but we do know that it is a future filled with hope, whether you ever remarry or not. And we know that if you seek His will for your life, you won't feel like you are missing out on anything, no matter which path He leads you to take.

The bottom line is that a heart fully open to loving God and others puts the will of God and the needs of others ahead of its own desires, its own fulfillment and its own pleasures. The scenarios outlined in the paragraph above may seem lonely, loveless and unappealing, but that's only when they are put through the filter of "self." *What do I get out of this?* is the underlying question. The healed, whole heart asks, *What can I do for God and others?* In light of an eternity that will be spent in complete joy with God in heaven, is surrendering your short lifetime on earth too much to ask?

Keeping Kids Whole

If you have children who are minors who have experienced loss because of death or divorce, you need to consider their needs before even entertaining thoughts of romance, dating and remarriage. Children's entire lives are turned upside down when they lose the daily presence of a parent in their home. In fact, many experience such profound devastation that they suffer the same effects as those diagnosed with post-traumatic stress disorder (PTSD). Divorce or death can cause their schoolwork to suffer, foster depression and anxieties, instill anger and fear, and can engage children in conflict with their friends and family. The change in their lives is huge, and adding a stepparent or potential stepparent can wreak additional havoc.

Children need time to heal following the death of a parent or their parents' divorce. They need to grieve the loss, and they need time to become familiarized with their new home life and routine. Children who now split time between parents have to learn the new "language" and "culture" of the two different households. They have to learn how to remember which stuff needs to go back and forth. They need time to get used to single-parent homes. Kids also need their hearts to be transformed.

They need to be led to Christ so that He can remove their fears, anger and anxieties. They need time to memorize key Bible verses with their parent and to meditate on His Word so that they can love their parents freely and without guilt.

 Memorize Psalm 127:3: "Behold, children are a gift of the Lord. The fruit of the womb is a reward" (NASB).

When a parent enters into a new romantic relationship, children's hearts can be damaged again. Remarriage shatters their dream of seeing their parents get back together. And if not enough healing time is given to them, their roots of anger or bitterness over the loss of their original family may grow deeper. As well, parents who are giddy over their new romance may not recognize or give enough credit to the negative emotions their children are experiencing.

While it may not be appropriate to give kids the full decision-making power over whether or not you will remarry, we would recommend seeking the state of your kids' hearts in regard to remarriage. On an age-appropriate level, ask them how they would feel about it, and let them know you will not be angry or disappointed with their answer. Give them permission not to feel guilty if they want you to stay single. They may like the person you are dating but not want you to marry. Let them know their feelings are important to you, and that you will seriously consider them before making any changes that will significantly alter their lives.

If you know in your heart of hearts that one or more of your children may suffer permanent damage if you remarry, our best advice is not to do it. You can't put your happiness ahead of your children's stability and expect your remarriage to be fully successful. We ask many divorced people who jump into new relationships without considering the effects on their kids two questions, and we ask the first question now of you: If your kids were in a burning building, would you try to rescue them, even if you knew it would cost you your own life? Unanimously, the answer is always a resounding "yes," and we expect that you are probably nodding your head right now. Now we ask the second question, one that is a lot tougher: So you are telling us that you would die for your kids; but will you live for them?

If it comes down to denying yourself the pleasures that come with a romantic relationship in order to keep your teens from rebelling or help your young children remain stable and whole, will you do it? You might be willing to die for your kids, but are you willing to live for them?

The Remarital Marriage Bed

When you are preparing your heart for remarriage, the subject of sex is also important to consider. In the Bible, God reserves sex for married partners, and He doesn't really give instructions on the challenges that may come with sex in remarriage. It's important for you to create boundaries while you are single that will protect you from sexual sin. Once you are divorced or widowed, you are legally and spiritually single again. Your body may crave sexual release like you knew in your marriage, but you are called to remain sexually abstinent until you are married again. That can be a tall order for people who have been married and have had an active sex life. Sex may not seem like a big deal, but it should. God expects you to surrender your sexual desires to Him, along with your heart and your life. The last thing you need in remarriage is to add the guilt of sexual sin to a relationship that will face enough challenges.

You want God to fully bless your sexual union in remarriage, free from guilt or recrimination, because remarital sex can also be accompanied by the "ghosts of marriages past." In order to cast these ghosts outside of your bedroom for good, it is important to consider a few questions and scenarios, such as the following:

- How will you feel if sex with your new spouse doesn't come as naturally or "feel" as good or intense as it did with your former spouse? If you are widowed, guilt may follow you into your remarriage bed. Or sometimes sex in a dysfunctional marriage was heightened in intensity because of the strong emotions that ran through the marriage. The tension between partners made sex a great release. What will you do if this is the case for you?

- What if you accidentally picture your former spouse in your mind during lovemaking in your remarriage? What if you unintentionally say your former spouse's name?

- How will you handle any awkwardness you may feel in the beginning of your remarriage over the differences in your new spouse's body? How can you keep from comparing it with the body of your former spouse?

• Can you talk openly about sex with your new mate without hurting each other's feelings? Will you be able to express your needs, your preferences, your likes and dislikes, without embarrassment or comparison?

• What will you do if one of you wants to know what sex was like "before," and the other wants to avoid any details from the past?

• How will you avoid comparing yourself to your mate's former spouse and wondering who was "better" in bed?

In first-time marriages between partners who have saved their virginity for each other, there is the uncomplicated joy of learning to please each other sexually without guilt or regret. The first-time lovers have no comparison, no fear that they are not living up to a sexual standard set by someone else. Remarital sex can be wonderful, but it is still complicated. Like all of remarriage, it can be challenging at first, and even for a long time. As you are preparing your heart for remarriage, consider your sexual side and see if you can have some frank conversation (preferably in a public place where you won't become aroused and tempted) about the remarital sex life that lies ahead. Frontloading the conversation now can help alleviate disappointment or disillusionment later.

Unequally Yoked

If you know you have taken the time to heal and have allowed God to transform your beliefs and heal your heart, you need to make sure that anyone you plan to marry has done this same spiritual groundwork. Your remarriage will have a difficult time succeeding if only one spouse is "sold out and surrendered" to a life focused on God and others. You will be missing a vital component for marital fulfillment if you can't worship God together and if you don't see things from the same worldview. Remember, everything we think, say and do is colored by what we believe. If you enter into a romantic relationship with someone who does not believe that God should take the top spot in life, then you will reap some serious consequences that can be excruciatingly painful. If you believe in Jesus Christ and have experienced His salvation, you must be obedient and remarry someone who also believes in Him.

How Can You Tell if You're Ready to Remarry?

Now that we've shared many of the challenges that need to be surrendered and overcome in order to prepare hearts for remarriage, how can you tell if you are ready to enter a new marriage? We offer the following seven guidelines for you to consider, all of which we believe are important for the best chance of remarital success:

1. *You may be ready for remarriage if you and your potential spouse love God first and fully.* You are actively involved in a local church; you are in fellowship with other believers; and you are meditating on His Word and spending time in prayer multiple times a day. You have allowed God the time it takes to transform your heart—and therefore your thoughts, actions and words. He has changed your beliefs.

2. *You may be ready to remarry if you would be perfectly fine remaining single.* You aren't ready to be together in marriage until you are completely fulfilled alone. Just you and God. Remarriage should complement your full, rich, satisfying, joy-filled life; you should not be dependent on finding the "right one" to be happy.

3. *You may be ready to remarry if at least two years have passed since the end of your previous marriage.* You don't have to like it, but there is just no getting around this one. You have read all of the reasons why we, and many other marital experts, believe that it takes at least two years to grieve the losses that come with divorce or the death of a spouse. There are no shortcuts in healing time.

4. *You may be ready to remarry if your Christian friends and family are in agreement.* If the people who love and know you best and who are also in right relationship with God see healthy growth and healing in you, and they are ready to embrace the person you want to marry, that can be a sign that you are on the right track. If one or more people who have loved you for years and whose advice you have previously trusted tell you to hold up, consider that a huge red STOP sign.

5. *You may be ready for remarriage if your kids are in agreement.* If your children are old enough to grasp some of the magnitude of what will happen in their lives if you remarry, and they are okay with it, that can be a sign that you are ready to remarry. It will still be a challenge, because there will always be issues none of you considered, but it will certainly help if your kids are not adamantly opposed to the idea.

6. *You may be ready for remarriage if you have prepared for it like you would study for your college finals.* Before remarriage, the two of you should soak up as much wisdom as you can by talking to others who have remarried, reading great books (like this one), taking parenting classes, going to workshops and seminars, worshiping in church together, developing a prayer life together, and getting wise counsel. Study like a $100,000 scholarship is on the line. The benefits of a healthy remarriage are worth much more! Know each other's love language, be well versed on the issues of love and respect, and discuss everything you can think of, from holidays to finances to sex to discipline.

7. *You may be ready to remarry if you are not blaming God for taking your spouse, or if you have forgiven yourself and your former spouse and have established healthy boundaries with your former spouse.* If the thought, voice or sight of your former spouse still makes you burn with rage or kindles a pang of longing, you have heart work to do before you should remarry. Memories of your former marriage should seem almost like a movie of someone else's life, with no pain, anger or desire attached. You also need to have proper boundaries around your relationship with your former spouse before you remarry. You can't live in your memories of the past with a spouse who is gone. Nor can you remain too close to a spouse you divorced. You can't serve two spouses at once.

Take this "test," honestly answering each question, before making the decision to remarry. If you have a green light on all seven points, you will have the best chance for a firm foundation in your remarriage. When storms hit, you are much more likely to be strong enough in your relationship to withstand them. If you have already entered remarriage and realize that you still have work to do, don't give up or convince yourself that your remarriage was a mistake. God takes marriage seriously; you should too. Get ready to dig in and do the heart work and healing necessary to get your remarriage on track. His promises are true, and He can transform single and remarried hearts and lives for His glory!

HEART PROTECTORS

1. How much time has passed since your marriage ended? Have you spent time alone with God, without dating or entering into any kind of romantic relationship? If not, are you willing to "back up" and spend that healing time now?

2. Were you surprised at how much time is recommended for healing? What amount of time do you think it takes to heal from a marriage that ended prematurely?

3. In this chapter, what sections stuck out the most to you? Where do you think you need the most heart work?

4. How ready are you for remarriage, according to the seven criteria listed in this chapter? If you have already remarried, what steps can you take to make your remarriage fit this list?

HEART MONITORS

List 10 ways you are "wonderfully made."

Try something new this week. Eat at a new restaurant, choose a new exercise or sign up for a new class. Challenge yourself to grow mentally and spiritually.

Ask friends and family members what they like best about you. Meditate on what they say, and believe it!

Put your romantic future to the seven-point test in this chapter. If it fails even one of the points, put your thoughts and plans for remarriage on hold until you can pass all seven points with flying colors.

PART TWO

ROLES IN MARRIAGE

7

The Heart of a
Remarried Husband

*Teach the older men to be temperate, worthy of respect, self-controlled,
and sound in faith, in love and in endurance.*
TITUS 2:2

Let's face it. In America today, men tend to get a bad rap. In movies and on TV, husbands are often lumped into two categories: abusive or comically stupid. We read stories in the news about deadbeat dads and watch fallen politicians and televangelists apologize for their sexual exploits. We want to reassure you right up front that we know there are still many intelligent men with integrity who want to embody the great character qualities found in Titus 2:2. We know there are a lot of men who marry the woman they love and stay faithful to her, men who plan to work hard to keep their marriage and family intact. If you're reading this book (or your wife is reading it to you), we applaud you for being one of those men, a husband who isn't afraid to learn how to love better and who wants to see his remarriage succeed. If we were standing next to you now, we'd give you a hearty handshake or a solid clap on the back. We know you want your remarriage to thrive, and we want to stand with you as you work toward that goal.

In the first section of this book, you learned a lot about the damage that has been done to your heart over the years and how to undo it by healing and guarding your heart. We pray that you are now (if you weren't before) firmly connected in a rich personal relationship with Christ and are allowing Him to transform your mind and beliefs by meditating on His Word and memorizing it. If you love God, and His love is flowing through you to your wife and family, you are off to a great start.

Now we want to take you a step further into the unique role that a re-married husband plays. We'll lay out some of the challenges and circum-stances you may face in your remarriage that could cause your heart to harden; and then we'll give you insight into your own feelings and behav-iors, as well as offer some practical ways to keep your heart, as a remarried husband, feeling like the safest place on earth (without getting overly mushy or anything).

The Remarried Husband's Need for Respect

A few years ago, a senior pastor named Emerson Eggerichs uncovered a biblical secret he says was a "truth hidden in plain sight for 2,000 years."[1] It is found in Ephesians 5:33, and you probably know it by heart. It's the verse that instructs husbands to love their wives as they love their own bodies. Pastors have preached this message to the men in their congrega-tions over and over again. Every Christian husband knows he is supposed to love his wife unconditionally. That means he loves her on bad-hair days, bad-mood days, bad-everything days. He has to love her, no matter what. The Bible tells him so.

What Eggerichs discovered was the second half of this verse, the part that is often glossed over but says, "and the wife must respect her hus-band." A lightbulb turned on when he realized the implications of this in marriage, and he went on to develop highly successful marriage confer-ences and write a best-selling book called *Love and Respect* from his revela-tion. Eggerichs believes (and we agree) that men were commanded by God to love their wives with no conditions attached because loving doesn't come naturally for men, yet their wives were created with a deep need to feel loved and cherished. The pastor then quickly connected the dots that wives must have been commanded to respect their husbands for the same reason. Wives are to respect their husbands unconditionally because re-spect does not come easy for women, but men need it, as Eggerichs puts it, "like they need air to breathe."

Men need unconditional respect from their wives, but a remarried hus-band may quickly feel like he's having a tough time getting it. We want you to know that your desire for respect is normal and okay. It's a deep-seated part of the way God wired you as a man. You need to recognize that, as a husband, you want your wife to respect you more than anyone else does. Her opinion of you counts the most, and you need to feel that she is your biggest cheerleader. In the workplace, at church and among male friends and acquaintances, respect is the code of honor you live by. But once you walk through the front door after work, respect may feel like it goes right out the window. When your wife hands you the trash you forgot to take out and complains that your ex-wife just called asking for more money that you don't have, the feeling of disrespect may rear its ugly head.

 Thank your wife for being your biggest fan.

You feel respected when your wife puts you first, ahead of the kids, her phone calls, her friends or her work. You are the head of your household, called by God to provide for it and protect it. But if your wife was a single mom before you two married, she may have been used to looking out for herself. Learning to live under your headship may feel unnatural, and you may interpret her discomfort as disrespect. As a remarried husband, you will need to work with your wife to define each of your roles in the home and distribute the balance of power so that you feel respected, and your wife doesn't feel stripped of her identity or purpose.

When men feel disrespected, their natural tendency is to do one of two things: (1) shut their hearts down, or (2) lash out in anger. Neither reaction is healthy, and both can do serious damage to a marriage. When remarriage occurs, the feeling of disrespect can be compounded because both spouses bring some of the emotional baggage from their former marriages with them.

If you are a remarried husband who experienced divorce, you may have felt disrespected by your former wife for years, so you may approach every encounter with your new wife with built-in wariness that she is not going to respect you. You may also be battling a loss of respect for yourself because of the damage divorce did to your children; for the financial comfort that was stripped away; or the behavior you displayed in your angriest moments. You may not respect yourself because you were unfaithful or did things in your past that you are not proud of, and that can create very shaky ground in remarriage. If you lost your former spouse to death, you may be afraid to open up to the possibility of pain again. You may fear becoming a caregiver. In any of these cases, the walls around your poor, disrespected heart may be high and almost impenetrable. It will be a top priority for you in remarriage to start dismantling those barriers and reveal the real you to your wife.

When you fell in love and remarried, part of what you fell for was the mirror image you saw reflected in your new spouse's eyes. She adored you, and that felt great. It made you stand taller, forget your mistakes and once again feel like you could conquer the world. When the routine and pressures of remarriage set in, you may think the stars in your spouse's eyes have faded and she can't possible respect you, the man she lives with every day. You have to ask God to remove the lie etched on your heart that your wife does not respect you and replace it with the belief that she deeply respects you—and that as a husband now living for God and his family, you are worthy of respect.

> *You have to ask God to remove the lie etched on your heart that*
> *your wife does not respect you and replace it with the belief that*
> *she deeply respects you—and that as a husband now living for*
> *God and his family, you are worthy of respect.*

Your wife also brings her emotional past to your marriage, and she may speak to you or look at you in ways that come across as disrespectful, especially in times of conflict. A disdainful look or sarcastic tone violates your code of honor as a man, and your heart clamps down. You will have to be vigilant in remarriage in guarding your heart from hardening when you feel disrespected. It is also important to determine whether your wife is truly acting disrespectfully or if you are seeing her actions through the lens of your past.

 In a time of non-conflict, talk openly with your wife about what specific actions, facial expressions, body language or speaking tones set you off or cause you to shut down.

You and your wife need to learn to recognize what triggers feelings of disrespect in you as a remarried husband so that you don't fall into the same unhealthy patterns that led to your divorce or develop a longing for your deceased spouse instead of the one you are married to now. When you feel respected, your heart can remain fully open and engaged. You will experience more satisfaction and will want to love your wife more.

Taming the Angry Beast

The emotion that remarried men generally battle more than any other is anger, and anger that goes unchecked destroys relationships. That's why Ephesians 4:26 warns us, "Don't sin by letting anger control you" (*NLT*). If one of the fruit of the Spirit is self-control, it must be employed by you as a remarried husband to keep anger from being unleashed in hurtful ways against those closest to you, especially your wife.

Anger is common in remarried husbands for a variety of reasons. Here are just a few:

- Your heart carries feelings of guilt or is scarred from being hurt. It's a lot easier to allow anger to fester than it is to admit your guilt or work through your hurt.
- You feel like circumstances are out of your control. If you could not keep your former wife from betraying you or control the lust that led you to destroy your previous marriage, you may harbor some deep-rooted anger.
- You can't "fix things" and make them all better for the ones you love. If you can't "fix" the pain your wife has from her past or control the emotional damage your ex-wife is doing to your kids, for example, anger is a natural response.
- You feel like a failure. Divorce feels like a big, fat *F* at the most important task in life. Death of a spouse feels like you've been cheated.
- You feel disrespected. If you have divorced or lost a spouse, friends and family members may have turned their backs on you. You may have been removed from positions of authority in your church or in civic organizations. Your reputation in the community may have been damaged.
- You were betrayed by your former spouse or feel betrayed by God.
- You can't provide as much as you want to. Remarriage often strains finances to the breaking point, when a husband must support a new family and a former one.

"I was very angry for the first years of my remarriage," Dan admits. "I was angry at what was happening to my kids and angry because I couldn't do anything about it. And because my wife, Marci, was right there, I was often angry at her, even when it wasn't her fault."

Many situations in remarriage can make a husband feel powerless and defeated, and this triggers feelings of anger. It's what you do with that anger that counts.

Not all anger is automatically bad. Anger at injustice is perfectly okay. In fact, righteous anger is important so that change can take place. Jesus was righteously angry when He saw unscrupulous people turning the temple into little more than a thieves' den. Moneychangers were fleecing God's flock, and Jesus in His anger tipped over tables and chased them out of God's house (see Matt. 21; Mark 11; Luke 19; John 2). The important thing to notice in this story is that Jesus was angry, but His actions were not sinful. He used His anger to bring about healthy change, to right a wrong.

You may be angry at the injustices you have experienced in your life, but is your anger fueling healthy changes in your heart? Whether you become angry and right wrongs or let rage rule you is the choice you have to make. You will never be able to control other people—your ex-wife or your prodigal teens, for example—but you can learn to gain control over the anger you feel so that you don't express it in destructive ways.

> *Whether you become angry and right wrongs or*
> *let rage rule you is the choice you have to make.*

If you want to succeed in your role as a remarried husband, you have to find healthy ways to release your anger so that it leads to good changes. Healthy anger, like pain, is a symptom; it's a sign that something is wrong and needs to be addressed. Unhealthy anger is a disease that doesn't inspire good change but instead corrupts and destroys. You must vigilantly guard your heart from becoming bitter or remaining enraged. *You must learn not to sin in your anger.*

Why is this such an important task? Because the target of a husband's anger in remarriage is usually his wife. Your anger may not have anything to do with your wife. It may have been sparked way back in childhood, adolescence or in your former marriage. But if it has been stored in your heart and is now a raging inferno, it will burn anyone in its path. And the one who is directly in your path on a daily basis is your wife.

Unhealthy, destructive ways of expressing your anger that we believe are sinful and must be eliminated from your remarriage include:

- Bullying
- Belittling
- Denigrating anyone, especially your wife
- Name-calling
- Using sarcasm to wound
- Bringing up past mistakes that have already been forgiven
- Yelling
- Hitting, kicking, pushing, pinching, slapping or any other form of physical battery
- Refusing to speak to your wife; shutting down
- Withholding sex as punishment
- Forcing sex
- Refusing to forgive
- Cheating on your spouse
- Escaping through substance abuse
- Spending no time at home
- Working too much to avoid going home

All of these unhealthy methods of expressing anger can destroy a marriage and family, some of them immediately (cheating) and some over time (yelling or belittling).

If you have deep-seated anger and have been taking it out on your wife, apologize to her now. Ask for her forgiveness, and show her you mean it by taking steps to change.

None of those actions brings about healthy change or helps you succeed in remarriage. While some of the items on our list are obviously very bad, others may seem fairly innocuous to you. Yelling is pretty common in many Christian marriages and families, yet we put it on the list because we don't think yelling produces any of the fruit of the Spirit, such as love, joy, peace and kindness.

Think about it this way: Have you honestly ever felt kindly toward someone who was yelling at you? As they stood there and yelled, did it open or close your heart? Were you moved to make positive changes in your life? If your dad yelled at you when you were a teenager for breaking curfew, were you instantly remorseful for your actions and able to embrace the error of your ways? Or did you glide right past the fact that you were late and think to yourself, *What a jerk!*? Chances are, you thought your dad was a jerk for yelling at you. His bellowing may have produced surface changes in your behavior, meaning that you may not have been late the next time because you didn't want to be yelled at again, but we think it's a safe bet to say that your dad didn't open your heart by yelling. He didn't soften your heart to do the right thing because it was the right thing. He merely caused you to obey curfew because you didn't want to feel humiliated. If you have never appreciated being yelled at by anyone, don't yell at your family.

If you have a habit of yelling, you have probably noticed that everyone tunes you out, yells right back or even yells over you and each other. So we offer this experiment to you: If you really want to grab your family's attention, the next time you are frustrated and about to yell, try dropping your voice to a whisper instead. Suddenly, everyone's ears will perk up. They will be surprised enough to want to know what you are saying, and they'll stop yelling in order to hear you.

Sign a contract with your wife or entire family stating that the members of your household will not yell from that day forward. Be the first to sign it, and hang it where you can all see it. Come up with a code word that can be used as a reminder when anyone starts to raise his or her voice. Or start a quarter jar that must be "paid" by family members when they yell. When the jar gets full, use the money to go out and create a memory that creates family togetherness!

Some of the ways you can defuse the anger in your heart in a healthy way may include any or all of the following:

- Praying daily
- Memorizing Bible verses about anger
- Exercising regularly
- Dropping your voice rather than raising it
- Walking away from conflict (until you calm down)
- Confessing your anger to a trusted (male) friend or mentor

- Listening to favorite worship songs
- Taking deep, cleansing breaths
- Getting solid Christian counseling
- Eliminating sugar and caffeine
- Talking honestly with your wife
- Making love to your wife
- Fellowshipping with other men
- Getting an accountability partner
- Asking those you've hurt to forgive you
- Forgiving those who have hurt you
- Finding something to laugh about

Dan found that praying and meditating on Philippians 4:6-7 helped defuse his anger. Read these verses out loud now:

> Don't worry about anything, but pray about everything. With thankful hearts offer up your prayers and requests to God. Then, because you belong to Christ Jesus, God will bless you with peace that no one can completely understand. And this peace will control the way you think and feel (*CEV*).

"I try to put things in perspective," Dan says. "The larger my thoughts are about God, the smaller my thoughts are about myself."

The next time anger flares, make it your goal to first determine what triggered your emotions, then formulate your plan to defuse your anger in healthy ways. It will take lots of prayer and practice, but you can do it. As your anger lessens, you will become a better husband, and your family's hearts will feel much safer.

Expressions of Love

Remarried husbands need respect, and they need to learn to deal with anger; but they also need to practice loving others and being loved. Loving well doesn't come naturally to many men. As we unpacked earlier when we looked at Ephesians 5:33, men have to be commanded by God to do it! We may think that love should come easy, but it takes study and practice to get the expression of love right, especially if we feel like the poster child for getting love all wrong in the past.

While humans can't manufacture love, as outlined in chapter 1, we do need to be able to let it flow from us in ways that our spouse can feel. We also need to recognize which actions and words from our spouse make us feel loved. As a remarried husband, you need to study your own heart and the heart of your wife as if you are going back to school to get a master's degree or a doctorate. If you do, the benefits of this kind of dedication will bear fruit in your marriage for the rest of your life. In fact, healthy expressions of love in your remarriage will continue to pay off even after you are gone. Healthy love in remarriage can erase the negative effects of divorce on spouses and children and leave a legacy for future generations of your family to follow. Isn't that exciting?

Healthy love in remarriage can erase the negative effects
of divorce on spouses and children and leave a legacy for future
generations of your family to follow.

In order to love well, you need to study up on what healthy love in marriage means, because your love for a new spouse will look different from the love you had for a spouse you lost. You may have loved well or never truly experienced love before. If you have opened your formerly untended heart to God's love and healing mercies, then you are now ready to overflow that love into your remarriage. Here's a good snapshot of what it looks like to fully love and engage in your marriage:

- A remarried husband loves well when he fully embraces the love his wife has for him.
- He lets down his guard and allows his heart to be vulnerable so that it can be open to her.
- He takes off any masks and reveals his true self to her.
- He shares his goals and dreams and opens up about his past hurts and sorrows.
- He admits his fears and anxieties, because he trusts that his wife will protect his heart.
- He is always honest with her.
- He receives her compliments and notices the things she does to please him.
- He accepts the gifts she gives him and brings her gifts.
- He enjoys spending time with her and desires her company over anyone else's.

- He likes to touch her and be touched and revels in her lovemaking.
- He gives his body and his sexual desires only to his wife.
- He confides in her as a best friend.
- He prays with her and reads the Bible with her.
- He works to provide for her.
- He stands up for her.
- He plans for the future with her.
- He works with his wife to nurture and raise their children.

That list sounds great, doesn't it? If you are doing all of those things, your remarriage can withstand any outside trials. Read the list one more time. Feel free to put a checkmark by the items you think you're doing pretty well, and circle the ones you need to work on. Show the list to your wife and see if she agrees. Together, you can make your hearts a safe haven. And you, the remarried husband, should take the lead.

Remarital Sex

Although we introduced the subject of remarital sex in the previous chapter, we'd like to unpack it more here. Maybe it's a subject that's hard for you to talk about, even difficult to read about here, but we believe it is too vital for a healthy remarriage and important for husbands to be left unaddressed. God created us as sexual beings, male and female, so that when we come together physically in marriage, we create a perfect picture of all the attributes, wonders, mysteries and characteristics of God. But for remarried partners, this act of love may be a source of deep shame. Remarried sex can be accompanied by confusion and conflict. For husbands and wives who are remarried, sex can be like Pandora's Box. You want it. It is exciting and enticing, but when you open it, it unleashes a lot more than you expected. For remarried husbands and wives, sex may be intertwined with guilt that is etched so deeply into their hearts that they feel the scars will never heal.

If you, your wife or both of you have always gotten sex "wrong," giving up your virginity too soon, having multiple sex partners, having sex with someone else during marriage, viewing pornography or having sex with each other before you remarried, your remarriage bed may be buried under that baggage. You may experience sexual dysfunction that can range from a lack of arousal to a dependence on fantasies or pornography to become "turned on." You may want to have sex very frequently as reassurance or avoid it altogether because guilt makes it such a hot button for pain and conflict. As a husband, you may climax too soon or feel inadequate in helping your wife reach her climax. And you may be at a sexual stalemate with all of this because you're afraid that talking about it might release something that's better left unsaid. Yes, the consequences of sexual sin can be all too apparent in remarriage.

When you have had more than one sexual partner (and you can do the math—anyone who has been married more than once has had at least two), the different body of your new spouse and the different style of lovemaking can feel just plain wrong somehow. Ask any Christian who has had sex outside of God's design, and he or she can attest to the truth of 1 Corinthians 6:18, which states: "Run from sexual sin! No other sin so clearly affects the body as this one does. For sexual immorality is a sin against your own body" (NLT).

You may feel insecure in your marriage bed, wondering if your wife's former husband was "bigger" or "better." If your former mate died, prepare yourself to feel like you are betraying her at first. Your wife may wonder if your former wife was sexier or pleased you more. If your wife had never been married before and waited for your wedding night to give you her virginity, you may have felt pain at being unable to reciprocate that precious gift. Your wedding night might not have been picture-perfect if your bride felt incompetent and awkward, knowing that you had prior sexual experience and she might not perform up to your expectations.

 Buy or make a wooden cross that's at least six inches tall. Get a few nails, a hammer, some paper and a pen. On scraps of paper, write down the sins that still haunt you and habits or addictions you want Christ to conquer. Fold the scraps and nail them to the cross as you ask God for forgiveness and pray to be released from them. Now bury that cross or throw it away as a physical depiction of your sins being permanently gone.

There is hope though. Jesus can take away your guilt and heal the hurt of widowhood. And every sin—including all sexual sin—has been covered by the blood of Jesus when He died on the cross. If you have received His salvation, and if you ask Him to forgive all of your sexual sins, He will. If you have already asked Him to forgive you, then your sexual history has been erased. Just like that. It's gone forever; your job is to start acting like it. Every time you allow guilt to creep in or insecurity to take root, you are acting as if your sin is bigger than the price Christ paid to redeem it. That's ridiculous! Nothing has more power than the blood of Jesus—certainly not your paltry, pitiful sins. Nail your past to the cross and leave it there.

Keep repeating the truth of your forgiveness with your wife until it takes hold in your heart, and enjoy the gift of sex with your mate. Awkwardness may still be there occasionally, and you can bet that Satan will try to worm his way back in with flashes of memories you'd either like to live in again (in the case of death) or would much rather forget (after divorce). He will continue to whisper the painful messages that were written on your heart. Take those thoughts captive and move on. Your wife's body was created for you, to be discovered and enjoyed in your remarriage bed; and your body was made for her. It may still take time (and lots of practice) to learn the best ways to please each other, but think of all the fun you can have along the way! Sex within marriage is just how God designed it to be. You can have plenty of healthy sex in remarriage, totally guilt-free.

Protecting Your Remarriage

Just as you have a built-in radar for respect, you are also hardwired as a husband to protect what you love. While your idea of protection may involve keeping other men away from your wife or installing deadbolts on the doors of your home to keep intruders out, what we have in mind are the ways you as a husband are called to protect your wife's heart and your own. It's your job as the husband to take down the fortress around your heart and rebuild it as a hedge of protection around your remarriage. You will need to carefully protect your marriage from the external forces that can drive you apart and the internal conflicts and unhealthy feelings that can put emotional distance between you.

Some of the external pressures on your remarriage can include conflict with former spouses, difficulties with children and stepchildren, legal battles, addictions, extended family loyalties, aging parents, strained finances, overloaded schedules, jobs, exhaustion, poor health, pornography, and other people who distract you from your spouse (either as potential romantic interests or friendships that take too much time or turn you against your mate). Internal pressures on remarriages may include "ghosts" of past relationships, old hurts, poor communication, division over discipline, lust, poor self-image, disrespect, anger, withdrawal, unrealistic expectations and sexual frustration.

As a remarried husband, picture yourself as a warrior in full metal armor, patrolling outside the fortress you have built around your marriage. Visualize yourself fending off all of these external *and* internal forces that Satan wants to use to tear your marriage apart. He doesn't want you to succeed at remarriage. If he can keep families in conflict, he effectively nullifies any good they can do for God. They are too consumed with their own issues to be able to minister to anyone else, and that's just the way the enemy wants it! Don't let him win. Don't let him even get a foot inside the door of your heart.

If reading time is hard to find or you just don't like to read, buy an audio Bible that you can listen to in the car or load onto your iPod. You can "read" good books this way too.

Dan and Marci were very tired of their quarreling and outbreaks of anger in the first several years of their remarriage. They had been praying over their marriage but felt stuck in some bad behavior patterns. Dan happened to run across a book about developing a powerful prayer life, and what he learned became life changing. As he read, Dan realized that God cannot bless a person and help him go forward until that person is willing to be transparent before a Holy God and confess and repent. Isaiah 59:2 says, "But your iniquities have separated you from your God; your sins have hidden his face from you, so that he will not hear."

Dan began to apply the principles in the book by being totally honest before God. He let God clean out his heart—stuff he had been harboring for more than 20 years. He confessed some things to Marci that he had hidden from her, and then she also confessed some things she had been hiding from him. For example, both spouses had given money to their grown children without telling each other. They had done this as a result of tremendous guilt and wanting to do something to bless their children, and they hid it from each other because they knew it would cause conflict. When they both confessed to each other the same exact sin, they agreed to start operating as one. The act of confession and repentance had a tremendous

I f your negative emotions or sexual guilt have led you down the path of addiction, whether it is addiction to substances, gambling, sex or pornography, your remarriage has very little chance for success until the stronghold of addiction is broken. Addiction is a huge heart blockage, one that can easily kill a marriage and even cost your life. You can't fully experience God's love or overflow love to your wife if you are caught up in any kind of addiction.

Seek outside, professional help; and get it now. Don't wait another day or even another hour. The best thing you can do for your wife, your children and yourself is to get the right tools in your arsenal to eliminate addictions permanently. There is no shame in admitting that you have an addiction, and seeking help for it. The real shame would be covering it up until it kills everything good in your life—or kills you.

If you have an addiction to drugs or alcohol, go to rehab and follow up with counseling and regular meetings. Get accountability partners, and cut off any relationships or friendships that feed your addiction. Stay away from places where you can get alcohol or drugs, and surrender your addiction in prayer to Christ every time you feel a pang of temptation. Limit the amount of money you have access to, and put in place every other safeguard you can think of to break addiction for good.

If you have an addiction to pornography or other sexual addiction, confess it and cut it off now. Turn off the Internet, throw out the magazines and get rid of every movie. Don't even let yourself watch a racy TV show or rated "R" film if a love scene would trigger your addictive behaviors. Likewise, if you have a gambling problem, stay far away from casinos, don't buy a single lottery ticket, and get rid of your Internet connection. Place your finances in the hands of a professional or trusted family member so that you have little or no access to cash or credit. Get support from others, and surrender your behavior to Christ.

Remember, the Bible says that the same power that raised Jesus from the dead now lives in you (see Rom. 8:11). And if you have enough power in you to bring the dead back to life, surely that power is strong enough to conquer your addictions and bring your blocked heart back to full flow. Only then can you love and engage fully and be the kind of husband in remarriage you were created to be.

impact on their remarriage. No longer did they set their own children above their relationship. Instead, they began to make decisions over their children by seeking God's will together.

You can protect your marriage from internal pressures by practicing the love list we outlined earlier in the chapter and by guarding and tending your own heart well. Set boundaries around your fighting style and practice conflict management. Keep your vertical connection with Christ strong by praying together as a couple every day, reading great books and studying the Bible together. Connect with a Bible-teaching church filled with Christians who are "real," who want to live for God in their marriages, and who love and accept you right where you are. Develop a ministry with your mate, so that you are serving God and others together. All of these things are weapons in your arsenal to fend off enemy attacks.

It wasn't long after Dan and Marci became honest with one another that they decided to have a small Bible study group in their home once a week. This also had a tremendous impact on their remarriage, as they knew they had a serious responsibility before God and the people attending their group. They had the responsibility of spending time in prayer, reading and meditating on God's Word, serving the members of the group and growing together. The extra-special blessing is that they wound up becoming the best of friends with all the people in their group, and remain so today.

Here's one more little weapon that can make a big difference in protecting your remarriage: Apologize often and forgive easily. Go beyond "I'm sorry" and ask for forgiveness. If you accidentally bump into someone or step on someone's toe, "I'm sorry" covers the misdeed and restores relationship because the injury was not intentional. Wounded hearts need more than that to reconcile. If you offend someone, if you act with malice and hurt a heart, you need to ask the one you've hurt to forgive you. As the offender, if you only say, "I'm sorry," you remain in control. It requires no humility on your part, and it can be difficult for the injured party to determine the true state of your heart. If you say, "I'm sorry. Will you forgive me?" it shifts the balance of power to the one who was offended. You have to humble yourself, and the control is handed to the one who was hurt. This humbling helps you to feel truly sorry for your actions, and it propels the injured party to forgive. When this cycle is completed, relationships have the best chance of being fully reconciled, quickly and with no lingering resentment.

Phone a Friend

On the popular game show *Who Wants to Be a Millionaire?* contestants are given three "lifelines" to try to keep themselves in the game if they don't know the answer to one of the questions. One of those lifelines is to "phone a friend."

As a general rule, men find it easy to hide things they don't like about themselves, bury things that go wrong, even deceive the ones they love because they don't want to be too vulnerable or because their fear and pride keep them from revealing the truth. Men don't like to be open, because it leaves them feeling exposed and vulnerable. But Christian husbands are called to be open, to deal in truth only, and to allow their hearts to remain soft and vulnerable. What if you just can't do that? What if you don't know how?

A remarried husband has two choices: (1) He can live behind a mask and run the risk of losing his marriage because he hides behind half-truths or outright lies, or (2) he can use his lifeline. He can phone a friend. A man may prefer to sing Simon and Garfunkel's "I am a rock; I am an island," and convince himself that he can go it alone, but the truth is that Christian men need trusted friendships and regular fellowship with other Christian men. Remarried Christian husbands need the wisdom and mentoring of other Christian husbands. You need a sounding board that has no potential to become a threat to your marriage, and you need to see other men who are trying to live honestly and openly with their wives. You also need someone who can hold you accountable when you face temptation or try to hide. When you develop strong friendships with other men, you can grow together in Christ by studying His Word and learning from each other's example.

If you don't know where to find that kind of friendship, choose a men's small group at your church or find a local men's Bible study. You may need to try more than one group or go more than a couple of times to feel a "connection" with one or more men. Clear your calendar at least once every other week, preferably weekly, when you can meet together to study, talk and pray. Set aside a specific amount of time for your meetings and stick to it, and then keep at it. Over time, your friendships will be the iron that sharpens iron (see Prov. 27:17), helping you become better husbands so that your marriages will make it.

Heart Monitors

1. Had you heard the message of "love and respect" before? If not, what did this reveal to you? If you had, what did you learn from hearing it again?

2. As a remarried husband, what in your past has caused you to feel disrespected? What triggers feelings of disrespect now?

3. How do you need respect to be shown to you in your remarriage? What specific things can your wife do to help you feel respected?

4. In what ways do you struggle with anger? What sets you off?

5. What five things will you add to your arsenal to help you defuse your anger?

6. Have you been forgiven for any past sexual sins? How can you improve your sex life in remarriage?

7. Name your three closest male friends. Do you spend time with them on a regular basis? Does that time include Bible study, prayer and open sharing? In what ways are your friends the kind of husbands you can learn from and grow with in a positive way?

Heart Protectors

Read or reread *Love and Respect* with your wife, or find a church using the video series.

If you don't have a regular exercise routine at least three times a week, start one this week. Cardiovascular workouts improve your physical health, strengthen your immune system and make a positive impact on your emotions and self-image.

Make a list of your family's "Fighting Rules." "No yelling" might be on there, or "We'll take a 10-minute break if we start to feel too angry." Start your quarter jar and add to it every time there's a violation of the rules.

Identify men you know who are good husbands. Spend time with one of them this week.

Note

1. Emerson Eggerichs, "About Love and Respect." http://www.loveandrespect.com/content/about_love_and_respect.php (accessed April 25, 2009).

8

The Heart of a Remarried Wife

The LORD God said, "It isn't good for the man to live alone.
I need to make a suitable partner for him."
GENESIS 2:18, *CEV*

A gorgeous white gown with a shimmery, ethereal veil. A sparkling dia-
mond ring. Breathtaking floral arrangements. The man of your dreams
standing at the front of a church altar in a tuxedo, beaming with adoration
and unable to take his eyes off you as you float toward him down the aisle.
Sigh. This is the dream most American women have of their long-awaited
wedding day. In remarriage, it's not often the reality.

As a remarried wife, you may have had the dream wedding the first
time around, but death snatched your husband, or your former marriage
quickly became a nightmare. Or you may have given up the wedding dream
to marry a man who already had an elaborate wedding to someone else.
Your remarriage wedding ceremony was most likely done quickly and eco-
nomically, without huge crowds and tons of fanfare. Even if you had a
fancy ceremony and reception, you may have caught yourself wondering if
it was as good as your spouse's "other" wedding. Or the day might have
had a damper on it because kids or stepkids were still grieving a mom or
dad they lost or were not allowed by former spouses to attend. It may have
been tense because relatives or friends weren't fully approving of the new
union, or worries and fear might have surfaced in you that this marriage
could end up one day just like your former one. (We actually know of one
remarried husband who jokingly sent a condolence card into the dressing
room of his bride-to-be on their wedding day. Yes, she still married him.)

No matter what your wedding day looked like, the picture painted in
the first sentences of this chapter capture what the heart of a wife longs
for: love and romance. To be more specific, most wives desire unconditional

love, and they want to be romanced long after the dating days and the "I Do's" are said.

It's perfectly natural for a wife to desire to be loved and cherished. In fact, God wired women this way. However, unconditional love and romance can be a tall order in remarriage, when wives, husbands and kids get caught in the loyalty triangle and a former spouse comes between you and your husband. The heart of a remarried wife can quickly get bruised or broken in the conflict and chaos that accompany remarriage. Emotional security is lost, and the "feelings" of love leave as the heart hangs out the CLOSED sign.

Love, Remarriage Style: What Unconditional Love Looks Like

If you read the last chapter, "The Heart of a Remarried Husband" (and we hope you did—if you skipped it, go back and read it before you go on to chapter 9—it will give you valuable insight into the heart of the man you married), then you know that God designed men to need unconditional respect. He also commanded wives to give it to them (see Eph. 5:33). In the same verse, God orders men to love their wives like they love their own bodies. The reason He commanded this was twofold: (1) Men don't naturally express love very easily, and (2) women need love as much as they need oxygen or, for many women, chocolate!

A wife with an open heart knows and believes she is adored. She knows she is special in the eyes of someone who loves her no matter what her mood. She feels like she comes first, placed in her husband's esteem above his work, the children and especially his former wife. She believes that she is physically attractive and that her husband desires her body. When a husband loves his wife the way God calls him to do in Ephesians 5:33, a wife's heart will have a much easier time staying open. But the remarried wife can't depend on her husband to do all her heart work. Her husband can't meet her need for emotional security.

No human can love perfectly, including your husband. Whether your husband falls on the short end of the measuring stick when it comes to outward shows of affection and romantic gestures, or he is the kind of guy who still brings you flowers regularly, plans date nights and continues to croon love songs in your ear (hopefully on key), he can't give you enough love to fulfill you.

The heart of a remarried wife requires proper tending, not only by her husband, but also by herself. That's right. Remember our advice in the beginning of this book about tending your own heart? The wife has heart repairs of her own to make in order to get rid of all the clogs that might keep her from overflowing God's love to her husband and family.

 When you feel like you haven't received a token of love lately, don't always depend on your husband to act, and then feel disappointed when he doesn't. Instead, give yourself a boost. Schedule a spa day, lunch with a good friend at a favorite restaurant, or indulge in a special treat. Consider it a kiss on the cheek from your Creator.

In order to have a fully open heart as a wife, you have to let God's love fill and heal you. Your husband cannot fill up your love tank completely. He will never be able to make you feel pretty enough, show that he desires you enough, or tell you he loves you enough to fill the void that can only be filled with a personal relationship with Christ. Your mate can never love you enough to bolster your self-esteem or make you believe you are a unique, beautiful woman created to live out a divine purpose. That kind of heart filling only comes from God.

Your husband can't heal the heart hurts that have been inflicted over the years by adolescent classmates, former boyfriends or spouses and the "mean girls" you've encountered. Only God's love can erase the damage done by Satan, who has whispered in your ear for years that you aren't worth anything, and that you will never be good enough, attractive enough, smart enough or talented enough to amount to much.

To experience true unconditional love, you must put time and energy into your relationship with Christ. He has to become your best friend, your comforter, the one from whom you derive your identity, your passion and your purpose. Then and only then can you believe the words of love that come from your husband and receive the gestures of love your spouse offers. Your husband is not—and never will be—your soul mate. (Sorry to burst your bubble once again.) Only God, who created your soul to long for Him, is your true soul mate. That's why He calls His followers His "bride."

The remarried wife who learns to love herself and her family by first loving God takes the pressure off of herself (for never feeling "good enough") and her husband (for never giving her enough). She will feel loved and will be able to be more loving.

According to 1 Corinthians 13, real love is a tall order for us humans. As we've noted before, love is patient and kind. It is not jealous, rude or self-serving. It is slow to become angry, does not delight in evil and doesn't keep track of wrongs. It always protects, trusts, hopes and perseveres. Phew! Have you ever loved or known love like that? We haven't. Yet that is the standard God sets of what "real love" looks like. It isn't when eyes meet across a crowded room or when a leg "pops" up during a kiss. It isn't even a happy ending. True love sticks around when things aren't great, when they aren't easy, when it seems easier to quit than to do the hard work to go on, and when others are not loving you in return.

Examine your bookshelf and DVD collection. Look at the romance novels and romantic comedy films and get rid of any that make you feel restless or breed discontent in you about your remarriage. Novels, in particular, can give you a warped sense of what romantic love entails.

When you connect with Christ and allow Him to speak healing into your heart, then you can finally know unconditional love. And you can outflow some of that love to your husband and family. The heart of a remarried wife is uniquely created. You are beautiful, cherished and adored. Don't believe the lies of Satan anymore. You have a special call on your life that only you can fulfill. Think of it this way: Out of all the women in the world, God chose you to be the wife of this particular husband, the mother to your particular children and the stepmother to your particular stepchildren. Why? Because God must have seen that you have a combination of talents, skills and gifts to share with them that no one else has. You are one of a kind, and your family needs your heart to be filled with love overflowing toward them.

Recognizing Heart Darts

When you grow your relationship with Christ and begin to see your value through His eyes, your heart begins to unfold. Old hurts finally heal. However, there are many "heart darts" in remarriage that the enemy aims straight at your emotional center, hoping to slam it shut again and again. If you

know what to look for, you can block the darts that come your way. If any
do get through and pierce you, you can dislodge them a lot easier if you recognize what just hit home.

Here are some of the common darts shot straight at the heart of a remarried wife:

- Verbal attacks from a former wife who hates you and teaches her
  children to disdain you
- Inappropriate attachment from a former wife who won't let go of
  your husband, expecting him to still meet her needs
- A former husband who verbally attacks you or turns your children
  against you
- A former husband who can't get over your divorce and who still
  tries to cling to you
- Guilt because you still feel attracted to your former husband
- Fear that your husband is still attracted to his former wife
- Feelings of insecurity because you are a first-time wife to a man
  who was married before
- Mistrust of your spouse because you've been betrayed before
- Feelings of inadequacy if you are a first-time wife expected to
  "mother" your stepchildren
- Children or stepchildren who rebel against you or your husband
- Financial pressures because of child support paid to another
  household
- Disappointment and unexpected feelings of being let down by your
  remarriage because of unrealistic expectations you had going into it
- Discomfort in social situations where there are friends of your for-
  mer spouse or friends you formerly had together
- Frustration over miscommunication with your spouse
- Feelings of hopelessness when you can't seem to get on the same
  page with your spouse
- Loneliness and isolation that you did not expect to feel in your re-
  marriage
- Feelings of being constantly misunderstood
- Feeling that you are invisible, that the kids or your spouse's job
  come first
- Difficulty making new friends as a couple or finding the right place
  to fellowship

These darts and others can do serious damage to a wife's open, healed heart, re-wounding it and closing its doors to the business of loving. If you recognize darts on the list above that may be sticking out of your heart now, pray that God will gently pull them out. You may not be able to change the actions or attitudes of your former husband or your spouse's former wife, but you can change your reaction to them. You don't have to be bowed or broken. You can choose to stand tall, basking in the love of Christ and filled with joy at the chance He has given you to experience love in your remarriage.

Face your fears and insecurities and share them with your husband. Ask him to hear your heart and remember that you were created to be emotional (so that he doesn't dismiss your words automatically as being overly dramatic). Talking about your anxieties and fears can help alleviate some of them. Ask your husband to pray for you, and make a plan together for handling situations that might trigger the release of any heart darts.

 Search Youtube.com for marriage counselor and comedian Mark Gungor's "Two Brains" video, describing the differences between men's and women's brains. Enjoy laughing together.

Be a Partner, Not a Dependent

Guess what? We've focused a lot on keeping an open heart as a remarried wife, but we also need to remind you that you are much more than just a wife in a remarriage. You have your own identity, individual calling and purpose that go beyond your role as a spouse. You are a woman hand-designed by God, created to be part of His plan. You may be a wife, mom and stepmom, but you are first and foremost a woman with a call to love God and live out the passions and purpose He has placed in you.

Your remarriage is a bonus—an extra blessing on top of the whole life God has already given you. You have a purpose, your husband has his own purpose, and together your marriage can serve God's purposes. With or without your husband, you need to recognize your own worth as a woman of God.

Many wives enter remarriage without a clear sense of who they are, how they are gifted and what their passions and purpose are. Or their whole identity was wrapped up in their marriage and family, which ended. They don't know themselves very well, and that can lead to insecurity and cause a wife to lean too heavily on her mate. As a remarried wife, you are your husband's partner, not his dependent. While you definitely need to respect him and his role as provider and protector for your family, you also need to know that you can stand on your own two feet.

If you married young, feel uneducated or do not bring an income to your marriage, you may feel insecure about your purpose. If you are a first-time wife to a man who was married before, you also may battle feelings of insecurity or dependency. You love being cared for by this big, strong man. Your husband enjoys being looked up to and relied upon. However, too much dependence shifts the balance of power in your marriage until a husband and wife who started as friends and partners are thrust into roles more like parent and child. Your husband doesn't need a wife who acts like a child. Nor do you want a husband who makes you feel like one.

To have a better partnership, you and your husband may need to handle your finances differently—paying bills together or dividing the money—so that each of you has responsibility and no one feels like a child receiving an allowance.

In order to restore the proper balance to your partnership, you need to take steps to uncover God's purpose for you. You might do this by taking quizzes that can reveal your personality, brain preference (are you logical and analytical or artistic and big-picture?), spiritual gifts and learning style. Once you know more about how you are hardwired, you can better see how your combination of skills and gifting translates into ministry, jobs and academics. You may discover a hobby you want to try, or you may decide that you want to earn a college degree. The point is to figure out what you love to do. When you are passionate about something, you will experience joy. When you are filled with joy, you overflow it to your family. Knowing more about your individuality can lift your mood, point you in the right direction to serve others, and help you be a better partner to your husband as he fulfills his purpose and passions alongside you.

R-E-S-P-E-C-T:
How a Remarried Wife Connects with Her Husband

While we've looked at ways a wife can become overly dependent on her husband, in remarriage the opposite happens just as often (maybe more). Remarried wives may have a hard time relying or depending on their husbands at all because they don't trust men or they have had only themselves to count on for a time before they remarried. Back when remarried wives were single moms, they had to adapt to being on their own.

You may have been a naïve, trusting young thing when you married for the first time, but after the catastrophe of your divorce or the death of your spouse, you quickly discovered that you could go it alone and make it just fine. In fact, you may have enjoyed the new sense of independence you found. When you remarry, the well-meaning ways your husband provides for you and protects you may begin to chafe against and irritate your independent spirit. Or you may get frustrated that he doesn't handle things the way your former husband did.

How can a remarried wife "submit" to her husband without subjugating herself to him? The answer, we believe, lies once again in Ephesians 5:33. Earlier in the chapter, we looked at how a husband is called to love his wife and how much a wife needs unconditional love. But in this verse, the wife is also called to unconditionally respect her husband. When she can grasp how easily this action on her part fuels her husband's desire to love her more fully, the marriage partnership feels more balanced. The issue of independence falls away as the wife feels valued and cherished in her role, and the husband feels esteemed in his.

 Make a list of the tasks you performed as a single or single parent. Cross off the tasks you hated that your husband now does for you. Appreciate him for relieving you of those unpleasant chores.

A wife heals her husband's heart and fosters his feelings of love for her by respecting him, even when he is not acting in ways that deserve a lot of respect. This is a foreign concept to American women in the twenty-first century, even Christian wives who desire to follow God's commands. The feminist movement has drastically shifted the way men and women are perceived. Prior to the 1940s, American men were the "bosses" of their homes and families. If they called, wives and kids came running. In television shows, films and radio series, men were authority figures who were obeyed and taken seriously. They provided for their families by working and bringing home a paycheck, while wives ran the home front, taking care of the house and tending the children.

World War II thrust many women out of the home and into factories and other jobs that needed to be performed while so many men were fighting in the war. After the war ended and the men came home, some women found it difficult to give up the respect, the paycheck and the adult routine they had slipped into when their husbands were gone. Fast-forward to the rebellion against all establishment in the 1960s and 1970s, and the old roles for husbands and wives were gone for good. In some ways, this was positive for women, letting them know they had value in and out of the home, and boosting their skill sets and self-esteem. It released them from being "trapped" under the authority of some husbands who believed they could mistreat or abuse their families. Television now started portraying women as smart and hard workers, while men were prejudiced, lazy or just plain mean.

But the feminist movement drove the desire for women to be treated as equals right past that original goal. By the 1980s and 1990s, total role reversal was in play. Men in the newspapers were "deadbeat dads," and the ones on sitcoms were downright silly. On the flip side, women were praised for their accomplishments, elected to higher offices and paid higher salaries. Men were no longer authorities, nor were men and women equal. Now, the women had the upper hand; and they weren't going to give it up easily.

For the next few days, pay attention to how men, especially husbands and dads, are portrayed on the TV shows you see, the programs your kids watch and in news headlines and stories. You may be surprised at what you discover.

Today, men in American culture are often regarded as foolish and unable to match a woman's strength of character, depth of love or intellectual abilities. Shows like *Sex and the City* taught us that women can "love 'em and leave 'em" just like a man and never bat an eyelash. Teen girls now flirt with each other in order to torment the boys around them and laugh at the young men's expense. There is a pervasive sense that men are extraneous. No woman needs a man, except as her own personal "boy toy."

As a remarried wife and Christ follower, you probably recognize how these cultural beliefs are based on Satan's lies. You probably see right away how damaging these lies have been and continue to be. And you probably believe that these lies about men's and women's roles have not affected you in the least. While you may recognize the inherent flaws in our culture's portrayal of men and women and see the damage it is causing, there is a good chance that you have been affected—or infected—by feminism more than you think.

We believe there is one good way to find out. Ask yourself the following question: Do I believe that I must show respect to my husband when he acts completely unworthy of my respect? Do I have to respect him if he drinks too much, leaves his dirty underwear everywhere or talks to me harshly? Should I show him respect if he flirts with another woman or never spends time with the kids? If you answered no to any of the questions in this paragraph, you may be following culture's commands, not Christ's.

We can hear you now, arguing that you still love your husband even when he does all of those things, but you will not respect him until he gets his act together and demonstrates that he is worthy of respect. Sorry, according to Ephesians 5:33, that doesn't cut it. As a wife, you are *commanded* to respect your husband. The buck stops there. The verse doesn't say another word. It doesn't say to respect him if he is a good husband or if he is holding down a job. It doesn't say to respect him if he "earns" it or if he is acting respectfully to you. It doesn't even say to respect him if he is loving you. Nope. Each half of the verse is a command directly to that spouse. Husbands are to love. Wives are to respect. End of story.

It would break your heart into a thousand pieces if your husband ever said he didn't love you because you were acting unlovable. However, many a wife feels perfectly justified in saying that she loves her husband but doesn't respect him. Yet a husband was created to need respect even more than he needs love. While that may be unthinkable to you as a woman, if God said it, we need to believe it. Therefore, in a healthy remarriage, a husband doesn't have to jump through any hoops to get the respect he needs, nor does the wife have to perform any certain way to be loved.

Maybe it's not fair to have to respect a man who isn't loving or respecting you, but God doesn't care about "fair." "Fair" is self-serving. God is much more interested in what is right and in what serves others. According to His standard, respecting your husband in any circumstance is right because it honors the man God created in His own image. And the benefit for you is double. Not only are you right with God because you are obeying Him, but the honor you show your husband (especially when he knows he doesn't deserve it) tugs on his male heart and pulls him toward doing the right things. A wife in remarriage who practices the fine art of respecting her husband will have a mate who wants to engage with her, for a respected husband desires to respond with love. Both spouses in remarriage are then living according to the Word, and its truth is strengthening their union and transforming their quality of life.

What does unconditional respect look like? Ask your husband what makes him feel respected, and take his words to heart. A wife can help her husband's heart stay open to her by making sure he knows she is his biggest fan. She needs to cheer her husband on in every one of his endeavors, letting him know how proud she is to be his wife. She should encourage him with words that describe how she respects him. She can empathize with how it feels to be the provider, husband and father. She should brag on him to others. Her husband needs her to align with him when there is conflict with others (even or especially her children; more on that in chapter 10), to always take his side and to support his efforts.

 Ask your husband if there are ways that you have continuously made him feel disrespected. If there are, apologize sincerely and tell him you will try to break your bad habits.

A wife who wants to show respect also needs to carefully consider her tone of voice and facial expression as she talks to her husband, especially about difficult subjects. Many wives don't realize how disdainful their looks and tone of voice can be. By softening her expression and gentling her tone, a wife can communicate any message to her mate without raising his defenses because he feels disrespected.

The Heart of a Remarried Wife Is the Heartbeat of Her Home

You now revel in the unconditional love of Christ; you have discovered who you were created to be; and you are well on your way to treating your husband with more respect. You have an open, loving heart that nurtures the relationships in your remarriage. As a woman created to give and receive love, nothing can replace your role as the heartbeat of your family. You play a large role in facilitating the emotional security your family needs to feel safe.

You operate from your emotions, and they can positively or negatively charge the atmosphere in your home. Therefore, the condition of your heart is vital to the success of your remarriage. When your heart tries to shut down because of hurt or anger (past or present), everyone in your family will suffer. A remarried wife must carefully guard her heart, because a wife that is shut down can shut down her family's hearts too.

When your heart is secure in God's love, and you are filled with joy as you fulfill your purpose, your family feels it. Surely you have heard the old expression: If Mama ain't happy, ain't nobody happy. There is a lot of truth in that statement. Your emotional state can lift or lower the mood in your household. Haven't you ever noticed how quickly irritation spreads? You get annoyed with your husband for once again giving the kids too much sugar right before dinner or for washing your delicates with his red shirts for the umpteenth time. He feels disrespected by your criticism, your angry tone and furrowed brow, and he unlovingly yells at you in return. Now your son wanders into the kitchen (and into the conflict) and one of you quickly turns on him, demanding to know why he ate potato chips on the couch instead of at the table. He stomps off and yells at his little sister for dumping her toys in his room. Conflict is contagious.

The heart of a remarried wife seeks to lower the level of conflict her family experiences. External pressures are tough enough in remarriage; adding internal chaos hardens hearts. Pay attention to your voice when you're feeling stressed or at odds with what's going on with circumstances or relationships, and if needed, practice softening your tone of voice. Offer encouraging statements often and pat your family members on the back every day. Your love cements your family together along its new seams. Each day, you are weaving a little more into the fabric of your remarriage. You can choose to weave threads of peace, passion and praise, or you can pull together strings of resentment, regret and rebellion. You can give love and respect generously, or you can withhold it and watch your remarriage falter. When the heart of a remarried wife overflows with love, her marriage can thrive.

HEART MONITORS

1. In what ways have you ever experienced unconditional love? What did it look and feel like?

2. What are your passions and purpose? What has God called you to do? If you are not sure, what steps will you take this week to discover your uniqueness?

3. What are some of the heart darts that have pierced you? How can you keep them from closing your heart's door?

4. Is the balance of power in your remarriage off-kilter? Are you too dependent or too independent? What steps do you need to take to become a true partner with your spouse?

5. In what ways do you show respect to your husband? List at least five ways here, and show them to your spouse. Does he agree? What would he add or subtract from your list?

6. How do you set the emotional tone in your home? How can you keep conflict from becoming contagious?

HEART PROTECTORS

Ask your husband to write down five specific things he wishes you would do or say (or not do or say) this week that would let him know you respect him. Think of five specific things your husband could do to make you feel loved this week. Exchange lists, and do them!

Make a personal goal for one month from now (try a new recipe, exercise three times a week), one year from now (perform in a play or vocal recital, travel to a foreign country), and five years from now (have a college degree, learn a new language). Put your goals where you can see them often.

Put together a romantic dinner or initiate an evening of romance. Surprise your husband with something he loves.

9

The Heart of a Remarried Dad and Stepdad

Stay alert! Watch out for your enemy, the devil.
He prowls around like a roaring lion, looking for someone to devour.
Stand firm against him, and be strong in your faith.
1 PETER 5:8-9, *NLT*

Some of my (Greg's) greatest childhood memories center around camping with my family. We all loved the outdoors and took advantage of the opportunity to camp as often as we could.

When I was about 13 years old, my dad and I heard about this unbelievable fishing river called Lee's Ferry in northern Arizona. Apparently, the fishing was so good that people were catching 12- and 13-pound trout. The mere thought of catching such a fish caused our mouths to salivate. As it turned out, however, the fishing was not the best part of this particular father-son adventure.

The trip to Lee's Ferry took about six hours, and we arrived there sometime late in the evening. Our hotel was about 40 miles from the nearest town, and we were surrounded by the Grand Canyon. The place was so remote and so vast that the sky was lit up like millions of tiny diamonds. The scene was breathtaking. Needing the perfect place to watch the stars, we decided to take our pillows and lie on top of a big stone wall behind the motel. We just lay there talking and watching the shooting stars.

"Hey, did you see that one?" or "Look over there!" were the only sounds. There were minutes when we didn't say a word. We just kept staring up at that beautiful sky.

While we were stargazing, without any warning, a stray cat leaped up and landed right on my chest. The sudden terror, along with my high-pitched scream, resulted in me flinging the cat straight up into the air and, unfortunately, right at my dad's unsuspecting head. He desperately tried to roll out of the way but lost his balance and fell off the wall. Needless to say, we never saw that cat again. We pulled the cactus needles out of my dad's body, and we couldn't stop laughing as we watched the stars well into the next morning.

Just like the cat that attacked us, in your role as a remarried dad, stepdad or both, you need to be prepared for some very serious "heart attacks," especially in the early years following your divorce and the beginning of your remarriage. During this period, you must carefully tend your heart to keep it from being clogged with anger or shut down by feelings of helplessness. You need to remain open to God's love pouring into you and flowing out from you to your wife, children and stepchildren.

In earlier chapters, we discussed every man's deep need to protect and provide. Men are created to keep enemies away from the ones they love and make sure they have their needs met. In remarriage, Satan tries hard to short-circuit remarried husbands' and fathers' efforts to do these two basic things. He wants remarried dads and stepdads to feel like failures at the very tasks they are hardwired by God to do. If you aren't prepared for these attacks by the enemy, the result can be heart damage.

The Heart That Protects

The dad and stepdad who loves and follows Christ stands ready to fight off any enemy that threatens or attacks the hearts of the ones he loves; but in remarriage it's tough to know who to protect first. The war is happening within your own family, and the attacks come fast and furious. In a stepfamily civil war, defending one heart means betraying another. Saving one relationship may cost the weary warrior dad and stepdad his relationship with someone else. It's almost impossible to keep everyone's hearts safe.

As a remarried dad/stepdad, you want to protect every member of your family; you want to make your home a safe haven for everyone you love. But how can you do that without creating a maelstrom of anger and resentment? If it's an issue, you must protect your wife from the haranguing of your ex-wife. You want to protect both your children and your wife, but they are often at odds with each other. You want to protect your stepchildren, but they want no part of you, and your kids resent it too.

When a remarried wife and her stepchildren square off, it's dad who gets caught in the middle. It's a no-win situation for everyone in the family.

Many dads and stepdads in remarriage shut down and withdraw, leaving wives and kids wounded on the battlefield of misery, and angry with him for not sticking by them. Some dads enter the fray to try to make peace, only to find that everyone turns on him. A remarried dad and stepdad's only other option is to choose to side with either his wife or his children or stepchildren, leaving the side he didn't choose full of resentment toward him.

When dads and stepdads can't figure out how to win the remarriage relationship war, they may lay down their arms and walk off the battlefield in total surrender. Or they may start slashing their sword with a vengeance, striking down any family member who gets in their way, hoping to defeat *something*. This is called the "fight or flight" reaction. When a dad and stepdad in remarriage can't fight for his family effectively, and he either withdraws or unleashes his anger, every member of the stepfamily loses.

> *The remarried dad and stepdad knows that Satan's favorite target is his family. Therefore, he stays fully engaged, prepared to fend off the true enemy of his stepfamily with the weapons God gives him.*

As a remarried dad and stepdad, you can protect your own heart from hardening by recognizing and remembering this truth in the heat of battle: *You are engaged in a spiritual war.*

You are not fighting your wife when she criticizes the way you handle your children or argues with you over the way you are handling *her* children. You are not battling your teenage daughter when she refuses to come to your house for visitation because she has more freedom at her mom's. You are not fighting your son when he bullies his new stepbrother. You are not fighting your stepchildren when they rebel against you. You are not even fighting your ex-wife or your wife's ex-husband when they refuse to co-parent and communicate with you. As a remarried dad/stepdad, you are to keep this truth in mind: Always, at all times, you are fighting Satan, the one the Bible says comes to "steal and kill and destroy" (John 10:10). The remarried dad/stepdad knows that Satan's favorite target is his family. Therefore, he stays fully engaged, prepared to fend off the true enemy of his stepfamily with the weapons God gives him.

As a remarried dad and stepdad who wants to love his family well and desires to tend his own heart and the hearts of his family members carefully, what are the weapons in your arsenal? First and foremost, your faith in Christ. The deeper your faith, and the more real and personal your relationship with Christ becomes, the longer you can stand and fight off the enemy with an open, loving heart, even when you feel bloodied and beaten. The strong faith of a remarried dad and stepdad can go a long way toward protecting the hearts of his family and making his home the safest place on earth.

 Imagine Satan as a little yippy dog. With the power of the Holy Spirit in you, the devil is little more than an annoying Chihuahua trying to nip your heels. The next time you feel the enemy trying to attack your family, picture him as a tiny dog and give him a good, swift mental kick. He can't defeat you. You already know you're on the winning team.

Your faith has to grow and change over time so that your armor has no chinks. The Bible promises that if you draw near to the Lord, he will draw near to you (see Jas. 4:8). How do you do this? You make your faith real and deeply rooted by praying continuously, studying the Bible regularly and with passion, and memorizing Scripture. You need to make sure you are growing in fellowship with other believers. You should be receiving instruction from knowledgeable Bible teachers and be plugged into a local church, where your wounds can be tended while they are fresh and your spirit can be renewed before you head back to the battlefield.

When a remarried dad and stepdad stands firm in his faith, he has the best chance of fending off enemy attacks and fulfilling his responsibility to guard all the wounded, bruised hearts in his family. While you can't heal the hearts of your family overnight, you can apply repeated doses of God's healing power when you exercise your faith. That's the best protection you can give the ones you love.

The Heart That Provides

In the movie *Forrest Gump*, the title character played by actor Tom Hanks refers to life as a "box of chocolates." Life in remarriage, however, more closely resembles a great, big tangled ball of string. Everything seems complicated. Providing for the ones you love is no exception.

Providing is a big challenge for dads and stepdads in remarriage because it often seems like there is never enough money to go around. (If you lost your spouse, your financial picture can vary widely.) If you have children who spend more time living with their mother than with you, you probably pay a hefty amount in child support. If your ex-wife had no income during your marriage or her income was significantly smaller than yours, you may be paying alimony to help provide for her after your divorce. You now have your own household to support and must provide for your wife and any children you have at home together, which may include your stepchildren. Add in leftover legal fees, consumer debt and the aftereffects of bankruptcy or ruined credit from divorce, and it's easy for a remarried dad and stepdad to feel like a failure, like he can't do enough for anybody, let alone everybody. Stress can mount, and the pressure can shut down your heart, rendering you ineffective at loving and connecting with your family.

The truth is, most people can't really afford to get divorced. If money is one of the primary reasons couples cite for splitting up, what makes them think things will get better if they create two households that now have to divide the same money pot? The numbers just don't add up. In remarriage after divorce, everyone's slice of the income "pie" gets smaller.

Dan and Marci lost everything in their divorces, and money became a huge issue in their remarriage.

"(Before divorce) I lived for money," Dan said. "I lived for making the big deals. Then when Marci and I were first married, we figured out how to eat at a Mexican restaurant with free chips and salsa. We would drink water and order a queso dip, and sometimes we'd ask if they would put ground beef in it, and that would be free. We'd make a meal of that. It was tough."

 Read all of Jesus' parables about money. Then study other places in the Bible that mention money. Take note of how money is treated and any advice given by God's Word.

The enemy works double-time to make you feel guilty or like a failure if you can't provide for everyone like you want to, or if one set of your kids doesn't enjoy the same lifestyle as your other set of kids. You may feel utterly helpless if your wife's desire is to stay home with your children and stepchildren, but she has to go to work each day to help make ends meet. Don't let Satan get even a pinkie toe wedged into the doorway of your heart. No matter how big your financial pressures seem, your number-one job as a remarried dad and stepdad is to keep your heart soft, pliable and overflowing God's love to your family.

So when money is tight and financial pressures build, a remarried dad and stepdad's plan of attack should be twofold: (1) Do everything you can to be a wise steward of what God gives you, and (2) wave the white flag of surrender. We can hear you thinking, *What do you mean? I thought you just told me never to give up. I'll never surrender. I'd rather die.*

When you are focused on protecting your heart and the hearts of your family from the devil's attacks, a remarried dad and stepdad never gives up. With God on your side, you remain willing to fight to the death to protect your family's hearts. When it comes to providing, however, surrender is your stealth weapon. You work hard to get your finances in order and do the job you have to the best of your ability, all the while handing the whole ball of wax over to the Redeemer.

Let's unpack this two-pronged strategy.

Do everything you can to be a good steward.
Wave the white flag of surrender.

While these two statements may seem like opposites, they actually go hand in hand. You give God the control of your money and you stop trying to manage it all yourself (surrender). At the same time, you uphold your responsibility to use everything He gives you for His purposes (stewardship). A remarried dad and stepdad who wants to be truly blessed in the area of money is hands-off in terms of power and hands-on in management. You have to be able to let go of your plans, your dreams, your goals, your vacations, your "climbing the corporate ladder," your desire to be rich, your need to please, your greed and your determination to prove you are a success. Instead, you ask God to replace that whole list of "yours" with a list of His.

Being a wise steward means changing your perspective about your money. You have to realize that it's not *yours* at all. We see you nodding, *You got that right. My ex and my kids take every penny!* But that's not at all what we mean. The definition of a steward is a servant. A steward works for a master, so everything he manages belongs to his boss. Every penny that passes through your fingers belongs to the Lord. He's the boss. It's all His. It came from Him and is owned by Him, even when it's in your hot little hands. God wants you to ask Him how you should use it. You need to see money as a tool, nothing more. It's not your source of joy or the rope that hangs you. It's merely an instrument that enables you to live, serve and give. It doesn't need to be hoarded; neither should it be wasted. It should be used to give God glory—like everything else you have, do or say.

The Bible talks a lot about money, evidently because God knows how much trouble we human beings have with it. In fact, 16 of the parables Jesus told had something to do with money. In Matthew 25:14-30, Jesus tells a story about a master who was going on a trip and left money with three of his servants to manage while he was gone. The first two servants took the money, did business with it and doubled it. The third steward buried the money. When the master returned, the stewards presented him with the results of their efforts. He praised the first two for making a profit but punished the third for returning the same amount that was given to him in the first place.

If you haven't been managing God's money wisely and your finances are in shambles, there are many steps you can take and should take toward becoming a faithful steward of the resources God gives you. If you have never been one to use a budget, get over it and start now. Not tomorrow or next week. Start today. It's past time to see where your money is really going and make a plan for where it should be spent from now on. You need clear, defined goals for getting out of debt, and you have to be willing to cut back and make sacrifices until debt is cleared. We know you've heard all this a million times, but if your remarriage finances are a mess and you aren't taking steps every day to fix them, they're just going to get worse. And if you haven't begun to see positive changes on your own by now, you're probably not going to be able to take the right steps by yourself (or you already would have done it). You need someone to help you formulate a game plan and put it into action, then hold you accountable to the plan.

Call the free ministry resources that are available for credit and debt reduction counseling. There are plenty of reputable companies and ministries that won't charge a thing to help you make a plan to become financially free. (There are also plenty of companies that will charge you a fortune. You should not have to pay for debt-reduction counseling.) Crown Financial Ministries (www.crown.org) is a great place to start. If you are serious about being a remarried dad and stepdad who provides well, you and your wife need to pray together about your finances, then work as a team to move forward. You may need to work overtime, or she may need to get a part-time job. You may decide that you need to work *less* overtime because your family needs time with you more than money, and you will cut back on entertainment or use coupons to make your grocery dollars stretch in order to keep the bills paid. Your budget has many pieces to the puzzle, and as a couple you can move them around until they make the right picture for your family. When you have financial breakthroughs such as a paid-off credit card or a raise in pay, celebrate. Stick within your budget, but pat yourselves on the back.

Teach your children and stepchildren early on how to handle small amounts of money. Have them pay God first and put some money in long-term savings. By the age of six or seven, kids can write down the money they receive in a check register and begin keeping track of what they spend and save. As a stepdad, giving allowances is also one easy way for you to be the "good guy" with your stepchildren. Make sure you teach your older children the dangers of using a credit card and the benefits of investing.

One vital financial puzzle piece is your tithe. Pay God back first. No excuses. The Bible says that the "tithe" is the first 10 percent of everything you earn or receive. It belongs to God. When you don't have enough to pay all the bills to begin with, it's easy to rationalize that God has enough. He doesn't need and won't miss the paltry few dollars you'd be adding to His pot. But that's not the point. The point is obedience. A holy God demands it. And remarried dads and stepdads need to be able to put away their pride and give it to Him. This is where your faith might really be put to the test each time you hand over 10 percent that your family really needs. The bottom line is: Do you believe that God will provide for you or not? He promises He will.

If you know the lengths you would go to as a dad to make sure your family never does without, don't you think that God—your dad—will do the same for you? Remember that white flag you're supposed to be waving. Do you trust Him, or do you exhaust yourself trying to do it under your own power? No matter how little you have, give back to God first and you will see a positive change in your finances because you are obeying Him.

One big no-no that plagues many remarriages is hiding financial information. It's easy to do, because many couples who come together when they are single parents keep their own bank accounts and pay their own bills even in remarriage. It takes a conscious effort to schedule time to create a complete financial picture together and to peacefully decide how any money coming in will be divvied up to meet the family's needs.

Never hide your financial situation from your wife. Deception is betrayal, and in a remarriage it can devastate and destroy. You are not protecting her by hiding the truth, borrowing money without her knowledge or taking out credit cards she is unaware of. Hidden debt is not protection; it's a trap that can pull your entire family down. We have no doubt that your motive is to ease your wife's worry and maintain her respect for you. We also understand how easy it is for spouses in remarriage to have an unspoken agreement that there are things "we just won't talk about." But hidden financial troubles can crush you under their burden and destroy your marriage as the pile of deception and debt rains down. Betrayal feels the same, whether it is an illicit relationship, a hidden addiction or a mountain of debt. When it comes to light, it hurts. And in remarriage, mates have usually experienced betrayal before, making trust tentative.

If you have not been honest with your wife about your financial situation, in a time of non-conflict, you need to come clean. Don't keep hiding it because you don't want to hurt her. The truth is, you've already hurt her; she just doesn't know it yet. The sooner she does, the sooner you can both decide what needs to be done to fix the situation. Our suggestion would be to have the conversation away from your home. That way, there's no chance of kids getting caught in the line of fire, and you don't "taint" your bedroom with the memory of your fights. Keep your bedroom a place of sanctuary. (It may be the only one you've got!) Take your fights to the nearest park, restaurant or shopping mall. In a public place, it's less likely that emotions will get the upper hand.

When you tell your wife what's going on, be humble and sincerely apologetic—keep an open heart. Don't defend your actions; simply admit what you've done and where you stand. Ask your wife to forgive you, and ask what you can do to make it right with her. Expect her to react to your news with tears and anger, and don't engage in conflict because you feel guilty and she's not taking it well. She may accuse you of hiding other things and ask if you are having an affair. Again, that's because women feel deeply, and all betrayal feels the same. Reassure her and let her know you will work hard to win back her trust.

Let your wife know that you want to be a team from now on, and that you need her help to make a plan for your financial future. Figure out ways to keep money matters out in the open, and try not to get frustrated if your wife questions your spending on a regular basis for a while. If she wants to see receipts, make sure you get them. If she needs the security of sitting down together to pay the bills, set aside time weekly to do it. Try to remember that your wife is not trying to disrespect you or make you feel like a child reporting to his mother. She simply needs to be reassured often that you are now managing money differently. If you remember the earlier truth that it is the devil you are fighting, not each other, and if you make changes and stick with them, you will make it through.

More + More = Less

Even if finances are tough for you, if you live in the United States, you have a lot. If you have electricity, a solid roof over your head and clean running water, you are better off than the majority of people on the entire planet. In America, we are so blessed with material things that we want what we want when we want it. And most of the time, we get it. When we don't get it, or when we can't give our kids what they want, it's a rude awakening. When you are blessed with money, providing still comes with difficulties because family members tend to keep a close eye on who is getting what from dad or stepdad. If your former wife and your kids with her go to Disney World while your second family is home with you eating Kraft Macaroni & Cheese, the enemy is going to try to work his way in and make tempers flare and resentment build.

On the other hand, if your children from a previous marriage or relationship are living primarily with a mom who can't afford much, they might feel deeply resentful on their weekend visits when they see the new Wii and all the toys that fill the home your "new" kids enjoy. Providing for everyone in remarriage is a constant tightrope walk for dads and stepdads.

Tilt too far in one direction or the other, and you are going to take a plunge. To alleviate some of the comparisons, remarriage is a great time to get back to the basics. You can have a wonderful life without a lot of stuff. In fact, the less stuff you have to maintain (houses, cars, boats, and the like), the more time you have to enjoy your family.

The paradox of more is that we actually have less. Our time is used up working to earn enough to maintain what we have or taking care of what we've got, and time is far more valuable than money. The bigger the house, the longer it takes to clean and the more it costs to live in. Decluttering five closets packed with unnecessary *stuff* takes more time than cleaning out one that contains the necessities. The trick is to learn to be content with less. Then when you are blessed with extra funds, ask the Lord what He wants you to do with them. Maybe He wants you to go on a missions trip, support a ministry or give to someone in need. When you give your money away to those who need it more than you do, it feels better than anything you get for yourself.

Ask your kids to come up with a family service project. You can feed dinner to the homeless or clean up the trash in your neighborhood. You might bake cupcakes for local firefighters or buy gifts at Christmas for a needy family. When you work side by side as a stepfamily to serve others, it takes the focus off of your family friction.

Your kids don't need more toys or entertainment. What they need is time with parents who are not distracted by their own troubles and can focus on them. They need a dad and stepdad who listens to them and plays with them. For remarried dads, it's easy to overdo it on the fun and the toys, especially if you want them to get past their grief or if you only get to see your children every other weekend. While remarried dads can never assuage their guilt or buy their children's love with more things, neither should stepdads try to gain their stepchildren's affections by giving them too much money or buying them too many things. You can't be held hostage by children who threaten not to visit or not to care about you or listen to you unless you entertain them or give them their way. It's okay to say no to what you can't afford. In fact, it's great self-discipline.

If you never say no, your children and stepchildren will have a difficult time delaying gratification, which can lead to troubles in school, jobs and their future relationships. It's not real life to get everything you want, so don't teach your kids and stepkids that you will meet their every desire. We know it's hard to say no to those cute little faces, and it's tough to turn down a teenager's demand when it feels like you're losing their love; but you aren't providing for or protecting your kids and stepkids when you overindulge them. You don't win their love; you lose their respect. Nothing material that you can give them will satisfy anyway. What they need is a heart-to-heart relationship with you and a personal connection with Christ.

Give your children and stepchildren a love for Jesus by showing them how real He is in your life and what a difference it makes to follow Him, and you will bless them with real treasure that lasts forever.

The Widowed Dad

If you've lost your wife, you need to be an active participant in your kids' lives, but you also need to be open to sharing your children if you remarry. You have to let your wife in, not to take the place of your former wife but to be the new helpmeet that God has provided for your family. You may have become overly sensitive and overprotective after the death of your wife, because you know how much your kids have been through.

It is typical in remarriage for new spouses to feel like they won't ever be able to live up to the memories of your former mate. A new wife may be putting her whole heart into her new stepfamily, while you and your children are still reserving most of your hearts for your lost loved one.

Seek out grief counseling for yourself or the kids if you have difficulty letting go of the past to engage in your remarriage. You, your wife and your children and stepchildren can learn to work together to create a safe emotional place that helps you become stronger after your loss. But you have to let your new spouse take on the role of wife and mother, even when at first it feels like that role still belongs to someone else.

How Dads Can Tug Kids' Heartstrings

Speaking of those cute little faces, a remarried dad needs to actively parent his adorable little children all the way through their not-so-cute teen years and beyond (and a stepdad needs to avoid actively parenting his stepchildren, but more about that in a minute). Once you're the dad, you're always the dad. You can't model Christ's love without getting involved in your children's daily lives. You can't abdicate the raising of your children to your former wife so that you don't have to deal with her, or hand off your parenting responsibility to their stepdad because he lives with them on a daily basis. Nor should you become passive in parenting when you remarry and let your wife do your job. Don't allow yourself to be pushed out of the parenting picture. Kids need their dad. They need you to be an active participant in their lives and walk beside them as much as possible.

Nothing replaces the emotional benefits of a strong relationship with a loving father. When dads are missing from their kids' lives, young children act out more in the classroom, have a harder time focusing and often feel sad. Boys may become aggressive and bully others or they may become clingy and overly dependent on their moms. By the time they reach their teen years, boys without a dad's positive influence and presence are often filled with rage that affects their academics, their friendships and their family. They lack respect for authority and may struggle to find their own identity.

 Have fun with your children. Do more than take them to their activities and stand on the sidelines watching. Play with them. Let them pick the game, sport or activity and throw yourself into the action. Show your children how excited you are to be with them.

Daughters without daddies may fare even worse. Little girls who grow up without a loving father have a void in their heart that they constantly seek to fill. They may try to stuff the hole by overeating, threatening suicide, self-harm (like cutting) or acting out sexually. If a girl never has a dad, she will go looking for love and attention from a male (boy or man) as soon as she is able. She is more likely to become pregnant as a teen and to have a very poor self-image. Ultimately, the kids who have never had a loving relationship with their father become parents who don't know how to have a loving relationship with their kids. The heart of a remarried dad needs to be dedicated to loving his children and being present in their lives so that he leaves a legacy of love for future generations of his family.

Your kids may not live in your home for much of the time, but they still need you to be clued in to what is happening in their daily lives. When their original family ended, they lost enough. Don't let them lose their connection to you. If you don't insist on actively parenting them after divorce, and if you drop into the "visitor" category, by the time they reach adolescence and teen years, your kids will be well aware that you are not part of the parenting plan. They will know that mom has the power and you are not to be taken seriously. Worse, if mom is an ineffective parent too, the kids will quickly realize that they get to call the shots. They will be far better at manipulating and pitting you and your former wife against each other while they slip through the cracks, because the two of you haven't stayed on the same page regarding their friends, grades, activities and issues.

In divorce, the legal system has traditionally limited local dads to only two or three days and nights with their children every two weeks, with some extra weeks during holidays and when they are out of school for the summer. If you live more than 50 miles apart, your time with your children is probably even less. You can't cram effective parenting into these short windows of time. Instead, you've got to think creatively and do the hard work to consistently reach their hearts.

If you have a good relationship with your kids' mom, negotiate for more time. If overnights aren't practical, see if you can pick them up after school or drive them to school. It may not be convenient for you, but drive time can be great conversation time that is worth the extra effort. If your children are very young and you can arrange your job schedule so that it differs from your former wife's, let her know you'd like to keep the children rather than have them put in daycare. It will save money and help you establish your role as their father as they grow. If you cannot negotiate for more time with your children, let your kids' mom know that you want to co-parent peacefully with her and that you aren't going away. You never want to create tense situations for your kids, but you also shouldn't accept getting shoved to the background of their lives. You want to be present at every event that you would have attended before you were divorced. That gives your kids the closest to "normal" parenting they can get post-divorce.

If you need more time with your kids, and the school allows it, go to their preschool or school for lunch at least once a week and be a classroom volunteer and field-trip driver and chaperone. Attend PTA meetings and parent-teacher conferences. Without being pushy, make sure that schools know you are involved. Visit the office yourself and get a school calendar, so that school officials know you. Don't just request a copy of your kids' report cards from your former wife; make sure you're on the school list to receive your own copies, as well as school calendars and events and sports schedules. Attend medical appointments, extracurricular activities and birthday parties. Don't just listen to your children's stories about their friends. Get to know their friends yourself. Even better, make sure you know their friends' families. When you have a relationship with the parents of your kids' friends, you can get in touch with each other directly if you have any concerns.

As the dad and stepdad, you are the spiritual leader in your home. Cover your household in prayer as often as you can. Make sure prayer with your family is not limited to before meals and bedtimes, and teach your kids that prayer is a real conversation, not a litany of rehearsed requests. Pray with your wife and children, pray over your wife and children, and pray for your wife and children. Let your family "catch" you often on your knees in prayer.

As your children grow and want to spend more time with friends, have the friends over to your home. Make your house the fun place to hang out, with movie nights, ice cream sundae bars and game nights. Work together with your wife to make your house feel like home to everyone. Your visiting kids (and stepkids) need their own space, and they need to be able to put their personal touch on that space. Family pictures should include all of the children, and the kitchen should contain some of their favorite foods, even if nobody else eats them.

Remarried dads can keep their children's hearts from clogging by putting encouraging notes on a bed pillow or in a lunchbox, and by giving plenty of hugs and kisses. As your children grow, physical displays of affection might start to feel awkward, but kids of all ages need to be lovingly touched. Adolescents and teens may shrug off your hugs, but keep trying. Pat their arms, clap your son's shoulder or back, or kiss your teen on the forehead. Give a quick shoulder massage or neck rub, "pound it" by hitting knuckles together, or pull them into a sidearm hug if a full-on embrace might be rejected. Every person needs to be touched, and if your teens aren't getting hugs from you, you can bet they're getting them from someone else. Children also need to hear words of love, approval and encouragement from you. Tell them "I love you" every time you see them. Let them know what a valuable member of the family they are and repeat often how no one could replace them in your heart. Praise their hard work and achievements. Be your children's biggest cheerleader. With dad's words inflating their sails, your kids will feel like they can soar.

 Keep yourself in good physical shape. Exercise improves your health, mood and immune system. It also makes you feel good about yourself, and that makes you a better dad or stepdad.

If you absolutely cannot be physically present in your children's lives on a frequent basis, because you live too far away from them, do everything you can to move. No, we're not kidding. You may have moved away from them for a much better job, or because you fell in love, or even to get some distance between you and your ex-wife. Your former spouse may have moved away with your kids for the same reasons, or to return to her hometown to be near her family for support.

It's natural to want a change after divorce. But the heart of a remarried dad has to be out for his kids above himself. He has to be willing to lay down his life for them, and by that, we're not talking about dying; we mean "lay down his life." The heart of a remarried dad needs to be so overflowing with love for his children and filled with the desire to see their hearts become whole, full and healthy that he is willing to give up his daily life to be a presence in theirs. You may have to let go of money, position or comfort in order to be able to parent them. But it's not about you. It's about your kids. If it is at all possible to change locations, do it as soon as you can. Your parenting season is a relatively short one, and then you will have the rest of your life to live where you choose without cheating your kids out of one of the two most important relationships they have in their formative years.

Long-distance dads who can't get geographically closer and local dads who can't see their children regularly because of legal restrictions, job schedules or any other reason will need to get creative to maintain healthy heart connections with their children. What other ways can you stay current with your kids? Today's technology offers a variety of easy ways to stay in touch on a daily basis, even multiple times a day. For very young children, ask your former wife if you can give her a CD with your voice or a DVD of you reading stories, singing silly songs and lullabies and saying bedtime prayers. You might feel ridiculous as you're recording it (to alleviate that, record it when your children are visiting), but your kids will have a part of you when you are not there.

If you know your former wife won't ever play a disc, schedule a daily phone call or see if you can set up a Skype account and get a webcam for her so you can have regular times when she will allow you to connect with your infant, toddler or preschooler. A webcam can also work well with older children. Work out a schedule, preferably nightly, when you and your kids can "visit" via the webcam. You can help them with homework, talk about their day and say bedtime prayers.

Other postmodern options for communicating with your kids include cell phones for phone calls and texting and the Internet for emailing, Facebooking, Tweeting, instant messaging and building a family website. You can also communicate the old-fashioned way by picking up a landline telephone or writing a letter. You can quickly type a note on the computer or pick up a greeting card and pop it in the mail at least once a week. Even better, write letters by hand. Not many people have words of love, encouragement and advice penned by their fathers. Those who do have them cherish them. Letters from Dad mean a lot.

 Set up a Facebook group for yourself and your kids (make sure your wife and ex-wife know about it first, so that no one feels threatened or left out). In that online space, you can post pictures and videos, instant message each other when you're apart, post messages on the "wall" for each other, respond to each others' posts and stay connected and current with each others' lives.

If your children do live with you, you still need to make sure you are actively parenting. Your wife, their stepmom, can't do your job. Even if you have other children with her that she is parenting, she can't parent her stepchildren. That's your job, and you need to work just as hard to make healthy heart connections as you would if you saw them less often. Just because they are under your roof and you pass them in the hallway on the way to the bathroom doesn't mean you are connecting with them. That takes face-time, conversation and a genuine interest in who they know, what they like and how they spend their time.

A remarried dad who wants to reach the hearts of the children in his home shares meals with them, shoots hoops with them or drives them to and from school. He makes it a priority to attend extracurricular activities and birthday parties and to know school officials and teachers. He does all the things that a "visiting" dad would do, but he gets the benefit and blessing of extra time to model what it looks like to be a man of integrity, and what it means to live daily for Christ.

The remarried dad works to keep his heart fully flowing with God's love, and he keeps a close eye out for any clogs that might be forming in the hearts of his children. A loving remarried dad applies emotional Drano at the first sign of any blockages in the hearts of his kids.

If you sense any of your children withdrawing emotionally from you, get to the root of the problem quickly. Make sure your kids know it is safe to share with you how they feel, even if what they are feeling is anger, resentment or hatred toward you, your wife or their other siblings. Try not to react negatively if they unleash on you. Their hurt may be over something real, or it may be that they perceived something wrong. It doesn't matter, because they are still hurt. Don't dismiss their feelings or get irritated by them. Listen closely, repeat back what you believe the problem is and figure out how you can take steps to resolve it.

It's crucial to confront rather than let conflicts simmer, because when kids have two households, it can be easy for them to run and hide. If they only visit you every other weekend, and you avoid the painful work of clearing the clog, your child's heart may harden to the point that he or she goes back to Mom's house one weekend and never comes back. If you have caused a heart blockage in your child, be quick to seek forgiveness and restore the relationship.

Grace: The Greatest Gift from a Stepdad to His Family

The role of stepparent is the toughest one in remarriage, because you can't play the part God meant for you to play in a nuclear family. You are not your stepchildren's dad, and everyone lets you know it. As a man, every step-dad longs for respect. He wants to be heard and obeyed, especially by the children in his home. After all, he is the authority in his household. Right?

Yes and no.

If you are a stepdad, of course you have authority in your home. But how you wield and exert that authority—whether with aggressive force or subtle grace—will determine the level of respect you get.

Stepparents enter a marriage without the benefit of history in their stepchildren's lives. They are not biologically connected or time-connected to the kids under their roof. They often missed the cute baby stage and adorable toddlerhood. They only get the energetic or sullen 'tweens or distant or outright defiant teens. When a stepdad steps in, he often wants to "help" his wife by whipping her kids into shape. After all, they have been single-parented by her for a while and may act more like she is a peer than their mother. The stepdad often sees the kids as lazy, mouthy or just plain rude to him and to his wife, their mother. The perfect recipe for stepfamily conflict is when a stepdad determines that he will get the kids "under control." The moment he lets them know who is boss, every member of his family is likely to turn on him. To his surprise, that usually includes his wife. After all, she is the mama bear, and he is after her cubs. Bitterness quickly builds, and stepfamilies can come tumbling down.

> *The perfect recipe for stepfamily conflict is when a stepdad determines that he will get the kids "under control."*

The wise stepdad steps up by stepping back into a support role. While dads need to step into active parenting, stepdads need to step out of it. That doesn't mean disengaging from your stepfamily, but it does mean that as a stepdad, you need to let your wife do the majority of the parenting and all of the disciplining of her children. Stepchildren will never, ever warm to "Sergeant Stepdad." They are likely to eventually respond warmly, however, to "Sold-out Stepdad," the man who loves Jesus in front of them and models grace and mercy.

The sold-out stepdad doesn't lay down the law. He listens and only offers advice when asked for it. If he disagrees with the way his wife is handling the kids or the way his stepchildren are treating her, he doesn't enter the battle and escalate conflict. Instead, he loves his family enough to wait and talk with his wife privately and work out their joint parenting style behind the scenes. His wife will administer the discipline, and he will stand behind his wife.

It is much easier said than done, because it feels like the balance of power in marriage is out of whack. When the wife is the primary parent in the home, it can feel disrespectful to the stepdad. However, the loving stepdad uses self-control. He doesn't interpret his stepchildren's relationships with their mom as rejection, nor his wife's protectiveness of her children as betrayal. The wise and loving stepdad knows his role is to be confident that he can protect his family the best when he protects them from his own judgment and covers them in heartfelt prayer.

It's a delicate dance when you are both dad and stepdad, especially when you spend lots more time with your stepchildren than with your own children. But you will keep the hearts of your wife and stepchildren open when you and your wife make parenting changes gradually, as a united front, and with these changes presented in family meetings, where kids have input.

The wise stepdad develops his relationship with his stepchildren at their pace. He does not try to force himself into their hearts or keep himself so distant that there is no relationship at all. Instead, he offers wise advice when asked for it and continually tries to befriend his stepchildren. He offers to take them on errands, invites them to breakfast or lunch, or steps up to take them back and forth to school if his work schedule permits. He asks open-ended questions at family dinners and initiates fun activities as a family. His goal is to be mentor and friend, not a second dad or authority figure. When he wins the hearts of his stepchildren and keeps them open, then his authority and advice will carry more weight.

Heavy-handed stepfathers may indeed whip their stepkids into shape—at least on the surface—if they try to take on the traditional role of dad-the-disciplinarian. But they will win only resentment in their stepkids' hearts. A loving stepdad will develop patience and self-control in himself by seeing his stepchildren's misdeeds and rebellion through the lens of grace and mercy and allowing his wife to bring the kids back into line.

Forming a "New Normal"

When you are a remarried dad and stepdad, there are a lot of people who need your time. Your wife needs you, your boss needs you, your kids from your previous marriage need you, your children from your current marriage need you, and your stepchildren need you (although they might not admit it). Your church needs you, your extended family needs you, and your aging parents need you. Even your ex-wife still needs some of your time to talk about the kids' schedules and money. It's a tall order to fit everyone in without somebody feeling cheated.

One of the toughest jobs for the remarried dad and stepdad may be figuring out how to give each individual family member the time and attention needed without dividing your family against itself. It's a balancing act that takes a lot of time and patience to achieve, but the payoff of a stable stepfamily is well worth every sacrifice.

Make it your habit to take one of your kids with you any time you run an errand. Rotate among your children when you need to fill up the car with gas, grab a gallon of milk or hit the home-improvement warehouse. It's an easy way to get a few minutes of alone time regularly with each child.

When you remarry, your wife moves into first position. She is your partner and your best friend, and she needs to be treated that way in your household. She needs your help around the house and with the daily schedules of your kids, her kids and the kids you have together. You, the remarried dad and stepdad, should show all of the children in your home how much you value your wife and her opinions. You need to back her and stand with her in front of your children. You need to make couple time a top priority. Your marriage is the foundation of your family. If the couple relationship falters, the kids get put through the relationship wringer again. So even if your kids are not thrilled with your remarriage, they need to know that you are. They may not think they like the new family setup, but it would be even worse for them if it falls apart.

While the remarried dad and stepdad shows his children and stepchildren how much he loves his wife and how important she is in his life, he also reassures the kids that they have not been displaced by his remarriage. They need to know that your heart expanded with love when you remarried; you didn't take anything away from them to give to anyone else. In order to keep healthy heart connections, work with your wife to carve out time alone with your children and, as they desire it, your stepchildren. The kids know your wife comes first now, and they probably resent it. After all, your biological children were part of your life before she was. Her kids were part of her life before you were. Plus, if you or your wife spent any time as a single parent following your divorce, your kids had you all to themselves for a while. Now they have to share you, and they need to know that they haven't been "replaced."

Whenever you feel exhausted because so many people depend on you and need your time, remember that loneliness and boredom are two obstacles you never face.

The heart of a remarried dad wants to give his children time alone with him so he can show them that the stepsiblings and half-siblings they may have acquired have not taken their place. Your children are likely to feel less resentment toward their stepmother or stepfamily if they don't feel like they've been pushed aside or lost you. So make sure you have regular times when it's just you and your kids. Treat your wife to a spa day or a trip to the mall, and let her know what a valuable gift she is giving you and her stepchildren by sacrificing her family time so you guys can be alone. Let her know how much you appreciate the role she is playing to help your children's hearts heal.

The heart of a remarried stepdad also needs to spend time with his stepchildren in order to grow into relationship, on an age- and gender-appropriate basis. (Stepdads probably should not spend extended periods alone with their teen stepdaughters right off the bat.) Your stepchildren may be the "newcomers" to your family, but that doesn't mean they get the short end of the relationship stick. Stepdads should take it slowly but should let each child know you want to get to know them and that you care about what they care about. Ask them what they would like to do and see if you can find an activity you can do together. Stepfathers can open the hearts of their stepsons by showing them their work, teaching them to fish, hunt or do woodworking or some other activity. If you are passionate about a hobby or activity, share your enthusiasm with your stepchildren. (Just don't get your feelings hurt if they don't get excited about your offers at first.) The slow and steady stepparent wins the race—and the hearts of his stepchildren.

Each of the children in your life needs individual time alone with dad and stepdad. A son and stepson needs to wrestle and play ball. He needs to be taught to work and shown how to be a gentleman. Sons need to learn how to discipline themselves to wait for what they want and work hard for it. They need to see from the time spent with their dad and stepdad what it looks like to be a man who loves Christ and serves his family. They need to be taught to protect the ones they love, even from themselves. As they grow, they need instruction in managing their tempers and reining in their sexual desires.

When a remarried dad and stepdad who loves Christ invests his time regularly demonstrating to his sons and stepsons how he lives a life of integrity, he can raise the next generation of men of integrity who serve Christ. While dads can speak directly into their sons' lives and shape them overtly, stepdads need to demonstrate by their own actions more than talking to their stepsons about the ways they need to improve. Live a life of integrity and great character so that your stepsons can "catch it" from you.

Daughters need to be daddy's little girls until they are grown. They need to have tea parties with him and learn how a lady should be treated by a gentleman. On daddy-daughter "dates," dads can hold doors open, pull out chairs and present her—his little princess—with flowers. Dads need to woo the hearts of their daughters so they can show their little girls how they deserve to be loved.

If you are not experienced in teaching the Bible, get a prepackaged curriculum or devotional book to help you be confident in studying the Word of God with your family. Lead devotions each day. Ask for prayer requests and keep a record of the answers so your family can look back and see God in action.

Daughters revel in time and attention from their dads, and they long for it when it is absent for a while. A daughter derives a lot of her self-esteem from the way her dad sees her and relates to her. If he holds her in high esteem and praises her often, she'll think better of herself. Girls need to talk, and they need dad to listen to their hopes and dreams. Daughters need to snuggle and cuddle with their dads, and he can throw an arm around his teen daughter's shoulder or hold her hand when they walk through the mall. Movies also provide a great opportunity for a daughter to rest her head on dad's strong shoulder. When a daughter has a healthy amount of love from her dad, she is less likely to go looking for it from another man too soon. When daughters are loved well by their dads and feel how Christ makes a real difference in his life, they learn how to love their own children well and are likely to want their own relationship with Christ.

Stepfathers can play an important role in their stepdaughters' lives, as well, especially if a stepdaughter's father is largely absent or if she lives in the home with you and her mother most of the time. Stepdads win the hearts of stepdaughters when girls see that their mothers are being loved well. Yes, they may feel some jealousy, but over time they will respect the man who takes good care of their mother. You keep the heart of your stepdaughter open when you act with integrity, and when you refrain from being overly authoritative and harsh. You can woo the heart of a young stepdaughter by finding activities that she likes, such as shopping and reading stories together. Adolescent and teen stepdaughters and stepfathers may have a more awkward time, but that's normal and okay. Take it slowly, and aim for courtesy and a mentor/friend relationship, not deep love. Over time (sometimes years), love can grow if the relationship is coaxed along, not forced.

> **Note:** It is advisable for a new stepfather not to spend too much time alone with teen stepdaughters. One way the enemy has destroyed many stepfamilies is to use a stepdaughter's anger to level false accusations of inappropriate behavior against her stepfather. Stepdads do not want to put themselves in a vulnerable position where bitterness can destroy their stepfamily in one allegation. In other instances, an inappropriate romantic or sexual relationship has developed between a stepdad and stepdaughter. Remember, this young woman has not been raised by you and may not feel like your child at all. She may just seem to be a young woman with many of the same qualities that caused you to fall in love with her mother. Your stepdaughter is impressionable and may idolize you. That can put the two of you in a vulnerable position when you begin having the inevitable stepfamily friction with your wife and your stepdaughter becomes an empathetic listener. Do not allow your stepdaughter to become your confidante. Remember that she is a child in your home, no matter how grown-up she looks or acts. While you do not want to remain standoffish, take your new relationship with a teen stepdaughter slowly, and build in safeguards to make sure everyone acts with integrity.

Think Big Picture and Leave a Legacy

Your sons and stepsons will be dads like you, so be the kind of man you want them to be. Your daughters and stepdaughters will choose a man like you, so be the kind of man you want them to find. Your choice of either making sacrifices in order to parent well or abdicating your job of being a loving, connected dad or stepdad will have a ripple effect on your family for generations to come. If you neglect, abuse or abandon the children in your life, you are very likely "paying it forward" to your grandchildren and great-grandchildren, who will suffer because of the damage their parents received at your hands and by your actions (or neglect). If you love Jesus wholeheartedly and ask Him every day to put a hedge of protection around your remarriage and help you be the best daddy and stepdaddy you can be, your grandchildren and great-grandchildren will carry on your tradition.

Parent each one of your children and stepchildren with your whole heart and your best efforts. Being a dad and stepdad is a huge responsibility and a precious privilege guaranteed to bring you some of your deepest heartaches, but also your greatest joys. If the hearts of your children and stepchildren remain open to you and you maintain a healthy outflow of God's love, they have the best chance of becoming healthy adults who can give love back to you and overflow God's love to their own families. Your big investment now will pay off big-time in a few short years when your children and stepchildren become not only your biggest achievement, but also some of your best friends.

HEART MONITORS

1. What will you do in the heat of the moment to remember that your enemy is Satan, not the family member you are fighting with?

2. What does your family's current financial situation look like? What can you do to improve it? How will you be a prudent steward?

3. In what ways are you maintaining healthy heart connections with your children and stepchildren? What can you do better to be an active parent and stepparent?

4. What time wasters can you eliminate from your day so you can spend more time connecting with your wife, kids and stepkids?

5. What is your big-picture vision for each member of your family? How are you coaching them toward their passions and purpose? What legacy do you want to leave?

6. As a stepdad, how can you win the hearts of your stepchildren without stepping on them? Does it feel unnatural to step back and not exert your authority? How can you get on the same parenting page with your wife that allows her to administer discipline, but you to feel good about her actions?

HEART PROTECTORS

Form new traditions. Take up a hobby as a family or build a collection. Each time you participate in something together that is non-threatening and fun, you strengthen stepfamily ties. When you start a collection, each member invests something in the hunt for new items, thinks about their family when they discover a new addition and enjoys joint ownership in something that belongs to all of you.

Create a family entertainment and dining-out envelope budgeting system. Hold a family meeting and show two envelopes to your children and stepchildren labeled "Family Fun" and "Dining Out." Explain that any money you put in the envelopes each month will be used for family fun and eating out. Make a list of their ideas on how to spend it. Teach your kids about opportunity costs—that every time they choose one thing they are giving up all the other possibilities those dollars could purchase. Some months, encourage them to delay gratification so they can save for something big, like a new video game system or mini-vacation. Show them how you can eat out a couple of times a month at fast-food restaurants or go out once to a nicer establishment. Invite your kids to contribute to the envelope, and give them the option each month of giving the money to someone in need.

10

The Heart of a Remarried Mom and Stepmom

For He Himself is our peace, who made both groups into
one and broke down the barrier.
EPHESIANS 2:14, *NASB*

If the heart of a remarried dad and stepdad wants to provide for and protect his family, the heart of a remarried mom and stepmom seeks to forge family peace and love. The verse above is every remarried mom and stepmom's dream, that barriers between both "sides" of her family will be broken down and they can all be united in peace. In the game "Monkey in the Middle," someone stands in the middle of two other people while the two on the ends throw a ball back and forth to each other, just out of reach of the "monkey." Life for remarried moms and stepmoms, at first, and often for a long time, feels like "Mommy in the Middle." Her dream of a peaceful, united home is always flying by right over her head. That's because remarried moms and stepmoms are women created by God to love. They do it well, and they don't see why everyone else can't just try a little harder. Remarried mommies and stepmommies love their children and are trying hard to love their stepchildren. They also love their husbands. Consequently, they hate it when all the people they love don't love each other.

Remarried moms and stepmoms want everyone to get along and act like a family, and they want it *now*. In fact, many attempt to make the ones they love look like a nuclear family from the moment the wedding ceremony is finished. The newly married wife, mom and stepmom eagerly lines up all her "ducklings" in front of their new "dad" for the first "family" photo. If you did this, we're not blaming you for wanting what you know is ultimately best for your family. But we challenge you to pull out your

wedding photo album now and look very closely at the expressions cap-
tured on each face that day. You know your husband and each of your children and stepchildren well. In fact, you probably can read them better than
anyone. As you look back now, what do you see?

If your kids and stepkids were older than 5 or 6, but under the age of
12, they probably pasted on slightly fake smiles that didn't quite reach
their eyes. If the children were 12 or older, they might not have done that
much. You may see blank expressions or slightly hostile glares. Come on,
look closely at your adolescents and teens. Are they frowning? Do their
eyes look vacant, worried, sad? What about your new husband? What is his
body language? Is he standing awkwardly? Does he look uncomfortable?
What are his eyes and smile really communicating? Now look at yourself,
the beautiful bride. Is it possible that you were gritting your teeth with the
effort to get this right?

First stepfamily photos, whether they are taken at the wedding or some
later date, often capture a couple who looks like they are going to throttle
somebody as soon as the picture is snapped. They are posed in awkward
positions close to a conglomeration of kids whose eyes bear witness to
their anger or deep sadness even as they force their lips upward in a smile
that, looking at now, you can see looks more like a grimace.

---

 *If you have recently remarried, forget your dream of the perfect family
Christmas picture. Let everyone off the hook this year. If you really want
one, give each child and stepchild (unless the kids are too young to care) the
choice of whether or not to be in the photograph. Make sure you give "visiting" kids the option too. If they want to be included, make sure you schedule the photo shoot during a time when they will be with you.*

The heart of a remarried mom and stepmom seeks to overflow so
much love to every family member that each one won't be able to help but
overflow love to each other. On the surface, that's a perfectly sensible strategy. The only trouble is, it doesn't usually work. The harder and faster a
mom or stepmom with an open, loving heart tries to push her husband,
children and stepchildren into warm relationship with each other and with
her, the more likely it is that her husband and all the kids will resist her efforts and refuse to forge a bond.

It's not a bad thing for remarried moms and stepmoms to have high hopes and expectations that their family members will come together as one, but it backfires on everyone when they expect it to happen overnight. Forging family bonds takes time, lots of it. Experts say that it can take as long as seven years for a stepfamily to feel bonded like a traditional family. Seven years! That can be supremely discouraging for a peace-loving mom and stepmom who takes that to mean that conflict will reign in her home for what seems like an endless amount of time. Her dreams dashed, the remarried mom or stepmom's heart may plunge into despair soon after remarrying.

Don't let your heart take a dive. Bring your expectations down to a realistic range. Give stepfamily members the freedom *not* to feel love for each other. Set your standard at the level of common courtesy, good manners and putting others ahead of yourself, as Christ-followers are called to do. Explain to your family that you would like to live in peace and expect each member to do the same. When you don't try to force feelings to grow, they will often begin to blossom on their own.

Tending Your Own Tender Heart

As a remarried mom and stepmom, you already know that your heart has to remain open and fully flowing before you can love your family well. Damaged hearts snap shut or "bleed out" all their love supply, and a remarried woman's heart can get depleted quickly. When children's hearts hurt, your heart gets hurt. When your husband is angry and tense, your heart gets injured. Your heart as a remarried mom and stepmom is going to get bumped, battered and bruised a lot, especially during the first two years of stepfamily life. If you are prepared for the pain, you will be able to heal much faster.

Some of the most common emotions that remarried moms and stepmoms experience on a regular basis are anger, rejection, jealousy, guilt, fear, sadness, loneliness and frustration. None of these is healthy, and each must be carefully weeded out of your heart. Your husband, children and stepchildren will make you mad. You may feel guilty that your children are undergoing so much change, that their new stepsiblings are unkind to them or that you are not spending enough time with your husband or each of your kids. You may feel guilty or afraid because you don't like your stepkids. You may feel jealous of the time your stepchildren take with your husband, and rejected because they don't want to include you or your children. Sometimes stepchildren make a stepmom feel like she is once again an eighth-grade misfit crying because the mean girls keep picking on her. You may feel overwhelming sadness because your family members hurt each other. You may even feel very lonely in the midst of the stepfamily crowd. All of these emotions are natural, but we'll let you in on the secret to being a mom and stepmom with a healthy, open heart: *Don't take parenting and stepparenting personally.*

Scripture says that "foolishness" is in the heart of a child, and kids and stepkids can say and do some pretty foolish things. Don't let their verbal arrows pierce your heart. Take your sorrows and worries to the Lord. Think of all the challenges that come with remarriage parenting and stepparenting as a stone that is sharpening you into someone with unshakable faith. If you keep your heart open, you will be blessed by learning to forgive easily, to love the unlovable and to achieve a sense of peace and joy that is not based on your circumstances. But how do you keep your heart open when stepfamily members are constantly wounding it? You need to handle your heart with tender, loving care.

Pick out a couple of praise and worship songs or Bible verses that comfort and encourage you and make them personal. Rewrite them as if they were addressed specifically to you. For example, the first part of John 3:16 would look like this: "For God so loved Mary that he gave Mary His only son . . ." Tuck these verses in your prayer journal or post them on your vanity mirror as personal reminders of God's love for you.

Your best preventive medicine is to keep your heart full through a personal relationship with Jesus that is vibrant and up-to-date. If you have never given your heart fully to Christ or asked Him to forgive your sins and take control of your life and your stepfamily, there is no better time than now. And there is no better gift that you can give yourself and each member of your family. Without Christ, there is no reason for family members to put each other first instead of themselves. There is no hope for eternal life, and there is little hope for a peaceful stepfamily life while you're still here on earth. If you have received salvation but you've never felt like God was real or very close to you, it's your job to get closer. As a believer, the Holy Spirit lives in you and is your power, your comforter and your teacher. When your faith is strong and real, your joy can return, even if your circumstances or stepfamily situation hasn't changed.

Fan the flames of your faith life daily. Keep up or begin a daily devotion and prayer time, and memorize Bible verses with your children (and stepchildren, if they are receptive). Connect with other Christians to go deeper into Bible study. Become an active part of the women's ministry in a local church, and if you aren't currently attending, ask your husband if you can all go to church on Sundays. Join a small group of women who will pray for you, encourage you, keep you accountable and hold you up when it's hard. Connections with Christ and with other believers play a big role in the care and keeping of the hearts of remarried moms and stepmoms.

Your woman's heart also needs lots of rich emotional connections, so you should build a circle of women friends to spend time with. A weekly lunch date or monthly mom's night out can quickly refresh your sagging spirits and shore up your heart when it hurts. With other women, you get to fulfill your need to talk, and you'll usually get an empathetic response. One warning about friendships: Be careful about over-sharing. Don't give out intimate or private marital or stepfamily details that would embarrass or shut down the heart of anyone you love. When you share your frustrations, make sure you keep the focus on *your* feelings and behaviors. Don't focus on your husband or kids and what they are doing or not doing. Choose your friends wisely by choosing wise friends. Make sure you don't spend too much time with any friend who tries to turn you against your husband, children or stepchildren. Friends help preserve families, not push them apart. Make sure some of your friends are older in the faith and more experienced than you so they can mentor you. And look for other remarried moms and stepmoms with whom you can swap stories and seek solutions. With the right support network of female friends, a remarried mom and stepmom will find her strength renewed and her heart prepared to withstand the pressures of her stepfamily life.

A remarried mom and stepmom also nurtures her heart when she spends time with her husband. You need romance, and you need to make it a priority to spend time together as husband and wife. If a weekly date night isn't in the budget, put kids to bed early once a week and cuddle on the couch. Try to schedule a weekend away at least every three months, and keep your communication current. If you talked to each other on the phone multiple times a day when you were dating but rarely touch base now, go back to your old ways. Remember what used to make your relationship fun and exciting, and make sure those elements remain in your marriage mix. Pray, worship and study God's Word together. Finally, don't forget to dream and plan together for the future.

For remarried couples, the honeymoon period comes after the years of parenting are done. Think of all the time you'll have for each other and all the fun you can have then, but only if you still like and love each other when you get there! A remarried mom and stepmom's heart overflows love when her relationship with her husband is in good shape.

 If you are a stepmom, especially if you did not have kids before, seek out at least one other stepmom to share with and learn from on a regular basis, preferably once a week. You can also join a stepfamily support group. Look for others who can share and encourage you with their experiences and wisdom from further down the stepfamily journey.

Finally, a remarried mom and stepmom tends her heart well if she makes sure she gets some time for herself. You need to think, reflect, sing, worship, take a walk, enjoy a hot bath, watch a sunset or go shopping without kids. Schedule times when you can be alone, and don't waste them cleaning the bathroom or putting away the dishes. Household chores will never be finished, and your heart health is far more important than a neatly made bed. If you can't afford a baby-sitter, and your kids are too young to be in school, trade childcare duties one day a week with another mom. Or find out if your church has a weekly Mom's Day Out.

You are more than a wife and more than a mom and stepmom. You are a unique woman with gifts, skills, talents and a calling. Take the time to keep growing and learning who you are in Christ and the ministry you were created to do. When you know, understand and embrace the woman God created you to be, you'll have a lot to share with your family. Don't feel guilty when you do healthy things to nourish your heart. Maintaining a healthy, loving heart is the best thing you can do for your family.

The Ideal Stepfamily

Hand in hand with keeping your heart healthy, as a remarried mom and stepmom, you also have to seek God's help in adjusting your unrealistic stepfamily expectations. Unless you are extremely blessed and your family is a major exception to the stepfamily rule, the people you love most aren't going to line up around the dinner table soon after the wedding is over and look like a Norman Rockwell painting. The more a remarried mom and stepmom cajoles her husband and kids into faking it, the more frustration every family member feels.

Moms, your husband and children love you. That means they want to please you and make you happy. Hold on to the hope that they will eventually work out their relationship with each other, because they don't like hurting you.

When members of two former families come together in marriage, a new normal has to be established for everyone. The remarried mom and stepmom's biggest challenge may be to adjust her expectations. She must accept that "new normal" is not the same as normal, and it never, ever will be. But that's okay.

A traditional, nuclear family (sometimes called a "primary" family) is formed when couples spend time together, fall in love and get married. They are usually young (in their mid-twenties), and they feel like they are "playing house" as they begin to build a life together. They experience sex for the first time and have plenty of romantic interludes. In fights, it's a battle of "I" versus the new "we." They build their careers, buy their first home, spend time with friends and often have significant time establishing their identity as a couple before they get pregnant. Pregnancy is a whole new, exciting adventure; and the couple eagerly dives into their roles as first-time parents. They learn together how to love, care for and discipline their son or daughter. In their first family photos, their eyes sparkle and their smiles are so big and genuine they look downright goofy.

Compare that chain of events to the formation of a stepfamily. A man and woman meet and spend time together, kids often in tow. Dates involve baby-sitters or movies on the couch after kids are in bed (with at least one kid interruption for a glass of water or due to a nightmare). The couple is usually in their thirties, and at least one of them has experienced a significant amount of betrayal, tragedy or loss when the first marriage ended in death or divorce.

Over the protests and warnings of some of their extended family members, friends, former spouses or children, the man and woman fall in love and get married. They have to figure out whether they'll live with the ghost of a former spouse in her house or his, or get a new place altogether. If they get a new house, they uproot their wounded kids again. There is no novelty this time in "playing house." Now it's just plain old chores. Sex isn't new for at least one spouse, and the new mates are likely to bring old baggage to bed. Oh well, between the kids and the jobs, there's not much time for romance anyway. Finding time for friends is nearly impossible, but they may not have many friends left after the divorce or remarriage.

Spouses with children come into the remarriage with parenting habits, family traditions and discipline styles already firmly established. They missed sharing the pregnancies and births of the other's children, and usually the cute baby stages as well. If both spouses are parents, they quickly discover that it's hard to get their parenting techniques and traditions in sync. The couple has little time to forge their own identity, because working, parenting and trying to adjust takes so much of their time and energy. Fights are battles of "I" versus "we," plus "my family" and "your family" versus "our family."

It's no wonder that eyes are dull or angry and smiles are pasted on in the first stepfamily photos! There has been such a huge amount of change for each person in a stepfamily that everyone is experiencing a kind of post-traumatic stress disorder. The husband, wife, children and stepchildren naturally need time to adjust. It's normal and perfectly okay to let them just be for a while, rather than trying to slot them into a role they're not ready for.

We didn't paint that stepfamily scenario to discourage you in your role as a mom or stepmom. In fact, we commend you for being willing to tackle the enormous task of being the loving woman in a stepfamily. We just want your eyes to be open to how different the two types of families are. You can't make a stepfamily into a nuclear family. Those days are already gone. In time, however, you can form what we think you really want: a stepfamily that loves each other and protects each others' hearts. You can have a stepfamily where children are friends and stepparents and stepchildren have a loving attachment. Your stepfamily can learn not to play "Mommy in the Middle" anymore. It isn't easy, and it takes lots and lots of time, but it can happen. You just need a different way of nurturing hearts to get there.

As a mom and stepmom, how do you nurture all the hearts in your home? In a word, individually. Each child and stepchild has a different personality, learning style, rebellion style and opinion about the new stepfamily. It takes a loving heart, listening ears and lots of patience and time to capture each heart in your stepfamily. The remarried mom and stepmom uses her emotional insight to evaluate the heart needs of each person in the family. She talks with her husband about where each child stands intellectually, academically, spiritually, physically and emotionally. She looks for problem areas that need to be addressed, progress that needs to be celebrated and milestones that have yet to be achieved. As she daily prays over each family member and evaluates and reevaluates their needs, she asks God to help her be His hands and feet to minister to her family members' hearts and point them toward a personal relationship with Him every day.

Moms: Learn to Let Go

As a remarried mom, the best way to gently nudge the hearts of your children toward opening to your husband, and the heart of your husband toward your kids, is to quit nudging. Give your children and your husband back to God, the one who gave them to you in the first place. Take your overwhelming desire to forge your family together straight to the Lord. Drop to your knees and drop your family at His feet. Tell Him they are His problem now. You can plead with Him to change hearts, but quit begging your family to do it on their own. If a remarried mom isn't purposeful in surrendering her husband's heart and her children's hearts to the Lord, her love can actually become the blockage that keeps them from loving each other. If they're getting plenty of love from her, they don't have to need or desire love from each other. To be perfectly blunt, remarried moms often need to be quiet and get out of the way.

Begin a prayer journal and start every morning with a specific prayer for each person in your family. Pray for the state of their hearts, and ask God to show you clearly how to guard and care for them without overstepping your bounds and taking over His job. He has given you the privilege of co-parenting these wonderful children with Him. Don't be so overzealous in your mothering that you push the Lord into the "visiting" parent role. As the Creator of everyone, He is the primary parent; you get to participate in loving and nurturing them under His guidance.

In your time with the Lord each morning, write down any thoughts you have, issues you are facing and requests for each family member. Be still and listen for God's still, small voice. While you are petitioning for the hearts of your husband, children and stepchildren, the Lord will minister to your mother's heart. He will be your strength and your shield, so your heart can withstand the enemy's attacks and keep you from running onto the battlefield to interfere. When you see a prayer answered or achieve a family victory, no matter how small or seemingly insignificant, go back to your prayer journal and write it down. Put the date on it, so you can chart your family's journey toward healthy, loving hearts.

If your budget allows, pick up a pretty new notebook or journal and some pens to begin your prayer journaling. Tuck them beside or under your bed.

For a remarried mom, surrendering her children is a super-huge task. We know you carried these little people literally under your heart and then watched them come into the world and take their first breath. You have been beside them every step of the way as they have grown into the unique creatures you are absolutely crazy about. Surrendering them to anybody—to God, to their school, to your husband's scrutiny and especially to the ex-husband you no longer trust—is hard and scary. Even the thought of letting them go makes your heart feel weak, because you know it makes your children's hearts vulnerable. You may even try to fool yourself into believing that if you can just keep up the illusion that your children are under your control, you can stop them from getting hurt. But you can't.

You don't have control of your children's hearts, and many times you can't stop the emotional curveballs life throws at them. Some "heart darts" are going to pierce them. If you are divorced, you have learned that lesson by now. In fact, after divorce, very little is in your control. When it's not your "watch," you can't control your children's schedules, the company they keep, the television shows they watch or the friends they visit. When your kids spend time at their dad's, he decides what happens on his time. And it's none of your business unless he wants to fill you in. Likewise, when they spend each day in a classroom, you don't know what conversations your children are having or what choices they are watching their friends and peers make.

If you don't hand your kids over to the Lord for safekeeping and keep handing them back to Him on a continual basis, you could go crazy with fear wondering what their hearts will experience. But fear is the opposite of faith. God commands us not to have fear but to trust Him wholeheartedly, even when we don't understand what's going on. Proverbs 3:5-6 reminds us to trust in the Lord with all our hearts, even when we don't understand. We are to acknowledge God's authority over every situation, and He will keep us on a straight path. When you surrender the ones you love the most, you release God to pour His love through you until you experience the peace you long for—the peace that "transcends all understanding" (Phil. 4:7). God is in control, no matter what the circumstances look like from your limited point of view.

Stepmoms: Marriage with His Children

If you were never married before or if you did not previously have children, and your remarriage package comes complete with first-time motherhood (stepmotherhood), congratulations! We really mean it. You have one of the toughest roles in a stepfamily, but you can do it. Stepkids don't come with instructions (and you can tell them that when you make a mistake), but there are lots of ways to learn how to be a great stepmom for the kids God has now placed in your life.

If you have never had children before, get as educated as you can. Read good parenting books, take a parenting class and get to know veteran moms and stepmoms. Your biggest challenges in being a stepmom will be to find the right balance of authority in your home and to manage your own emotions. Your stepchildren may push you away again and again. They may try to interfere with your relationship with your husband, disrespect or defy you, hurt your feelings repeatedly, and reject your best efforts at every turn. Still, as the woman in the home, you may end up cooking, cleaning and chauffeuring for them. Stepmoms have to guard their hearts carefully so that they do not take their stepchildren's ungratefulness personally.

Authority in a stepfamily is a toughie. If you have older stepchildren, you can't square off against them if they don't like you, yet you should not be bullied either. Kids are excellent manipulators, and if they don't like your relationship with their dad, they will try their best to pit you against each other. You and your husband will need to create a parenting plan together so that you can decide how conflict will be handled and discipline administered before the need arises.

When conflict occurs between you and your stepchildren, try to defuse it with grace. Walk away, go outside or let your stepkids know you will get back to them to resolve the issue later. Try very hard not to get lumped into the role of "tattletale" to your husband about their bad behavior. Your stepchildren will probably challenge you and act out against you, but never in front of their father. So when you point out the faults he does not see in his "angels," cracks start to appear in your couple relationship.

This is especially true with stepmoms and stepdaughters. You both love the same man, and like any love triangle, that spells trouble. Let your stepkids know that you want a good working relationship with them. If they are little, you can lavish love on them without consequences. The older they are when you come into the picture, the more distance there may be to overcome.

Stepmoms, make this your daily mantra: I will pray for my stepchildren today. I will show my family Christ's love today. I am making a positive difference in my stepchildren's lives today, even if they won't see it for a long time.

If you have never been a parent, you and your husband need to make sure that you don't jump in too fast. It is very common for a newly wed, first-time wife who marries a dad to try to instantly run the home front and take care of the kids the way a mom in a traditional family would. She wants to please, and it's comfortable for her husband if his former wife did a lot of the housework and childrearing. She may have been the one to make the haircut and doctor's appointments and bake the cookies for the class party. Because the first-time wife wants to be a helpmate to her husband and show his children that she cares about them, she may dive in too quickly to her maternal duties.

While taking care of the ones entrusted to you is not wrong in a stepfamily, it can make waves. If a stepmom does too much, her stepchildren will feel disloyal to their mom. Their mother may get upset, too, if you walk into your stepson's classroom with cookies at the same time she walks in with her cupcakes. You and your husband will find the stepfamily journey easier if your husband remains the one to primarily parent his children. He needs to administer the discipline and do most of the parenting duties. Ease into your new role by doing some parenting duties with him, like running the kids to school. When everyone is used to this, then you can see if it works well for you to take them on your own.

Being a stepmom is also a delicate dance, and you can expect many missteps and crushed toes in the first years. In the beginning of your stepfamily, try to assess what your stepchildren would like from you. Stepfamily meetings can be very helpful in establishing ground rules for relationship, alleviating overly high expectations and reassuring everyone that your job is just to do the best you can to get along as you get to know each other. Let your stepchildren have a voice in chores, discipline, rules and even fun planned activities. When kids can take ownership in the process, they are much more likely to go along with the plans and uphold the family standards. Again, aim for common courtesy and respect at first, and maybe for a long time. Let love come later, at its own pace. You will never be their mother, but you can become someone they love deeply. And you will learn and grow in ways you never imagined.

Stand By Your Man

Women with children who remarry used to be single moms, and it can be a tough transition in remarriage for a mom to move her husband into his proper place in her heart and her home. Once a mom remarries, her relationship with her husband should become the primary relationship in her heart. The remarried mom needs to stand by her man, but that can feel like crowding out the kids. Let us reassure you that you are not throwing your kids or stepkids over when you honor and show respect to your husband. When you and your husband love each other fully, you are demonstrating for the children in your home what a healthy couple relationship looks like, so that one day they can replicate it in their own marriages. Still, even when a remarried mom knows that putting her husband first is the right thing to do for all, it can be difficult.

 Do something for your husband today that you know will make him feel loved, whether it's straightening the house before he comes home, telling him how proud you are of him, watching a sporting event sitting next to him or preparing his favorite dessert. Let your family see you honoring your husband.

That's understandable. It was just you and your children for however long you were a single parent. You formed a tightly knit unit in order to heal after death or divorce. Your hearts were hurting, and you probably clung to each other just to make it through. If divorce devastated you emotionally, your kids may have been your lifeline, the only thing that spurred you to get out of bed each morning.

As a single-parent household, you called all the shots in your home. You may have enjoyed slumber parties in mom's bedroom and spontaneous trips to the convenience store or video store at odd hours of the night. Routines, structure and discipline didn't seem all that important to enforce when it was just you and the kids. After remarriage, everything's different, and it takes some getting used to. Picture yourself pre-remarriage, standing in a circle with your children, clasping each other's hands tightly. You held each other together. Now picture your husband trying to take his place in the family formation. In order to welcome your husband in, either he has to pull your hand from the hand of your child, or you have to make the choice to drop your son's or daughter's hand. Either way, you may feel an unexpected flash of resentment. Your child undoubtedly will. If your child highly resents the intrusion, you may have to pry the fingers off or somehow fold your hand over both of theirs. It's awkward and a bit uncomfortable, even though you want your husband to be part of your circle.

The remarried mom needs to stand by her man,
but that can feel like crowding out the kids.

The family circle reforms itself with your husband in it, but now there is at least one of your children holding the hand of a man who may still feel like a stranger, not a dad. Everyone is aware of the difference. We like the way that Association of Marriage and Family Ministries (AMFM) stepfamily experts Don and Kathy Coryell put it in their *Basic Training for Marriage and Stepfamilies* manual:

> New stepfamily members are each like dots in a connect-the-dot picture. After the remarriage occurs, the adults and the children must begin to connect the dots, in order to complete their unique stepfamily picture. They must work backward from instant family to growing the connections. . . . If the couple connection is not solidly outlined, the rest of the drawing won't be inside the lines of stepfamily connection.[1]

To have a successful remarriage, your marriage must come first, and your kids need to know it. You have to treat your relationship as a couple tenderly. In a primary family, the couple relationship came first and it is the strongest bond in the family. In remarriage, the couple relationship was inserted into an already-existing family, and it is the weakest link.

A remarried mom needs to be vigilant about guarding her family members' hearts from her tendency to overprotect. As the mama bear, you have early detection sensors that instinctively pick up the first faint whiff of anyone's frustration, resentment, irritation or disapproval of your children. Instinctively, your claws come out to protect your cubs. Anyone who even looks at your children funny may hear your roar of displeasure. Too often, when a husband comes too "close" to his wife's cubs, trying to discipline them or give them a command, mama bear steps in between them to shield her babies. Many a remarried mom steps in to "protect" her children from her husband when they don't need to be protected.

As soon as the children pick up on what mom is doing (and it only takes once or twice—kids are savvy little manipulators if it gets them what they want), they become experts at continuing the conflict, playing up the complaints their stepfather has made about them or telling their mom how "mean" he is to them. Once again, when a husband and wife disagree about the children and stepchildren, the stepfamily triangulates. Picture a triangle with the kids standing on one point, mom on another point and her husband on the third point. Instead of functioning like a "team," they're all fighting to maintain their position with each other, not realizing that there

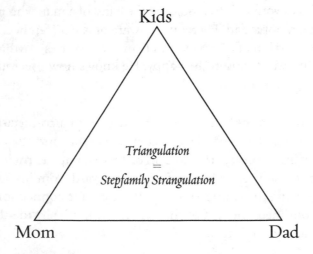

is plenty of love, respect and room for all in the hearts of family members. Once triangulation begins to occur, it can become a vicious cycle that the stepfamily finds very hard to stop. Triangulation quickly leads to strangulation of the stepfamily. It's a dangerous place for a remarriage to be.

Dan and Marci experienced a lot of triangulation within their remarriage and stepfamily that almost tore them all apart.

"When Dan and I were first married, Dan missed his 11-year-old son, Sam, and invited him to stay with us for three weeks. My 20-year-old son, Michael, was also staying with us," Marci says. "Sam had heard nothing but terrible things about me and was very angry over his parents' divorce. Sam believed that his father hated him. He didn't understand why Dan had left him. He was hurt, confused and jealous of Michael. Sam made faces at me when Dan wasn't looking and was very disrespectful. He played us against each other. Michael noticed it too, but Dan didn't believe us.

"One day it got to me, and I lost my temper and started yelling at Sam. Dan yelled at me for yelling at Sam. Then my son Michael yelled at Dan for yelling at me. Before you could blink, Dan and Michael were on the verge of a fight. Michael marched right to his room, packed his bags and was gone the next morning. I was upset that my son left. Sam felt he had won. And my relationship with Dan was damaged. This was a whole new scenario for all of us, and our emotions were fueled by deep-seated resentment. None of us was prepared enough or wise enough or mature enough to know how to handle it."

Remarried moms must avoid triangulation, practice the fine art of surrender and put their trust in the Lord first, but also trust their husbands. You need to remember that you married a good-hearted man who loves you. Even if he doesn't yet feel love for your children or see that you love his, he will try hard to do what he thinks is best for all of you because he loves you and wants you to be happy. He knows how precious your children are to you, and although he may seem to be too heavy-handed, you need to let your husband and your children spar a little as they settle in to stepfamily life. Remember that your husband is hardwired to need respect, and you disrespect him when you strip him of control by shielding your children—that's triangulation. You also send a clear signal to the kids that their stepdad's words are of little importance, because mom will quickly countermand them. If you want your children to respect your husband (and you should—he has been chosen by God as your mate to provide for them and protect them), then you have to stand united with him.

You can't come behind him to "clean up his mess" or make excuses for him to your children either—that's triangulation. The moment your children pick up on the fact that you also thought he was being "mean," they will feel justified in their disrespect or disdain.

Even if your husband does come down on your kids too hard, in your opinion, keep your lips buttoned until a time of non-conflict when you can approach him behind closed doors. We can't stress enough how important it is for remarried couples to stand together and back each other in front of the kids. If you strongly feel a decision needs to be changed or punishment softened, you need to discuss that with your husband outside of the kids' listening ears. Ask yourself if the punishment is really going to hurt your child, even if it was a little harsh or unfair. Will 25 sit-ups permanently injure your admittedly mouthy adolescent son? Will unloading the dishwasher every night for a week truly overtax your eight-year-old daughter? Probably not. Will causing your husband to feel disrespected in front of your children permanently damage the tentative bonds in your stepfamily? There's a good chance it will.

Keep your heart physically fit, as well as tending it spiritually and emotionally. The daily tasks of mothering or stepmothering a stepfamily are exhausting, but you still need a regular exercise routine. It will greatly improve your outlook and give you extra strength for stepfamily struggles.

If you share your thoughts with your husband in a time of non-conflict, and in a tone that communicates respect for his role in your family, he may realize that he was a little rough. If the punishment is to be lifted or lightened, the adult who laid down the law has to be the one to lift it. When your husband faces your children and lets them know he jumped to the wrong conclusion or got on their case too hard, then lifts the punishment, your stepfamily takes a great step forward toward forging bonds of love and respect. You're probably not there yet, but you're in a lot better place than you would have been if you had stepped in and short-circuited the process. A remarried mom needs to remember that her husband's and children's hearts are ultimately damaged, not protected, when she triangulates the family.

Remarried moms and stepmoms who adjust their expectations, surrender their families to the Lord, take care of their own hearts, demonstrate respect for their husbands, ease into relationship with their stepchildren, and hold the line with their own kids are taking the quickest route to stepfamily success. The garden of their family's hearts is well manicured, tended and ready to bloom. As her family flourishes, a remarried mom and stepmom gets to shine in her role as nurturer.

HEART MONITORS

1. How can you keep yourself from jumping in the next time your husband and kids begin to fight?

2. In what ways are you tending your own heart now? How will you ensure that you are keeping your heart free of clogs?

3. What parenting plan have you formulated with your husband? Have you reached agreement on how repeated "offenses" will be handled, and by whom?

4. What opportunities for fun have you presented to your stepfamily? How can you encourage members to take ownership in your family without pushing them?

HEART PROTECTORS

Call a family meeting and let the children come up with a list of fun activities to do and meals they want to have. Put them on the calendar and invite each person to participate, but don't force anyone to join.

Schedule a day with your husband to dream about what you hope your family will look like one day and what steps you'll take to get there. Make a list of goals for what you'd like to see in each child and in your own lives in one year.

Be the head cheerleader of your stepfamily team. Encourage each person every day.

Note

1. Don and Kathy Coryell, *Basic Training for Remarriage and Stepfamilies: A Unique Faith and Grace-Based Approach* (Riverbank, CA: Creative Connections Ministry, 2008), p. 163.

The Hearts of Children and Stepchildren in Remarriage

For his Holy Spirit speaks to us deep in our hearts,
and tells us that we are really God's children.
ROMANS 8:16, *TLB*

Children are a gift from the LORD; they are a reward from him.
PSALM 127:3, *NLT*

When Dan and Marci left their spouses to marry each other, the doors of their five children's hearts slammed shut with a resounding bang. The damage of years of being exposed to their parents' stressful or dysfunctional marriages, topped off by the betrayal that came with Dan and Marci's affair and subsequent marriage, erected barriers in their children's hearts that would take many years to heal and take down.

"Let's just say they were not singing from the same songbook that we were," Dan says dryly.

When kids lose their traditional family, their hearts hurt. No matter how it happens, kids and stepkids just plain hurt. When a family is turned upside down and inside out, kids pay the most. They lose their innocence, grow up too fast, step into roles they weren't made for, and turn into manipulators. For a while, following the end of their primary family, some of their needs (physical, emotional or spiritual) go unmet as their wounded parents try to pick up the pieces of their own lives.

While remarriage and stepfamily stability can bring many benefits to children over time, in the beginning it's all about loss for the kids. Think about it. Remarriage is great for the two adults. They are getting physical companionship, sexual intimacy, a conversation partner, a best friend and someone to share the parenting duties and household tasks. They feel attractive again and get to put behind them any stigma of divorce, widowhood and single parenting. It seems like such a win-win for the couple that they often do not realize the impact it will have on their children and stepchildren. It feels like everyone should be excited and able to see all the pluses. And what really throws new stepfamilies for a loop is that the kids may have been excited during the dating phase. But things usually change dramatically once the ceremony is over and the new stepfamily settles under one roof. The sudden emergence of tension, anger, rebellion and sadness that kids themselves may not have expected to feel quickly throws many stepfamilies off-kilter.

As you prepare for remarriage or experience remarriage, try to step into your children's shoes and view your marriage through their eyes. When you remarry, the kids lose their dream of ever having their biological parents reunite. (And nearly every child's heart longs for his or her parents to be like the Disney movie *The Parent Trap*.) They lose space in their own home, as they no longer have the freedom to enter mom or dad's bedroom and may have to share their own room with new stepsiblings. If the stepfamily moves into a new home, the children lose the familiarity of their neighborhood and friends, and may even have to change schools. They lose time with their formerly single parent, too, as they now have to share mom or dad with their new stepparent and stepsiblings. If the parent moved his or her child into the position of friend and confidant after the loss of their marriage, the child loses that "special" role that the stepparent now fills.

Give your kids the help they need to succeed. If their actions are self-harming or dangerous, seek professional counseling or treatment. If they have fallen behind academically, hire a tutor or spend extra time helping them with their work. If they are struggling with loss, get grief counseling. Recognize that this is a time of transition when they will not function in top form, so give them what they need to recover.

That's a lot of loss, isn't it? No wonder your kids and stepkids slam their hearts shut and take it all out on you! That's why the best phrase to repeat to yourself when you are a parent in a stepfamily is, *It's not about you.* That one little phrase can help you keep your hearts open to your kids and stepkids when they are acting the most unlovable and creating the most chaos. How? It reminds you of two things: (1) You are called as a Christ-follower to love others unconditionally, even when it costs you; and (2) you can't take your children's and stepchildren's behavior personally. Parents and stepparents have to be the adults and try not to get their feelings hurt, no matter how many buttons their children and stepchildren push.

Parents and stepparents can also prepare their children ahead of time for the changes that come with remarriage and listen carefully to their fears and concerns. Accept their anger and help them grieve. Pray with them and over them often. Lead them continually to Christ their Savior and creator of their heart, and help them discover the Holy Spirit, their Comforter.

Children Are a Gift from God

Kids and stepkids need their parents and stepparents to remember Psalm 127:3. Each and every one of the children and stepchildren in your life is a gift and a reward—not a punishment! And they should be treated that way. When hurting kids and stepkids vent their feelings—even the ugly ones—and find grace and mercy at the end of their bad behavior, their hearts begin to soften. In time, they can heal. Children and stepchildren in remarriage desperately need their hearts to be nurtured tenderly and lovingly by all of their parents and stepparents. They need, like all of us need, unconditional love. Think about those two words we often say so lightly: *unconditional love*. What does it really mean? It means loving and accepting your children and stepchildren *exactly the way they are right now*. It means acting lovingly toward them whether they bring joy to your stepfamily or wreak havoc daily. It means accepting them even when they are filled with bitterness, anger, rebellion, defiance, grief and hate. In fact, unconditional love is needed the most when kids' hearts in remarriage are the most hardened, when their actions are delivering the most damage.

Reassure your children and stepchildren that there is nothing they could do to make you love them any more, and nothing they could do that would make you love them any less. Just like your feelings for your spouse, you choose to love your children and stepchildren. Period.

For parents, and especially for stepparents, it is crucial to demonstrate unconditional love over and over again, without any judgment, even when your emotions aren't lining up with the love you're asking God to help you give. As a stepparent, don't condemn yourself for not feeling as crazy about them as you do for your own kids. You can't manufacture love for them, but you can remind yourself that God can love them through you. You must act lovingly toward your stepchildren. If children and stepchildren see a model of unconditional love, over time their heart health will improve and they can recover from the loss of their primary family and form loving bonds with their new stepfamily (or stepfamilies).

As you practice keeping your own hearts open and filled with God's love so that it pours out to your family, you must also teach your children and stepchildren how to tend their own hearts. They have experienced permanent loss that has taken its toll. The way their hearts are handled from today forward may determine how well they love their own families for generations to come. The great news is that children are just that—children. They have a long time to learn, grow and heal. And because you now know the truths about the heart, your children and stepchildren can receive early training about the importance of their heart, how to fill it with the love of Christ and how to keep it open and attached to others.

Finding Common Ground in a Foreign Land

For children and stepchildren whose parents divorced, going back and forth between their families is similar to traveling back and forth to different countries. Each time they move from one household to the other, the kids have to remember to adjust. Each of their families has its own rules, ways of communicating, traditions, tensions, standards and schedule. Switching gears every few days or every other weekend often causes kids to act out when they return from their other family. Compassionate parents and stepparents who want hearts to remain open try to keep conversation light and demands few when kids first return home. Kids have to "switch skins" when they switch houses. The children whose hearts suffer the least damage when primary families end and new stepfamilies form are the ones whose parents and stepparents in both households learn to work closely together and keep the same standards, so that the households run similarly. (We will take a look at ways to connect with former spouses in chapter 12.)

Try to carefully discern which misdeeds come from closed hearts and which ones are mistakes or misunderstandings. For example, if on a regular basis a child comes back to your home after visits to his other parent's home without his backpack, you need to figure out why before you decide what action to take. He may just be forgetful, or he may not want the pain of separation and the discomfort of transition, so he leaves his backpack in an effort to communicate his desire to stay. He may be leaving it purposely to hide school reports, or he may feel like he will displease or disobey his parent in the other home if he brings it back to your house. If you don't get to the heart of the behavior, you may take the wrong course of action.

To help children and stepchildren adjust to remarriage, make it your policy to conduct family meetings. Get everyone's input in regard to family activities, menus, policies, curfews, chores and household rules. You can even ask the kids what they think punishment should be for different offenses. Let your children and stepchildren know you will take their suggestions seriously, and implement policies that are as fair as possible to everyone. Make your expectations clear but not too strict. Children and stepchildren assimilate into stepfamily life best when they have a say in the new standards and schedule. Be willing to hear their hearts, and use as many of their suggestions as you can. Slow and steady forward progress wins the stepfamily race.

Learn how foods affect mood and brain chemistry. For instance, angry kids find release when they can crunch their food. Get them some carrot sticks. Potassium also helps alleviate their stress, so bananas and applesauce are great snack choices.

Great Expectations

So what should stepfamily members expect of each other? What standards should a stepfamily set? When a stepfamily first comes together, loving bonds and deep trust do not exist between all the members. Stepparents and stepchildren are leery of each other, as are stepsiblings. Trust has to be built over time. Remember the truth that when battered hearts come together, they can remain partially closed, tentative about loving fully, afraid to expose themselves to the possibility of that intense pain again.

So when parents and stepparents immediately try to set a lot of ground rules or come down hard on kids' and stepkids' bad behavior, conflict and tension are likely to escalate, especially with adolescents and teens. Children and stepchildren won't open their hearts to their stepfamily if they are burdened with what seem to be arbitrary new rules and discipline.

The one standard that doesn't change is God's standard, and that should be your stepfamily's default mode. If you want your stepfamily to follow Christ, then let your kids and stepkids know that you are asking them to be responsive to God's authority, not yours. Use the Bible as your family guidebook. Show your family what it says about how to treat each other, with kindness and brotherly love. Explain to your children and stepchildren that you are not trying to force them to have loving feelings for each other or for you, but that your family will try to live by the Golden Rule. You should aim to treat family members like you want to be treated, respecting each other's property and speaking politely. Explain that because relationships are new, a lot of grace and mercy need to be given to each other.

Your kids and stepkids need your permission *not* to feel love for all their new family members. At the same time, children and stepchildren need to know it's okay to love everyone too. They should not feel guilty for loving a stepparent or stepsibling. It's a good thing when children's hearts are open enough to love new members of their family; they should be able to do so without loyalty conflicts between their two homes.

One important tool in the stepfamily toolbox is forgiveness. Teach your family the fine art of forgiveness, and let it start with you. If you divorced, ask your children to forgive you for the losses they have experienced. If you were not faithful in your marriage, and your children know it, ask them to forgive you for not following God's standards. Don't divulge details; simply ask them to forgive you for hurting their other parent. Let them know that you have asked for God's forgiveness, and show them biblically what happens when we ask God to take our sins away. If you have been too impatient, distracted or demanding as a parent or stepparent, ask your children and stepchildren to forgive you. In fact, ask your kids and stepkids if you have caused their hearts to close against you in any way. Believe us, they'll let you know! Give them permission to tell you honestly how you have hurt their hearts. Listen carefully, make no excuses and ask their forgiveness. Let them know that you want to make changes, that you want your family to live in peace.

If you have put your children in roles they were not made for, tell them you need to reestablish healthy boundaries. Your daughter should not be your confidante, and your son should never be your caregiver. If you put them there when you were a single parent, it's going to create friction when you need to assert your authority. Expect children who have been parented outside the lines to resist being pushed back inside. They aren't going to appreciate being treated like kids again, but you can't help that. It's your job to parent them all the way to adulthood. If you don't, your whole family will pay the price. Explain why the way you've been relating to each other isn't healthy for your hearts. Seek their forgiveness, but don't be shocked if they have a hard time giving it to you for a while.

When you have apologized for the ways you've hurt your stepfamily, ask them if there is anything they need to apologize for. If family members confess to anything, be quick to forgive them. Remind them that once we give our sins to the Lord, He never brings them up again. Stepfamilies should do the same for each other. Once an offense has been confessed and apologized for, it should never be thrown back in the offender's face again. Pray together, asking the Lord to give your stepfamily a fresh start.

Find creative ways for your family to make restitution to each other and right wrongs. Children and stepchildren's hearts respond best when punishments fit the crime, when they can understand the correlation between what they did wrong and the discipline they received. For example, two months' grounding from all friends, electronics and activities might not be the right punishment for a teen who took $20 from his stepmother's purse. However, stealing is a serious offense that should not be taken lightly. A better fit might be for the teen to give back $40 to $60 in restitution, either in cash or by doing chores to work it off. A stepchild who mouths off to a stepparent should not be yelled at or spanked by the stepparent. Instead, the parent might require their child to find and write 15 verses in the Bible that talk about the power of words.

The goal in expectations and discipline is always to find ways to reach the heart, not just to correct behavior. It's fairly easy to force outward behavior to change in a child or stepchild, at least for a time; it is much more difficult to reach the heart and get them to want to do the right thing. Set the example by making sure your heart is in the right place. Are you trying to make your kids and stepkids get along or obey, because it's the right thing for them to do, or because you want your stepfamily to look good to others? Do you administer discipline in anger or out of fear, rather than with the goal of reaching the heart? If so, learn the fine art of surrender. Your children and stepchildren belong to the Lord. They are His children.

Take the pressure off of your family by giving them back to Him and allowing Him to work in their hearts.

Work hard to eliminate a critical spirit from the way you parent. Think about how you respond to criticism. Does it inspire your heart to change? Probably not. Think back to when you were a teen. Weren't you already well aware of the faults your parents criticized? Most people, even teens, already know what they are not doing well. Criticism just fosters resentment or lowers self-esteem. Encourage your kids and stepkids 10 times more than you criticize.

Stepfamily Structure and Discipline Duties

While stepfamilies should allow relationship bonds to develop at their own pace, the family needs some kind of framework from which to operate, because there are so many pieces and personalities to fit together. If there is chaos, anarchy rules and stepfamily hearts lack the opportunities to form solid heart connections. Stepfamily members need structure in order for hearts to feel safe. If nobody knows what the rules of the game are, how can they follow them? For children, this is especially important, because if rules are not clear and consistently enforced, they won't know when they've broken them. Their hearts may be bound by the fear that their next step might be their last, or hardened in rebellion and frustration because they feel like they can never get anything right.

Stepfamilies can experience a great deal of difficulty with discipline. As we've talked about before, the husband, in order to gain respect from his family, may feel like he needs to start "keeping the kids in line." The remarried mom may give him the job of disciplining her children because she believes that's the way to show respect. The reverse can happen as well. Stay-at-home stepmoms are right there with their stepchildren when an offense occurs, so naturally they administer the discipline right then and there. Right? Not always.

It may feel "normal" for the head of the household or the one at home with the kids to run the show but, in stepfamilies, the old rules don't work. Parents may be glad to hand over to stepparents the unpleasant duty of discipline. Guilt may have left them unable to make their kids unhappy, so handing out punishments isn't their strong suit anyway. But when the stepparent issues orders or expects obedience from the kids, he or she will most likely be unpleasantly surprised. Young children may jump to attention because they easily accept authority for the most part, but older ones need relationship before they buy in to authority. They feel this stranger has no right to tell them anything. He's not their dad or she's not their mom, and never will be. Remarried moms or dads are once again in the middle, and everyone's unhappy.

It may feel unnatural, but the hard-and-fast rule that stepfamilies *must* follow above any other if they want family members to have a chance of forming healthy heart bonds is this one: *Biological parents MUST be the ones to administer discipline.* This might feel backward, but it's your best chance for success. That doesn't mean that stepparents play no part in raising the children; it just means that they are largely silent partners in front of the kids, at first. A wife can back her husband or he can back her. You can be each other's sounding board, but stepparents can't call their stepkids on the carpet. If a stepparent is going to be alone with the children and may have to discipline, the parent should transfer his or her authority to the stepparent in front of the kids, so that everyone knows it. This is similar to the way parents would act with a baby-sitter, letting the kids know that when they are away, the baby-sitter will be in charge.

Stepcouples should expect conflict in their stepfamily. It's absolutely normal, just not much fun. To promote stepfamily peace, choose your battles as wisely as you can. Try to overlook minor offenses so you are not constantly correcting. Stepfamilies need fun before too much friction. As a couple, talk through just about every parenting situation and potential disciplinary scenario before you get there, so you will already know how you have agreed to handle it. What are the most important values you want upheld? What behaviors could do permanent damage or would wound deeply? Try to figure out what are the "minor" and "major" offenses so you are not too hard or too soft on the kids. Maybe you will both agree that a teen's hair color or messy room doesn't matter, but hitting a stepsibling or smoking cigarettes does. Figure out what you will do to praise and reward progress as well as how you will punish misbehavior.

While children are never the cause of divorce in primary families, they are often seen as the biggest reason remarriages don't make it. Conflict over the kids can become a permanent division in the stepfamily. When a parent and stepparent disagree on how to handle a child's behavior, the focus shifts from the child's misdeed to the couple's conflict. The child gets off the hook while the stepcouple goes at it. That triangulation can destroy a stepfamily. Wise stepcouples decide early on what the rules will be for everything they can think of—from dating to disrespect and from drinking to disobeying—and they stick to them! Talk about the forms of punishment you believe in and what tones of voice you will use. If you know before an offense occurs what your plan of action will be, and if you follow through with the agreed-upon course of action on a consistent basis, issues with children can be addressed properly and without additional stepfamily conflict erupting.

 In most stepfamilies, the stepparent's natural tendency is to administer the law, while the biological parent gives out the grace. In truly successful stepfamilies, the adults make sure they function just the opposite. The biological parent lays down the law, while the stepparent gets to form bonds by giving out grace.

Remember that you are accountable before God for the way you parent and discipline your children and stepchildren. Your kids are not your friends yet, but if you parent them with proper boundaries and handle their hearts lovingly, they will be someday.

Kids' and Stepkids' Heartfelt Needs

As you learn to "step" together, get to know your children's and stepchildren's heartfelt needs. First, children in stepfamilies need to know that they are still a priority to their parent and that their parent's love has not lessened or changed. The best reassurance is time spent together. Biological parents and children need time alone, and the wise stepfamily creates a structure that builds that time in. Stepparents can also reassure their stepchildren that they are not trying to take the children's parent away from them. As children and stepchildren grasp the way God's love flows into people and then outflows to others, they will better understand that their new stepfamily members are not taking any love from them but are actually giving them more opportunities to love and be loved!

Stepchildren need their stepparent to pursue their hearts, even if they are pushing the stepparent away. The stepparent that wins his or her stepchildren's hearts listens well, mentors, befriends and lets the kids set the pace of their relationship. Stepparents can court their stepchildren by finding something fun they have in common, such as a recreational sport or hobby. Stepparents bring new skills, talents and passions into the stepfamily mix, which also gives their stepchildren the opportunity to enjoy something new.

Let your stepchildren know upfront that you do not intend to try to be another mother or father to them, but that you will perform the same duties a mom or dad would in your home. You will take care of whatever needs they have while they are with you, just as you would anyone that Christ placed in your life. Let them know you are willing to be a listening ear, a homework helper and chauffeur when needed.

Children and stepchildren need be able to talk about their feelings, and they need parents and stepparents to validate them. They need to understand what happened to their primary family without the gory details of breakups or legal battles. Kids need to be kids, and healthy parents do not need their children to take their side. They try at all times to keep their children and stepchildren out of the middle of any parental disagreement or conflict. Children and stepchildren also need to know that they are not the cause of the changes in their family. No divorce between two adults was ever a child's fault; however, many, many kids believe it was.

Finally, the hearts of children and stepchildren need to feel safe. They need to be safe from verbal, physical or emotional abuse from anyone in their stepfamily. They need to be safe from teasing and sarcastic remarks. And they need time to believe that the new stepfamily they have is safe from destruction, that it won't fall apart.

Halves, Steps and Other Siblings

When a mom and a dad marry, they often expect their respective children to consider themselves siblings as soon as the wedding ceremony is over. But the kids at best may be friends and are more likely to feel like strangers.

Stepsiblings need to know that it is their actions toward family members that are important, not their feelings. Because God's love flows through them and outflows to others, they should treat each other courteously, respect each other's things and look for some common ground so they can have fun together.

To prevent some stepsibling battles, it is very important for every child and stepchild to have his or her own space. If they can't have a whole bedroom, then they need to have their own drawers, closets or other place to keep their belongings. Again, this is important for all the children in the stepfamily, even the ones who may only visit occasionally. They need to be part of the team, not made to feel like outsiders. Allow kids to decorate their own side of a shared bedroom to reflect their personalities and so they feel at home. Make sure that the kids don't invade each other's space or take each other's belongings without permission. Everyone in a stepfamily needs to work hard to help hearts feel safe and to help build trust. And if a child's "stuff" isn't safe, he or she won't feel safe. Anyone who helps himself to his siblings' or stepsiblings' possessions should have to replace double what has been taken.

 Get to know other stepfamilies and collect some of their "best practices" when it comes to parenting.

Have patience with competition and territorial battles, and be very careful that your words and actions as parents and stepparents do not pit your children against each other. If you are bringing together older children and younger children, make sure that older stepsiblings are charged with protecting the younger ones, not taking advantage of them or torturing and teasing them. Do not rely on the teens to baby-sit unless you know they will be loving to their stepsiblings. Even if they do act lovingly, don't wear out their affection by putting the baby-sitting responsibility on them too often.

Watch carefully for any imbalance of power, as it is easy for older kids to act cruelly to younger ones if they feel the little ones have "invaded" their family. Stepsibling conflict can quickly set the remarried couple at odds, because each adult has the tendency to side with his or her children. Unless any of the children is in real physical or emotional danger from the others, try to allow the kids to work out their own differences. Allowing them to work it out keeps your couple relationship stronger, prevents children from becoming habitual tattletales, and keeps kids and stepkids from going "underground" with their bad behavior so they won't get in trouble.

As you teach your family how to care for their own hearts, it's a natural fit to share ways they can care for each other's hearts too. Help your children come up with creative ways they can have fun, whether it's buying a game they can all enjoy, going places together, planning and cooking family meals or just saying encouraging things. Help them to restore relationship after conflict occurs by apologizing and seeking forgiveness. Allow them to purchase their own gifts for each others' birthdays and other occasions so they have a stake in the relationship. Encourage them to cheer each other on in their respective sports and extracurricular activities.

 Speak as politely and courteously to your children and stepchildren as you expect them to speak to you.

If you have adolescents or teens of both genders, make sure that your stepfamily institutes rules for privacy, and be careful about leaving teens of the opposite sex alone on a regular basis. You and your spouse may see them as siblings, but they know very well that they are not. Do not be naïve. When a young man and a young woman spend extended periods of time alone together, romantic interest and even sexual experimentation can naturally occur.

Be careful not to accuse your children of doing anything wrong, but make them aware of the reasons why privacy and hanging out in groups is important for your stepfamily. If they are not forewarned that they could develop romantic feelings for a stepbrother or stepsister, they can feel deeply guilty, ashamed or that there is something weird about them if it happens. Let them know that a crush might be normal, but that they need to protect their hearts from acting on any romantic feelings while they live together as brother and sister in your home.

Your children may not have chosen to be together, but if they believe that God can bring good out of any circumstance, then there must be something good their stepsiblings can contribute to their lives. Share with your kids that their siblings, stepsiblings and any eventual half-siblings will be the only people on earth who will have the same memories of childhood that they do. Even their future husbands and wives won't be able to look back with them and laugh at the silly things the parents did when they were growing up. Only their siblings and stepsiblings can really understand. If they grow into a healthy relationship as kids and teens, as adults they will always have someone on their side, aunts and uncles and cousins for their children and others with whom to carry on family traditions.

If the wife becomes pregnant with a half-sibling to any of the children, the stepfamily dynamic shifts again. Some stepfamilies find that the new baby helps unite them, because this cute, helpless little person is someone they are all related to and can share. Other stepfamilies find that the new addition brings out a whole new set of negative feelings in their children, including jealousy, resentment or even sadness and rejection. Alleviate any fears children may have about being displaced by the new baby. Remind them how love works once again, so they remember there is plenty to out-flow all around. Let teens know you won't curtail their social lives by expecting them to baby-sit all the time, but encourage their involvement.

On an age-appropriate level, include your children and stepchildren in the preparation for the baby and discuss their feelings and what they think will change when the new arrival comes. Let them help set up the nursery, shop for baby items or throw their mother or stepmother a baby shower. Again, the more children and stepchildren are invited to take ownership in the stepfamily without being forced into it, the bigger the bond they are likely to have.

The biggest challenge for stepcouples who have a child together often lies with their own behavior, not the kids' and stepkids' attitudes. It is easy for the husband and wife to gush and glow about the impending arrival, to the point that they alienate their existing children. They are so excited that it makes their kids feel pushed out of the limelight. A child of their own is easier for stepcouples in many ways, because they share in this life from the very beginning. They can discipline together, and their child will never be a visitor in their home. Because everything is "natural" with this new child, it can shine a spotlight on how unnatural some aspects of parenting the stepfamily are. You must guard your hearts from hardening against your other children, just because parenting them is more challenging or difficult. Ask the Lord to keep you from appearing to favor your children's half-siblings, so that you do not foster jealousy among your children.

Heart Connectors

The stepfamily that forges loving bonds and keeps everyone's hearts safe gets to know each other and grow together best by focusing on faith and fun.

Parents and stepparents should make it their goal to help each child develop his or her identity and faith in Christ, pray with their family frequently, study the Bible and go to church together. They can also bring their stepfamily together by unpacking each member's strengths, talents and unique personality and gifting. Everyone in a stepfamily can contribute something to the other members, because God handcrafted each of us and put us together for a purpose.

Print out a spiritual gifts test, personality type quiz, learning styles assessment, love languages test or other self-assessment tool. Gather your stepfamily and take these quizzes together. The questions are easy, and they can actually be fun. When you have tallied the results, share them with each other. Talk about how each family member's unique combination of personality, gifting and learning style makes him or her bond with some people and clash with others. Help your children and stepchildren see how their gifts and talents can be used in school, in a career they might enjoy and in their relationships.

Encourage stepfamily dialogue about what your family's purpose might be. What does God want you to accomplish together? Out of everyone on the planet, you are together as a stepfamily for a reason. Determine to discover what that reason is. Get input from children and stepchildren about ways you can serve others. When you serve someone else, you work together as a team. Your external focus on a project together takes the spotlight off your internal difficulties.

It is much easier for stepfamilies to add in positive experiences than it is to try to eliminate challenges. Take your stepfamily where they can see others' needs and meet them by working in a soup kitchen, serving at a homeless shelter or going on a missions trip. When you see firsthand what real need looks like, petty squabbles and jealousies seem much less important.

Get buy-in from every stepfamily member as much as you can, so that everyone takes a turn planning and preparing meals, choosing activities, rotating chores and even picking what to watch on TV. Give plenty of incentives to motivate your kids and stepkids. Are you motivated to work really hard without a paycheck or pat on the back? Your children and stepchildren need rewards too.

Uphold your children's and stepchildren's primary family traditions, but also form new ones within your stepfamily. If your stepchildren traditionally spend Christmas morning opening presents and having stockings at their other home, maybe your new tradition can be to enjoy your stockings and drink hot chocolate on Christmas Eve. If children have a traditional birthday party with one parent (and if you can't combine efforts to put on a party together), maybe your tradition will be a special birthday lunch outing for just the birthday child and parent.

Give your kids and stepkids the freedom to preserve the best memories of their past while encouraging them to also participate in the present. Gently let them know that they are not betraying their primary family if they enjoy special times with their stepfamily. Make it fun to be a member of your family. Put music on and dance around the living room. Run outside and jump in the pool after bedtime, just because. Wake kids and stepkids up to see shooting stars or the first snowfall of the season. Put encouraging notes in lunchboxes and speak each family member's love language. Celebrate the little things, and praise your children and stepchildren often.

When stepfamily members' hearts are handled lovingly and love is flowing freely, the benefits to the children and stepchildren can be enormous. Here are just eight of the many benefits stepfamily life can bring:

1. Childless stepparents have the chance to make a permanent investment in the life of a child. Biological parents of sons or daughters may have a chance to co-parent stepdaughters or stepsons.

2. Children learn how to have healthy relationships by watching how the adults closest to them relate to each other. If their parents couldn't stay married, the children can benefit from seeing a healthy remarriage last.

3. Stepfamily members have a chance to experience different customs. When two families merge, each unique family culture can enrich everyone's understanding and experience. ("We've

never gone camping . . . watched a baseball game . . . eaten Thai food . . . been to a museum before.")

4. Children living in a remarried family often have increased maturity, coping skills, ability to accept differences, cooperation and flexibility.

5. Members may get to experience a different family configuration. For example, an only child may gain stepsiblings or half-siblings. Children may get a stepsister or stepbrother close in age as a companion and playmate. They may get a different family role or "birth order" (no longer the youngest or the only boy anymore, for example).

6. The typical stepfamily has many more members than a traditional family; thus, they have more people to care for them and on whom to rely for support in times of need.

7. The stepparent can be an appropriate role model for the stepchildren. As the children grow, the stepparent may give support, skills and perspectives that the parents can't.

8. A single parent's remarriage can be a blessing for parent and child by restoring the two-adult household structure, stability, closeness and security that were lost through divorce, separation or death.

The benefits of a healthy stepfamily are many, and you can rest as parents and stepparents in the knowledge that when you learn God's truths and apply them to your stepfamily, you are doing the very best you can. Still, some stepfamily members may never bond or believe their stepfamily was a good thing. They may fight you every step of the way. Do not grow weary or allow your heart to clog under the continual assault. Remember that you are engaged in a spiritual battle. Satan wants your children to have only the legacy of death or divorce. He does not want them to experience healthy family life that they can replicate in their future. Instead, he comes to destroy. Understand that you, as parents and stepparents, can love with all your heart, apply everything in this chapter, pray fervently and make every effort to open a child's wounded or resentful heart. But some children and stepchildren will choose not to love their stepparent or stepsiblings. Or they may bond with some members, but not with others. If they allow resentment and unforgiveness to clog their emotional arteries, some children's hearts will never open to their stepfamily.

As children become teens and young adults, your influence over their hearts wanes. The state of their hearts becomes an issue directly between them and God. Your job is to teach them God's truths, lead them to Him and release them. They must choose for themselves whether they will let go of their anger and pain and accept His healing. Always keep the door of relationship wide open, but surrender your children and stepchildren to Christ. Pray that they will meet sincere Christ-followers who will draw them to Him; ask the Lord to woo them, and seek His protection of them. Then let go.

There may be no greater agony than watching a child or stepchild turn away and reject you. But God is faithful, and He will not waste your pain. With each stepfamily experience, the Lord teaches and refines your heart. As your stepfamily evolves, you have the privilege of learning and growing as a parent and stepparent. God can use every stepfamily battle to draw you closer to Him.

HEART MONITORS

1. Before reading this chapter, what did you know about the losses children feel in remarriage? What surprised you?

2. What family rules have you and your spouse established? How well have you covered the ways you will discipline and the standards you want to keep?

3. What behaviors can you overlook in your children and stepchildren, and what offenses are major?

4. How can you help your children keep their hearts open to stepfamily members? How will you help stepsiblings bond?

5. How is your household fun? What have you celebrated lately, and what surprises have you pulled off? What will you plan, to keep your stepfamily serving others and working together as a team?

HEART PROTECTORS

Go on a "benefit hunt." Gather your family together and invite each willing person to identify one or more benefits they feel your stepfamily provides them, either recently or long-term. It may be helpful to get people started by inviting them to complete sentences like these:

- What I appreciate about our stepfamily recently is . . .
- This family feels better to me than (another family) because . . .
- Something our stepfamily offers me that I never had before is . . .
- If we lost our stepfamily, I'd really miss . . .
- When I'm old, I'll probably be glad that our stepfamily . . .
- Something my friends like about our stepfamily is . . .
- Compared to other families, we . . .

Encourage comments and discussion, and when you feel "done," encourage awareness and feedback by asking your family to reflect and comment on "What are you aware of now?" or "How did you feel about this exercise after we all finished?" or "What, if anything, did you just learn about us?"

Surprise your stepfamily with "date nights." Grab the kids out of bed and take them to the movies in their pajamas; get everyone up to look at the stars; or get all dressed up and treat them to a fancy restaurant.

Open Hearts Toward Former Spouses

If it is possible, as far as it depends on you, live at peace with everyone.
ROMANS 12:18

In the movie *Stepmom*, talented actress Susan Sarandon plays Jackie, a divorced mom of an adolescent daughter, Anna, and a son about eight years old named Ben. Jackie loves her children and is a great mom, but she is bitter about her divorce and blames it on Isabel, the younger woman her ex-husband is marrying (played by Julia Roberts). Throughout this sometimes painfully realistic film, Isabel and the kids attempt to form the awkward first bonds of a healthy stepparent-stepchildren relationship, while Jackie's displeasure is apparent.

Jackie can't stand the fact that Isabel is in her children's lives, yet she remains smiling and upbeat in front of her children. Still, her anger comes through, and Anna and Ben get caught in the middle, as portrayed brilliantly in one horseback-riding scene. As Jackie rides across a lovely meadow with Anna and Ben, Anna asks her mother if Isabel makes a lot of money as a fashion photographer. Ben then makes an offhand comment that he thinks his new stepmother is attractive. Jackie's responses, delivered in a light tone and with a smile, contain subtle digs at her children's new stepmother. The effect they had on her young son was immediate and profound. His mother's words lodged straight in his heart. The short conversation went like this:

Anna:	Does Isabel make a lot of money?
Jackie:	Well, people like Isabel, who think only of themselves, often do make a great deal of money.
Ben:	I think she's pretty.

Jackie: Yeah, if you like big teeth.
Ben: Mommy?
Jackie: What, sweetie?
               [Here, the camera zooms in on the little boy's
               earnest face.]
Ben: If you want me to hate her, I will.[1]

The message communicated to Ben's heart was this: Slam the door shut against any interloper. You are mine, and that woman has no right to have a relationship with you. And Ben heard it, loud and clear.

What messages are you communicating to your children and step-children about your ex-spouse or your mate's former spouse? What attitude are you revealing toward your children's and stepchildren's other biological parents through your body language and facial expressions? How do you talk to each other on the telephone and act when you're in the same room?

Open Hearts with Former Spouses

To keep their hearts open, the number-one need of children and stepchildren in remarriage is full permission from their parents and stepparents to love, accept and bond with you all and to see you all love each other with a Christ-like love. *Ha!* you might be thinking. *We divorced because we don't love each other anymore.* But if you have allowed Christ to perform the necessary "heart surgery" we have been sharing in this book, then you have asked for forgiveness and given it, grieved your losses and developed a relationship with the Lord that has healed your hurts so that you can outflow His love. He can remove your heart blockage toward your former spouse and help you live out Romans 12:18, which commands us to do everything within our power to live at peace with everybody.

The absolute best thing a parent can do for his or her children is to love their other parent. That's an awfully tall order after divorce, but it can be accomplished with Christ. First, you must forgive everything that happened in your marriage and during its demise. You must let go of your resentments, past and present, and determine not to harbor them in the future. If you don't want to forgive, start by asking God to give you the desire to forgive. Keep asking until you are ready to do it. Once you have forgiven, keep forgiving. Your former spouse will still irritate and anger you often.

You most likely will not see eye to eye on many things. After all, if you were in perfect harmony, you probably wouldn't have divorced. Still, if you want to live for Christ with an open heart, you have to let Him outflow His love to your former mate. When you want to hate instead of forgive, keep the following in mind: This person you hate created those beautiful kids with you. Furthermore, God says you have to forgive or He won't forgive you.

Bitter, unforgiving parents permanently damage their children's hearts and relationships. Most children long to get along with all their family members, if they can be assured that it is okay to do so. Here is how Susan Clark put it in *Raising Children in Blended Families* by Maxine Marsolini:

> It wasn't that I didn't want to be a part of Dad's new family. I desperately wanted this to happen. But Dad and I, once close, were torn apart by my new sisters and my stepmother Janis—all wanting time with him, too. The constant attention and doting I had received previously was now divided among so many. I was left feeling abandoned and betrayed. . . .
>
> When our son was born, Mom came to care for me and help me with all the first-time mom things I was uncertain of doing. Naturally, Dad and Janis also wanted to share in the birth of our first child. Mom wouldn't hear of it! "If she sets foot in this house, I'll leave," she said, leaving me with the difficult and unfair task of telling Dad that, while he could visit, Janis could not. That one phone call will haunt me the rest of my life.[2]

Give your children permission to love their stepfamily members. It won't cost you anything, and it will help keep your child's heart open and able to connect with others in a healthy manner throughout his or her life.

 Ask your children and stepchildren in what ways they feel caught in the middle of parents and stepparents. Give them permission to speak freely, and ask them what changes they would recommend. Let them know you will do your part to live in peace.

Some people refuse to forgive because they feel it lets their offender off too easy. However, forgiveness releases you, not your former spouse. It unclogs your heart to be in right relationship with God and others. If you forgive your former spouse, he or she does not have to reciprocate. We do the right thing because it is the right thing, no matter how others are acting. That's what we teach our children. We must follow our own advice.

To forge a positive co-parenting path with your former spouse, you also need to ask forgiveness for any wrongs you committed or ways you hurt him/her in the past. Go beyond "I'm sorry" and ask your former spouse to forgive you. Let him/her know you want to work together in peace for the sake of your kids. This puts your co-parent in the position of having to make a conscious decision to put the past behind and go forward peacefully as co-parents. If he/she will not listen to you or refuses to forgive you, be okay with that. Just continue to treat your former mate with courtesy. You can't control anyone else's heart flow, but you can choose to do your part to be at peace.

Children and stepchildren whose two homes are not on the same page are easily destroyed. They live under the constant stress of trying to keep both parents happy and the guilt of knowing that every time they please one parent, it displeases the other. They are used as messengers between parents and either harden their hearts in order to numb their pain and avoid feeling their parents' pain or carry the excruciating weight of everyone's pain. When one or both parents' bitterness and desire for revenge is deeply entrenched, children can become completely alienated from one or both parents. And when children completely reject a parent, one of the two most important relationships in their formative years, they can find it difficult to sustain any relationship for the rest of their lives. They are likely to feel unable to love, undeserving of love or both. Don't create this heart malfunction in your own kids. Do the hard work of seeking forgiveness and extending it. Let your kids off the emotional hook.

When former spouses cannot or will not co-parent effectively, the kids get to run the show. They know that when they want something and mom says no, they can just tell dad she's being mean and he will give it to them. And vice versa. Manipulation becomes ingrained in children's behavior, which creates even more conflict and blame between the two households. Children who can manipulate to get what they want because their parents do not uphold each other's standards or communicate well are completely beyond either parent's control by the teen years and are often on a path to self-destruct.

Your heart towards your former spouse should strive for peace and effective co-parenting. To co-parent with a former spouse whose standards and values you may not like or agree with, you have to remember that you are doing it for your children. It's about them, not you. Your children need both of their parents, and they need them to work together. When you divorced, you may have thought you were getting out of your relationship with your former mate. Wrong. If you have children together, divorce got you out of the fun, friendship and sex that you had in marriage, but you get to keep the miscommunication, frustration, power struggles, financial disagreements and all the other things that led you to divorce in the first place!

Living out Romans 12:18 for your children's sake means talking to your former spouse a whole lot more frequently than you'd probably like. It means training your facial expression not to turn sour when kids tell stories about their other parent and stepparent. It means refusing to retaliate when your former spouse creates conflict, even when he or she is causing emotional damage to your relationship with your children. It means to politely end phone conversations that get heated and walk away if an argument begins in the presence of your children. Speak in soft, warm tones, and pray for peace prior to any encounter with your former spouse. Your healthy heart should continually seek to defuse any disagreement, find a compromise and work together.

 If you know you must discuss a topic with your former spouse that may cause friction, think about all the possible reactions and responses you may get and what your responses will be before you place a call or get into conversation. If you can already predict how a conversation will go and plan how you will act, you will more effectively be able to control any negative feelings.

Living in stepfamily peace means forging a bond with your spouse's former mate, too, for your stepchildren's sake. If your husband or wife was treated badly by their former spouse, you may find that your heart harbors more of a grudge toward them than toward your own ex. Ask the Lord to help you release your dislike to Him and give you the strength to see your mate's former spouse as simply an imperfect person who also needs the love of Christ flowing through his or her heart. Make any and all contact as friendly as possible so that your stepkids don't draw dividing lines in your stepfamily and reject you as a stepparent out of loyalty to their parent.

Even if your former spouse or your mate's former spouse remains bitter, badmouths you to your kids and stepkids and tries to ruin your relationship with them, don't fight back. Your kids will feel every ugly word and every harsh tone go through their hearts like piercing arrows. You can't shoot through your kids to get at each other. Instead of reacting with anger toward your exes every time the same old, emotional triggers are pulled, determine not to get worked up in future encounters. Again, you will never be able to control your former spouse or your mate's ex, but you can allow the Lord to change your response and keep your heart flowing with His love.

Creating a Co-Parenting Plan

When you are establishing your co-parent structure, look at the big picture from the kids' perspective and choose what will be the most comfortable and normal for them, not the most convenient for you. For example, you may not want to see your ex-husband or ex-wife every Christmas Day until your last child together turns 18, so you decide to take every Christmas Eve and let your former mate have every Christmas Day. But is that the most normal for your kids? Isn't it likely that they want to see both of their parents on Christmas Day rather than experience the pain of missing one of you every year? You may want to meet your ex-spouse to exchange the kids at a McDonald's or other public place rather than let them pull into your driveway, but is that the most comfortable for your children? If they forget something, wouldn't it be easier for them to run back inside the house to get the item rather than driving all the way back for it or having to do without until the next visit?

In order to co-parent well and live in peace, you have to give a lot. If your former mate does not share your standards or your faith, you may not get much in return. Your ex may take everything you give and ask for more. With each demand, you will have to decide whether this is something you can give gracefully or if giving in will set a precedent you are not willing to set. You have to count the cost to your kids if you give in or if you hold your ground. If you let your former mate have the children on your Thanksgiving weekend, for example, you miss the chance for them to attend the family reunion on your side. However, if you don't, you know she will make the children feel guilty for leaving her alone on the holiday. Which decision is best for them? There is no easy answer. You can take your kids' preferences into account, but let them know you will ultimately make the decision with their other parent. That keeps them from feeling disloyal over having to choose one of you over the other.

Even if you don't want to, pray for your spouse and your mate's former spouse on a regular basis. Pray that their hearts will be healed, even if they don't deserve it. If their hearts get filled with God's love, your children and stepchildren will be blessed and their relationships improve.

When you want to co-parent peacefully, be respectful and courteous. Make plans for the children only on your own time, not on the other parents' visitation time. You can't call the shots during your children's time with their other parent, but you can and should try to agree on some ground rules that you will both stick to, so kids can't easily pit you against each other. For example, you might agree on what movie ratings are acceptable, how much TV time is okay and whether Internet access will be available in a child's bedroom. You should try to stick to a common bedtime and the same sleepover rules. If one parent disciplines the child, the other parent should keep the punishment in place too. Keep each other informed of significant events, challenges, academic troubles and even friendships you don't trust. The more each of you knows about your children's lives, the less your children can hide from either of you. Co-parenting well takes an enormous amount of effort, but in the long run it is less work and a lot less painful than seeing a teen become pregnant, turn to drugs, get into legal trouble or even lose his or her life.

If you have more time with your children than your former spouse, make an extra effort to help your ex stay involved in the children's daily lives. It might be easier for you if your former spouse dropped out of the picture, but it would be devastating for your kids. Even if you don't approve of your former spouse's lifestyle, the negative effect of the lifestyle on the kids is usually less damaging than a parent's absence would be.

When Your Efforts Are Not Enough

When you try everything you know to make peace with your former spouse and co-parent together, and your ex still refuses to have any kind

of communication or relationship with you, release the conflict to the
Lord. Determine to do your very best to guide your children according to
God's standards when you are with them and surrender them to His protection when they go to their other parent's home. You are going to have
to trust the Lord. Pray fervently that your children's hearts will be protected, and keep praying that your former spouse's heart will soften so you
can work together. You will probably have a rockier stepfamily journey
than you would if you could co-parent effectively, because your children
can rebel against your rules if they know they can get their way with their
other parent. Your children can even emotionally blackmail you, withdrawing their love and possibly their visits when they don't get their way.

Don't give up. If you come to a stepfamily impasse, get a good counselor to work with you to find some common ground. Find a Christian
counselor who can help your children develop their own survival strategies
for negotiating their two worlds.

Setting Healthy Boundaries

In some stepfamilies, figuring out how to get along and co-parent is not
the biggest issue between former spouses. The problem some remarriages
face is that former spouses still get along too well and new spouses feel
they are too close for comfort. Some former spouses have never properly
cut ties with each other. For a remarriage to make it, healthy boundaries
need to be set firmly in place with former mates. Keep in mind that the
goal of a boundary is an open heart. The very reason we put boundaries in
place is because the boundary is needed in order to keep our heart open to
the other person.

The most common scenario is when a man has remarried, but his former wife has not and she continues to heavily depend on him. Because he
wants his children to be comfortable, and out of guilt that their marriage
ended, some remarried husbands and dads remain at their ex-wife's beck
and call. While a husband can be courteous, even act friendly toward his ex-
wife, he cannot be her close friend, confidant, hero or, of course, her lover.

Remarried men need to put their wife first, their children next and
their former wife way down the line. In order to do this, conversations with
his former wife should be limited to the children only. Extra financial support should not be given, household repairs made or advice shared. If you
are remarried, personal conversations are reserved for your current wife,

not your ex. If your ex-wife has a flat tire, she can call an emergency road-side service or law enforcement officer to fix it. If she wants to cry about her love life (or lack thereof), she can turn to any one of her girlfriends. If she wants to make an orthodontist appointment for your daughter to get braces, then she can talk to you.

The same goes for a wife's relationship with her ex-husband. No matter how close you once were, that friendship cannot be maintained or reestablished without putting your remarriage in jeopardy. Whatever mess your ex-husband gets into, it's not your job to clean it up. If you or your spouse find yourself attracted again to your former mates, that's pretty normal. Emotions tend to cycle, so with ongoing contact it is not unusual for feelings to resurface. If they do, stop contact immediately except strictly about the kids. Even then, keep it short or try to communicate through texts and emails. Your affections, attention and allegiance are to your current spouse, not your former one. You closed that door when you made new marriage vows. If you and your ex are too close for your spouse's comfort, pull back from your former spouse for the sake of your marriage. Your spouse needs reassurance that your love and romantic attention are his or hers alone.

The Best Is Yet to Come

Remarriage is hard work, but when you undergo the painful heart surgery required to reshape your relationships and allow God's love to flow properly, you create a stepfamily that feels like the safest place on earth. It's a warm and welcoming place where heart connections can grow. If you never give up, and put best practices in place, you'll eventually find great satisfaction in the challenges you've overcome and discover joy in the friendships within your family.

Remember that in remarriages, the honeymoon comes way down the line. The first few years are usually the toughest, but that means you can truly create a happy ending. Remember that old farmhouse with the porch swing and the children playing in the yard we talked about in the beginning of this book? It's waiting for you in your future as a remarried couple, if you lay the groundwork and do the heart work to get there.

Dan and Marci are a living example. Even after emotional devastation, plenty of mistakes and significant heart damage, Dan and Marci persisted in letting God's love heal their hearts and outflow to their families. And what's the payoff for years of pain and rejection? A legacy of love and their sweet granddaughter named Hope (it's a fitting name for what this couple finally feels). Today, their children and stepchildren have forged their own bonds with family and stepfamily members. They don't all look the same or connect at the same levels. It isn't picture-perfect, but affection and attachment are present. Their children are now grown, and Dan and Marci are living the honeymoon years as best friends; their marriage is stronger than it has ever been. Their story touches others going through the same difficulties, and the benefits of their hard work can be seen in their grandchildren's lives.

"Now there's Hope," says Dan. "Here's my granddaughter, the daughter of my stepson, and she doesn't know any difference. For her, there's no 'step' this or that. She only knows that I am her grandfather."

HEART MONITORS

1. What is your relationship with your former spouse like? Have you established healthy co-parenting habits and boundaries? If not, what changes will you make?

2. How have you put your children and stepparenting in the middle of co-parenting conflict? How can you make changes so that they can freely love all of their family and stepfamily members?

3. What issues are unresolved with your former spouse? What apologies do you need to make to bridge the gap toward reconciliation? What do you wish your former spouse would apologize for?

4. In what ways have you surrendered your children and stepchildren to the Lord? How can you trust that He will protect them when they are not with you?

HEART PROTECTORS

Have an open discussion with your spouse about your former mates and your relationships with them. If either of you is uncomfortable or there is conflict between you because boundaries have not been set, make a plan together of how you will handle your communication and interactions with your former mates. Reassure each other that your marriage comes first.

Have a stepfamily confession session in which you clear the air with your children and stepchildren about any conflict with their other parents. Ask them what they think you could do to work together better. Pray together that the Lord will lessen conflict and strengthen your connections.

Notes

1. Gigi Levangie, *Stepmom*, Columbia/TriStar Pictures, 1998.
2. Maxine Marsolini, *Raising Children in Blended Families* (Grand Rapids, MI: Kregel Publications, 2006), pp. 47,49.

PART THREE

HEART CHANGERS

13

Heart Checkups

Each of the interactive tools in this chapter is designed to give you a "heart check-up." They can enlighten you to new ways or remind you of familiar ways you can take better care of your own heart and the heart of your mate. They are NOT meant to condemn or judge you, and they are not here for you to use as a weapon to wield to judge or criticize your spouse. See them as bearers of information that you both can use to help your remarriage be the safest place on earth.

The State of Your Marriage Quiz
Dr. John Gottman

How strong is your marriage? For the last 25 years, Dr. John Gottman of the Family Research Lab at the University of Washington has been studying what he calls the "masters and disasters" of marriage. He listens to married couples talk about each other and their marriage as he measures their heart rates, observes facial expressions and evaluates how they describe their mate and their marriage. Based on Gottman's findings, he created a free marriage quiz that is designed to provide you with results that can arm you with knowledge you need to strengthen your marriage.

Gottman is able to predict with 90 percent accuracy which couples' marriages will make it over the long haul, and which will not. Test the strength of your marriage by taking this 22-question relationship quiz. Don't let it scare you into thinking your marriage is doomed if you bomb. Take it as a challenge to enjoy discovering each other at a much deeper level.

I can name my partner's best friends.
___ yes
___ no

I can tell you what stresses my partner is currently facing.
___ yes
___ no

I know the names of some of the people who have been irritating my partner lately.
___ yes
___ no

I can tell you some of my partner's life dreams.
___ yes
___ no

I can tell you about my partner's basic philosophy of life.
___ yes
___ no

I can list the relatives my partner likes the least.
___ yes
___ no

I feel that my partner knows me pretty well.
___ yes
___ no

When we are apart, I often think fondly of my partner.
___ yes
___ no

I often touch or kiss my partner affectionately.
___ yes
___ no

My partner really respects me.
___ yes
___ no

There is fire and passion in this relationship.

___ yes

___ no

Romance is definitely still part of our relationship.

___ yes

___ no

My partner appreciates the things I do in this relationship.

___ yes

___ no

My partner generally likes my personality.

___ yes

___ no

Our sex life is mostly satisfying.

___ yes

___ no

At the end of the day my partner is glad to see me.

___ yes

___ no

My partner is one of my best friends.

___ yes

___ no

We just love talking to each other.

___ yes

___ no

There is lots of give and take (both people have influence) in our discussions.

___ yes

___ no

My partner listens respectfully, even when we disagree.
___ yes
___ no

My partner is usually a great help as a problem solver.
___ yes
___ no

We generally mesh well on basic values and goals in life.
___ yes
___ no

Now add up the number of times you checked "yes" and then use the following guide to help you interpret your score. Yes: _____

16 to 22: Green Light
If you scored in the 16-22 range, your relationship is probably in good or even great shape *at this time*. But we emphasize *at this time* because relationships don't stand still. In the next 12 months, you'll either have a stronger, happier relationship, or you could head in the other direction. To visualize where your remarriage stands, think of yourself as currently driving down the road, going through a green light. There's no need to stop what you're doing. Keep cruising along, making the most of your marriage. But remember that you're moving all the time. Keep moving together, and don't stop working to make your relationship all it can be.

8 to 15: Yellow Light
If you scored in the 8-15 range, you're approaching a yellow light in your remarriage. You need to be cautious. While you may be happy now in your relationship, your score reveals warning signs of negative patterns you can't afford to let take hold. Check your heart for hardening and review the chapters in this book for keeping your quality of life high. Keep your heart flowing with God's love as the wellspring of life. If you landed in this range, you should take steps now to protect and improve what you have together. Expend some extra effort on your marriage right now and you'll avoid a lot of heartache in the future. You can have a lifetime of love together if you nurture each other's hearts now.

0 to 7: Red Light

Finally, if you scored in the 0-7 range, it's like approaching a red light. You must stop and think about where the two of you are headed. Your score indicates the presence of "germs" that have infected your marriage and could put your relationship at significant risk. You may be heading for trouble or you're already there. Don't give up! As long as there is life left in your body, there is time for your hearts to heal. You know what you need to do. Get your focus off your own happiness and turn your eyes back to God. He can turn your hearts back to each other.

So, how did you do? We hope your high score indicates that your hearts are overflowing love freely. But if you think you are suffering from some hardening of the love arteries, go back to the greatest surgeon of all, the God who created you, and let Him do some major heart surgery.

Safety Rating Scale
Dr. Greg Smalley

In the Safety Rating Scale I (Greg) developed, you can quickly determine how safe each spouse feels in your remarriage. It's a good barometer to measure how well you are guarding your hearts.

Below is a list of behaviors. Place a checkmark next to the behaviors that *your spouse* has exhibited to some degree over the last three months. Be sure to work the columns horizontally, that is alternating from the left column to the right column and back.

Column A	Column B
____ Acted in kind and caring ways	____ Judged your behavior
____ Initiated a spiritual relationship (e.g., prayer, Bible study, church, and so on)	____ Gossiped or talked to other people about you
____ Communicated how valuable you are	____ Nagged or hassled you
____ Gave you gift(s)	____ Talked about divorce or leaving

____ Served you or gave unexpected acts of love

____ Affirmed love for you verbally

____ Showed patience

____ Sought to understand you

____ Looked past your behaviors

____ Provided words of affirmation

____ Asked about your feelings

____ Empathized willingly

____ Expressed curiosity and interest in you (i.e., your feelings and thoughts)

____ Gave you his/her undivided attention

____ Provided compassion

____ Shared his/her feelings

____ Made strides to be healthy

____ Acted cheerful or pleasant

____ Used sarcastic humor

____ Had an angry outburst

____ Avoided you or withdrew from you

____ Tried to solve or fix situations

____ Forced or demanded conversation

____ Looked for your negative traits

____ Acted needy or clingy

____ Used information against you later

____ Did something else while listening to you

____ Criticized you

____ Tried to be right or win

____ Judged your feelings

____ Reacted defensively toward you

____ Belittled you

_____ Attended to your needs/love language

_____ Spent quality time with you

_____ Validated your feelings

_____ Provided affection and touch

_____ Engaged in meaningful conversation

_____ Showed a slowness to anger

_____ Listened without trying to change you or fix the issue

_____ Valued your personality differences

_____ Provided unconditional love and acceptance

_____ Encouraged you

_____ Verbalized things that he/she appreciates about you

_____ Respected your boundaries

_____ Acted gentle toward you

_____ Complimented you in specific ways

_____ Ignored you

_____ Verbally attacked you

_____ Refused to listen

_____ Rejected or abandoned you

_____ Disrespected you

_____ Wasn't honest about something

_____ Was too busy (e.g., work, family, friends, hobbies)

_____ Manipulated you

_____ Acted in a controlling way

_____ Tried to "fix" you

_____ Broke a promise or didn't follow through on a commitment

_____ Intimidated you or physically threatened you

_____ Brought up the past

_____ Absence of a desire for God/spirituality

____ Sensitive toward you	____ Violated his/her own integrity
____ Trusted you	____ Showed a lack of appreciation
____ Made you a priority	____ Displayed a superior attitude
____ Laughed with you	____ Assumed the worst about you
____ Asked you about your day	____ Betrayed your confidence
____ Protected you	____ Acted selfishly

**Total number of checks
in column A** _____

**Total number of checks
in column B** _____

Here's how to score the Safety Rating Scale: Take the total number of checks in column A and record that number in the space below. Next, take the total number of checks in column B and record that number in the space below. Next, subtract the column B total from the column A total and record that number in the "total" space.

Column A _____ − Column B _____ = Total _____

Finally, plot your total score on the Safety Scale continuum below.

Completely Unsafe	Somewhat Unsafe	Somewhat Safe	**Completely Safe**

-38   -28   -21   -14   -7   **0**   7   14   21   28   **38**

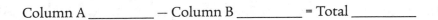

Now that you know your number, what do you do next? Again, we strongly encourage you to use the Safety Rating Scale as "information"

and not as a report card on your marriage or your spouse. No matter how you and your spouse score on this scale or any of these quizzes, you still have the opportunity to make your marriage feel like the safest place on earth.

The best way to use this scale to help your relationship grow is to talk about the behaviors in column A that you would love to see take place more often in your marriage. The reality is that you both possess a gold mine of information that can increase the safety your hearts feel in your relationship. Make sure your conversations focus on adding behaviors that will help you feel safe. Try not to focus on the column B behaviors. However you use this scale, do it in a way that honors your spouse and glorifies the Lord.

Top Relational Needs
Drs. Gary and Greg Smalley

Wherever you are in your marriage journey, the following exercise can give you a powerful picture of what you both want from each other in order to feel loved. We always ask couples, "If things were a '10' in your relationship, if things were ideal, what would that look like? What would your marriage contain?" Don't worry—it won't be as hard as you might think. For the most part, you'll be working from a list we've developed over the years in our work with thousands of couples. Why a list? Because if you're at all like us, it's easier to work from a list than to start from scratch. If you were to ask me, "Gary, what do you really want or need in your relationship?" I'd more than likely say, "I don't know." I'm pretty laid-back and easygoing, so without a list I'd tend to struggle. So use the list (with our blessing) to discover the contours of your own great remarriage relationship.

To understand which of the following needs are most important to you, rank each need from 0 to 10. If you have any needs not listed, write them on the "other need" lines at the end of the list.

Little Importance   **Extremely Important**

    1   2   3   4   5   6   7   8   9   10

In my relationship with my spouse, I need to . . .

____ Feel connected through talking.

____ Feel connected through sharing recreation/fun times together.

____ Be touched nonsexually.

____ Make love.

____ Receive verbal tenderness.

____ Receive physical tenderness.

____ Live by the laws of man with my spouse's support.

____ Live by the laws of God with my spouse's support.

____ Know that we'll stay together and feel secure in our love.

____ Know that we'll stay together and feel secure in our finances.

____ Feel accepted and valued for who I am.

____ Feel accepted and valued for what I do.

____ Feel safe when I share who I am.

____ Be included in most decisions that affect my life or marriage.

____ Gain agreement and harmony in decision-making.

____ Know that my spouse needs me.

____ Know that my spouse supports my desire to give money away.

____ Know that my spouse supports my desire to give gifts to others.

____ Know that my spouse supports my desire to serve others.

____ Receive genuine praise and affirmation.

____ Have alone time and know my spouse understands this need.

____ Be seen as physically attractive.

____ Be seen as honest and trustworthy.

____ Know that my spouse supports my desire to assist the younger generation in developing and leading useful lives.

____ Receive gifts.

____ Receive acts of service.

____ Develop a future plan together for our marriage.

____ Feel like we have developed complete faith in each other.

____ Become emotionally healthy and have an emotionally healthy spouse.

____ Know that my spouse wants us to maintain a mutually vibrant spiritual relationship.

____ Know that my spouse will apologize and seek forgiveness.

____ Know that we can resolve differences/conflicts/arguments.

____ Engage in mutually satisfying communication.

____ Know that we can cope with crises and stress.

_____ Feel that my spouse understands my personality and gender differences.
_____ See my spouse demonstrate a willingness to change (flexibility).
_____ Know that my spouse agrees on how to raise our children.
_____ Be passionate and romantic.
_____ Socially connect with others.
_____ Maintain careful control over my expectations.
_____ Know that my spouse notices our positive relational history.
_____ Know that we strive for mutuality and equality in our relationship.
_____ Share negative and positive feelings without delay.
_____ Know that my spouse accepts my influence.
_____ Periodically update my spouse's knowledge of my greatest needs.
_____ Receive genuine appreciation for my service.

Other need: _____.
Other need: _____.

From the preceding list, determine your top 10 needs, in order of importance (with #1 as your most important need).

1. _____
2. _____
3. _____
4. _____
5. _____
6. _____
7. _____
8. _____
9. _____
10. _____

In order for your mate to completely understand your top 10 relational needs, it's necessary to explain what each need means to you. If one of your top needs is to "engage in mutually satisfying communication," for example, then you must explain what that means to you. If your mate gives you "satisfying communication," what does that look like? What would your spouse be doing or saying? Explain your need as specifically as possible. Tell your spouse what specific behaviors would provide mutually satisfying communication. You ranked your top 10 needs; now take the time to unpack and define them.

1. _____
   _____
   _____

2. _____
   _____
   _____

3. _____
   _____
   _____

4. _____
   _____
   _____

5. _____
   _____
   _____

6. _____
   _____
   _____

7. _____
   _____
   _____

8. _____
   _____
   _____

9. _____
   _____
   _____

10. _____
    _____
    _____

Personality Profile
Dr. Gary Smalley and Dr. John Trent

The better you know yourself and understand how uniquely you were made, the easier you will find it to communicate your needs to your spouse. When you know how your personality is hardwired, and you compare it to the way your spouse was designed, you can identify where your strengths and weaknesses complement or clash.

In the space provided, identify the degree in which the following characteristics or behaviors most accurately describe you at home or in your relationships with your loved ones.

0 = not at all; 1 = somewhat; 2 = mostly; 3 = very much

I	II	III	IV
__Likes control	__Enthusiastic	__Sensitive	__Consistent
__Confident	__Visionary	__Calm	__Reserved
__Firm	__Energetic	__Undemanding	__Practical
__Likes challenge	__Promoter	__Enjoys routine	__Factual
__Problem solver	__Mixes easily	__Relational	__Perfectionistic
__Bold	__Fun-loving	__Adaptable	__Detailed
__Goal driven	__Spontaneous	__Thoughtful	__Inquisitive
__Strong willed	__Likes new ideas	__Patient	__Persistent
__Self-reliant	__Optimistic	__Good listener	__Sensitive
__Persistent	__Takes risks	__Loyal	__Accurate
__Takes charge	__Motivator	__Even-keeled	__Controlled
__Determined	__Very verbal	__Gives in	__Predictable
__Enterprising	__Friendly	__Indecisive	__Orderly
__Competitive	__Popular	__Dislikes change	__Conscientious
__Productive	__Enjoys variety	__Dry humor	__Discerning
__Purposeful	__Group oriented	__Sympathetic	__Analytical
__Adventurous	__Initiator	__Nurturing	__Precise
__Independent	__Inspirational	__Tolerant	__Scheduled
__Action oriented	__Likes change	__Peacemaker	__Deliberate
_____Total	_____Total	_____Total	_____Total

Now graph your scores on the following table.

Personality Profile

I	II	III	IV
"L"	"O"	"V"	"E"
60			
58			
56			
54			
52			
50			
48			
46			
44			
42			
40			
38			
36			
34			
32			
30			
28			
26			
24			
22			
20			
18			
16			
14			
12			
10			
8			
6			
4			
2			
0			

The personality inventory you just took is like a fingerprint. It helps identify you and reveal your tendencies. Unlike fingerprints, however, you can change your tendencies. Discovering your personality tendencies in relationships helps show you where your strengths and weaknesses exist. Each of us has these personality strengths in combinations, which are variable and adjustable. They need to be brought into balance. Therefore, the goal is to help you understand where you are "out of balance" in terms of your personality. We've found that our greatest personal strengths—when pushed out of balance—become our biggest weaknesses. For instance, let's say you have the strength of tremendous enthusiasm that draws others to you. It can become a weakness if your enthusiasm turns into manipulation.

If a particular character trait of yours is too extreme, to the point that it irritates your mate or your children, you can decide to tone down that trait and turn up other traits. Let's take a closer look at the four different personality types and see what happens when our strengths are pushed out of balance:

L is for Lion

Strengths	Strengths Pushed Out of Balance
• Problem solver	• Too busy
• Bold, direct communication	• Insensitive
• Decision maker	• Not thoughtful of others' wishes
• Strong-willed	• Stubborn
• Independent, Self-reliant	• Avoids people and seeking help
• Action oriented, persistent	• Inflexible, relentless, unyielding
• Likes authority	• Too direct or demanding
• Takes charge	• Pushy, impatient—do it now!
• Confident	• Cocky, overlook others' feelings
• Enterprising	• Big risks
• Competitive	• Cold blooded

Lions tend to have direct or blunt communication within a relationship. It is usually one-way communication, so they can be poor listeners. In their relationships, Lions need such things as personal attention and recognition for what they do, areas where they can be in charge, opportunities to solve problems, freedom to change and challenging activities within a relationship.

What does a balanced Lion look like? Since Lions are naturally hard on people (and tough on themselves), their greatest relational need is to add softness to their personality tendencies to keep from being too tough on those they love. Also, Lions may need to learn that meaningful communication takes time. They need to slow down and discuss decisions with others, not simply charge ahead on their own.

O is for Otter

Strengths	Strengths Pushed Out of Balance
• Enthusiastic	• Overbearing
• Takes risks	• Dangerous and foolish
• Visionary, inspirational	• Daydreamer, phony
• Fun-loving, infectious laughter	• Not serious, obnoxious
• Motivator, promoter, initiator	• Manipulator, exaggerates, pushy
• Energetic	• Impatient
• Friendly, group oriented	• Shallow relationships, bored
• Likes variety, enjoys change	• Scattered, lacks follow-through
• Spontaneous	• Not focused enough
• Enjoys creativity or new ideas	• Unrealistic, avoids details

Otters can inspire others through their communication. They tend to be optimistic or enthusiastic in the way they relate to others. It is usually one-way, and their high energy and charm can manipulate others or wear them out. In a relationship, Otters need such things as approval, opportunity to verbalize, visibility and social recognition within a relationship.

What does a balanced Otter look like? One of the greatest relational needs for Otters is to practice more follow-through. Otters tend to make all kinds of promises and think all things are possible, but they need to make good on their promises and stick to their commitments. Otters also need to develop sensitivity to the feelings of others and weigh the consequences of their words or actions before jumping into something impulsively.

G is for Golden Retriever

Strengths	Strengths Pushed Out of Balance
• Sensitive feelings	• Easily hurt
• Loyal	• Missed opportunities

- Calm, even-keeled
- Undemanding, patient
- Peacemaker, hates confrontation
- Enjoys routine, dislikes change
- Warm and relational
- Accommodating
- Sympathetic, good listener

- Lacking enthusiasm
- Pushover, taken advantage of
- Misses honest intimacy
- Stays in rut, not spontaneous
- Fewer deep friends
- Too indecisive
- Holds on to another's hurt or pain

Golden Retrievers' communication style tends to be more indirect. They usually have good two-way communication with others; thus, they make great listeners. However, they tend to use too many words or provide too many details. In a relationship, Golden Retrievers need such things as emotional security and an agreeable environment. They are easygoing and calm, and they usually don't like conflict.

What does a balanced Golden Retriever look like? Because Golden Retrievers have an eagerness to please others, they have a hard time saying no. Therefore, their greatest relational need is to set limits and boundaries essential for their own well-being. Further, Golden Retrievers need to practice confronting others. They need to turn their ability to internalize negative things into positive outward behavior, where they think and act decisively.

B is for Beaver

Strengths	Strengths Pushed Out of Balance
• Perfectionist	• Too controlling
• Detailed, enjoys instructions	• Hard time finishing; slow
• Accurate, precise	• Too critical and too strict
• Consistent, predictable	• No spontaneity or variety; boring
• Controlled, reserved, orderly	• Too serious and stuffy; rigid
• Practical	• Not adventurous
• Sensitive	• Stubborn
• Conscientious	• Too inflexible
• Analytical	• Loose overview
• Discerning	• Too negative on new opportunity

Beavers tend to be factual and precise in their communication. They usually have good two-way communication with others and also make good listeners—especially in relation to tasks. However, their desire for detail and precision can frustrate others. In a relationship, Beavers need such things as quality and exact parameters and expectations. They need to live "by the rules."

What does a balanced Beaver look like? Because Beavers tend to be extreme in their thinking, it's important for them to realize that nothing is ever as bad as it seems or as good as it appears. They need to be more relaxed and let some things remain unfinished or undone. Letting go of the need to have everything exactly right is important for a Beaver. They need to learn to put events in the right context, instead of magnifying small problems way out of proportion.

When you and your spouse understand each other's personality bents and can see how your weaknesses are really strengths pushed out of balance, you can sharpen each other's strengths and help tame each other's weaknesses. When you do, you will have fewer personality conflicts down the road.

For additional insight, answer the following questions:

1. How do you feel about the results of taking the personality assessment? Do you agree with the results?
2. Which of your own personality strengths do you most honor or treasure?
3. How do these strengths benefit or enhance your marital relationship?
4. Describe a time when you said or did something you later regretted, and you now realize that the problem was one of your strengths that got pushed to an extreme.
5. How does understanding your spouse's personality bent help you relate better to him or her?
6. List at least five personality characteristics that you admire about your spouse.
7. How do these strengths benefit or enhance your marital relationship?
8. What are some weak areas you would like to develop?
9. How do your spouse's strengths expose your weaknesses?
10. What qualities of other personality types would you like to develop? Why?
11. What can you do to affirm and complement your spouse's unique personality? How can you blend your strengths with your spouse's?

12. Do you see where your weaknesses may hurt or irritate your spouse?
13. How will this personality knowledge be helpful in parenting?

Remarriage Mission Statement

*A remarriage mission statement creates in peoples' hearts
and minds a frame of reference, a set of criteria or guidelines,
by which a couple can govern themselves.*

STEPHEN R. COVEY

Creating a remarriage mission statement helps to protect and enrich your remarriage. It gives you a goal and a shared sense of purpose that can cement the bonds that brought you together. It can be especially helpful in remarriage because it helps you form your own identity as a remarried couple and creates a "new normal" for your stepfamily. It moves both of you away from your past and gives you hope of a fulfilling future.

You and your spouse can begin creating your remarriage mission statement by identifying what is truly important in your lives. Many remarriages gain a sense of who they are from the opinions and perceptions of those around them, from the lessons they learned in their previous marriages. As a result, couples can end up allowing judgment, habits or even insecurities shape who they are and what they accomplish. The most effective remarried couples, however, fashion their own future. Instead of letting other circumstances or people determine their destiny, effective couples plan and create their own positive results. A mission statement sets them on the right path and keeps them from straying away from it.

A remarriage mission statement does these things:

- Helps you and your spouse "begin with the end in mind"
- Encourages you to think deeply about your life
- Helps you examine your innermost thoughts and feelings
- Clarifies what is really important to you
- Expands your perspective
- Imprints self-determined values and purposes firmly in your mind
- Provides direction and commitment to values
- Enables you to make daily progress toward long-term goals
- Provides a picture of your desired results for your life and marriage

How to Create Your Own
Remarriage Mission Statement

Creating a remarriage mission statement begins with exploring what your remarriage is about and examining the principles you live by. One of the best ways to do this is to envision you and your spouse at the end of life. Imagine that it's your fiftieth wedding anniversary, and you're gathered with your children, stepchildren and all your grandchildren. They are throwing a big surprise party for you. Your extended, blended family is telling stories, reflecting on the many twists and turns of your life together. With that thought in mind, answer these questions:

- What memories do you want your family members to have?
- What accomplishments do you want to be able to look back on—relationships (with God and with others), impact on the world for eternity's sake, service to your fellow man, career achievements, and so forth?
- What character qualities do you want your family to remember about you?
- What taught values do you want your children and stepchildren to be passing on to their children?
- What kind of legacy do you want to leave?

Next, discuss with your spouse your values, hopes, dreams and ideals. This goes deeper than, *One day I hope we can buy a boat and a camp on a lake in the country.* It should be more like, *I want us to achieve harmony as a stepfamily. I want our remarriage to erase all negative effects of our divorce. I want our marriage to be an example of lasting love that our children can replicate. I want to be a family that is radically committed to Jesus Christ in every way.*

It can also be something like, *My dream is that it will be said of us that we poured out our lives in love and service to God and people.* To understand what your remarriage is about and to outline your operational principles, answer these kinds of questions:

- What is the purpose of our remarriage?
- What kind of stepfamily do we want to have?
- How do we want to resolve our differences?
- What kind of parents and stepparents do we want to be?
- What kinds of things do we want to do?
- What kind of relationship do we want to have with one another?

- How do we want to treat one another and speak to one another?
- What things are truly important to us as a couple?
- What are our highest priorities and goals?
- What are the principles and guidelines we want our remarriage to follow?
- What marriages inspire us and why do we admire them?
- How can we contribute to society as a couple and become more service-oriented?

With these ideas on the table, you're now ready to refine and pull them all together into some kind of written document that will reflect the collective hearts and minds in your remarriage. To give you some direction in writing your remarriage mission statement, here are a few examples to get you and your spouse inspired:

The Smalley family mission is to honor and serve God, others and ourselves. We will create a nurturing place of order, integrity, love, happiness and relaxation. We will believe in each other. We will foster responsibility by teaching our children to love, learn, laugh, and to work and develop their unique talents.

Our mission is to be devoted to living our lives as a Christian family, focusing on the teachings of Christ. We will work together to strengthen our community through our active involvement in charities and Christian outreach programs. We will set strong examples for our children and raise them with the proper amounts of nurturing and discipline. We are committed to considering each others' feelings always and put others' needs above our own. We will give praise to the Lord each day for bringing us together.

We will encourage others to become like Christ through loving relationships, healthy lifestyles and stimulating experiences.

We will love each other, help each other, believe in each other. We will wisely use our time, talents and resources to bless others. We will worship together forever.

Our marriage is great—as equal partners, we want to love, have fun, teach and learn. We are a great team.

It is our belief that the other is never wrong. Rather than blame or accuse, we will ask, "Will you help me understand?" With love and understanding, we will grow our lives together.

Once you have created the mission statement for your remarriage, make it something special. Print it on bordered paper or have it done in professional calligraphy. Frame it and hang it in a place of prominence. Memorize it. Recite it together each and every day until you know it by heart. Let others know what your mission statement says. Sharing it with friends and family will only serve to strengthen your resolve to follow it daily. As you write your remarriage mission statement, you will become more aware of your family's potential, natural talents and tendencies. Don't rush the process. Instead, take time to craft the mission statement that will guide your remarriage. Finally, don't be afraid to revise it if needed. Your remarriage mission statement is your "Constitution," the living document that provides a framework for your family.

Not to us, O LORD, not to us,
But to Your name give glory
Because of Your lovingkindness,
because of Your truth.
PSALM 115:1, *NASB*

ACKNOWLEDGMENTS

First and foremost, we thank our Lord Jesus Christ, who fills our hearts with His amazing love.

This book could not have been completed without the help of many family, friends and colleagues.

Thank you to our families who have always cared about and supported our hearts and passions. Thank you to the Smalley children—Taylor, Maddy and Garrison—for the special gift of being your father.

Thank you to Natalie Gillespie, an exceptionally gifted writer, for being our collaborator.

Thank you to Kim Bangs for being an amazing editor.

Thank you to Roger Gibson for his outstanding help in bringing this project to reality.

Thank you to Greg's colleagues at the Center for Relationship Enrichment—Gary Oliver, Jan Phillips, Jackson Dunn, Sherri Swilley, Judy Shoop and Stew Grant—for your support in the writing of this book.

And, finally, thank you to Regal Books and the Gospel Light team who have engaged in copyediting, internal design and layout, cover design and the myriad of details required to bring this book to press.

ABOUT THE AUTHORS

Dr. Gary Smalley is president and founder of the Smalley Relationship Center, which presents conferences nationwide and provides resources for families and churches. Combined, his books have sold more than six million copies. *The Blessing* and *The Two Sides of Love* won the Gold Medallion Award for excellence in literature, and *The Language of Love* won the Angel Award for best contribution to family life. Gary has been a guest on numerous national TV shows, including *The Oprah Winfrey Show, Larry King Live* and NBC's *Today*. He is the co-author, with Ted Cunningham, of *The Language of Sex* and *From Anger to Intimacy.*

For more information, visit **www.GarySmalley.com**

Dr. Greg Smalley has a passion to help premarital and married couples learn how to enjoy a lifetime together. He earned his doctorate degree in clinical psychology from Rosemead School of Psychology at Biola University in Southern California. He also holds two masters degrees: one in counseling psychology from Denver Seminary, and the other in clinical psychology from Rosemead School of Psychology.

Dr. Smalley is the director of marriage ministries for the Center for Relationship Enrichment on the campus of John Brown University. He is an assistant professor of marriage and family studies at John Brown University. He is also on the teaching team at Fellowship Bible Church.

Dr. Smalley helps lead marriage seminars around the world and, together with his wife, Erin, does intensive relationship coaching for both married and engaged couples. He also helps train pastors, professionals and lay leaders on how to effectively work with married and premarital couples.

Dr. Smalley is the author or co-author of 10 books, including *The Wholehearted Marriage, Before You Plan Your Wedding, Plan Your Marriage, The DNA of Relationships for Couples, The Marriage You've Always Dreamed Of, The DNA of Relationships, The DNA of Parent and Teen Relationships, Men's Relational Toolbox, Life Lines: Communicating with Your Teen, Winning Your Wife Back* and *Winning Your Husband Back.*

Greg and his wife, Erin, along with their two daughters, Taylor and Maddy, and son, Garrison, live in Siloam Springs, Arkansas.

For more information, visit **www.SmalleyMarriage.com**

Dan and Marci Cretsinger live in St. Charles, Illinois, and are members of Willow Creek Community Church, where they are small-group leaders.

Dr. Greg & Erin Smalley
smalleymarriage.com

visit our website for

{
- marriage tips
- free resources
- additional books
- speaking request
- marriage blog
}

smalleymarriage.com

SMALLEY
relationship
C E N T E R

The Smalley Relationship Center provides conferences and resources for couples, singles, parents, and churches. The Center captures research, connecting to your practical needs and develops new tools for building relationships.

resources include:

- Over 50 best-selling books on relationships
- Small Group curriculums on marriage & parenting
- Church-wide campaign series with sermon series, daily emails and much more
- Video/DVD series
- Newlywed kit and pre-marital resources

www.garysmalley.com website includes:

- Over 300 articles on practical relationship topics
- Weekly key truths on practical issues
- Daily devotionals
- Conference dates and locations
- Special events
- Weekly newsletter
- Free personality & core fear profiles
- Request a SRC Speaker

To find out more about Gary Smalley's speaking schedule, conferences, and to receive a weekly e-letter with articles and coaching ideas on your relationships, go to www.garysmalley.com or call 1.800.8486329